BONNIE SCOTLAND

LECTOR HOUSE PUBLIC DOMAIN WORKS

BONNIE SCOTLAND

ASCOTT ROBERT HOPE MONCRIEFF

ISBN: 978-93-5614-320-3

Published: 1912

LECTOR HOUSE LLP
E-MAIL: lectorpublishing@gmail.com

BONNIE SCOTLAND

That I for poor auld Scotland's sake,
Some usefu' plan, or beuk could make.

Burns.

BENEATH THE CRAGS OF BEN VENUE, PERTHSHIRE

BONNIE SCOTLAND

DESCRIBED BY

A. R. HOPE MONCRIEFF

**PAINTED BY
SUTTON PALMER**

1912

Published November 1904
Reprinted 1905, 1912

NOTE

THE author does not attempt elaborate word-pictures, that would seem pale beside the artist's colouring. His design has been, as accompaniment to these beautiful landscapes, an outline of Scotland's salient features, with glimpses at its history, national character, and customs, and at the literature that illustrates this country for the English-speaking world. While taking the reader on a fireside tour through the varying "airts" of his native land, he has tried to show how its life, silken or homespun, is a tartan of more intricate pattern than appears in certain crude impressions struck off by strangers. And into his own web have been woven reminiscences, anecdotes, and borrowed brocade such as may make entertaining stripes and checks upon a groundwork of information. The mainland only is dealt with in this volume, which it is intended to follow up with another on the Highlands and Islands.

CONTENTS

LIST OF ILLUSTRATIONS

BONNIE SCOTLAND

CHAPTER I

THE BORDERS

THE dawn broadens, the mists roll away to show a northward-bound traveller how his train is speeding between slopes of moorland, green and grey, here patched by bracken or bog, there dotted by wind-blown trees, everywhere cut by water-courses gathering into gentle rivers that can be furious enough in spate, when they hurl a drowned sheep or a broken hurdle through those valleys opening a glimpse of mansions and villages among sheltered woods. Are we still in England, or in what at least as far back as Cromwell's time called itself "Bonnie Scotland"? It is as hard to be sure as to make out whether that cloudy knoll on the horizon is crowned by a peat-stack or by the stump of a Border peel.

Either bank of Tweed and Liddel has much the same aspects. An expert might perhaps read the look or the size of the fields. Could one get speech with that brawny corduroyed lad tramping along the furrows to his early job, whistling maybe, as if it would never grow old, an air from the London music-halls, the Southron might be none the wiser as to his nationality, though a fine local ear would not fail to catch some difference of burr and broad vowels, marked off rather by separating ridges than by any legal frontier, as the lilting twang of Liddesdale from the Teviot drawl. Healthily barefooted children, more's the pity, are not so often seen nowadays on this side of the Border, nor on the other, unless at Brightons and Margates. The Scotch "bonnet," substantial headgear as it was, has vanished; the Scotch plaid, once as familiar on the Coquet as on the Tweed, is more displayed in shop windows than in moorland glens, now that over the United Kingdom reigns a dull monotony and uniformity of garb. Could we take the spectrum of those first wreaths of smoke curling from cottage chimneys, we might find traces of peat and porridge, yet also of coal and bacon. Yon red-locked lassie turning her open eyes up to the train from the roadside might settle the question, were we able to test her knowledge whether of the Shorter Catechism or of her "Duty towards her Neighbour." It is only when the name of the first Scottish way-station whisks by, that we know ourselves fairly over the edge of "Caledonia stern and wild"; and our first thought may well be that this Borderland appears less stern than the grey crags of Yorkshire, and less wild than some bleak uplands of Northumberland.

TANTALLON CASTLE, ON COAST OF HADDINGTONSHIRE

**THE BASS ROCK, FIRTH OF FORTH,
OFF THE COAST OF HADDINGTONSHIRE**

What makes a nation? Not for long such walls as the Romans drew across this neck of our island, one day to point a moral of fallen might, and to adorn a tale of the northern romancer who by its ruins wooed his alien bride. Not such rivers as here could be easily forded by those mugwump moss-troopers that sat on the fence of Border law, and—

> Sought the beeves to make them broth
> In England and in Scotland both.

Is it race? Alas for the ethnologic historian, on its dim groundwork of Picts and Celts—or what?—Scotland shows a still more confusing pattern of mingled strains than does the sister kingdom! To both sides of the Border such names for natural features as Cheviot, Tweed, and Tyne, tell the same tale of one stock displaced by another that built and christened its Saxon Hawicks, Berwicks, Bamboroughs, and Longtowns upon the Pens and Esks of British tribes.—Is it a common speech? But from the Humber to the Moray Firth, along the east side of Britain, throughout the period of fiercest clash of arms, prevailed the same tongue, split by degrees into dialects, but differing on the Forth and the Tyne less than the Tyne folks' tongue differed from that of the Thames, or the speech of the Forth from that of the Clyde mouth. So insists Dr. J. A. H. Murray, who of all British scholars was found worthy to edit the Oxford English Dictionary, that has now three editors, two of them born north of the Tweed, the third also in the northern half of England. Scottish "wut" chuckles to hear how, when the shade of Boswell pertly reported to the great doctor that his post as Lexicographer-General had been filled by one who was at once a Scotsman and a dissenter, all Hades shook with the rebuke, "Sir, in striving to be facetious, do not attempt obscenity and profanity!"—or ghostly vocables to such effect.

Is it loyalty to a line of princes that crystallises patriotism? That is a current easily induced, as witness how the sentiments once stirred by a Mary or a Prince Charlie could precipitate themselves round the stout person of George IV.—Is it religion? Kirk and Covenant have doubtless had their share in casting a mould of national character; but the Border feuds were hottest among generations who seldom cared to question "for gospel, what the Church believed."—Is it name? Northerners and Southerners were at strife long before they knew themselves as English and Scots.

By a process of elimination one comes to see how *esprit de corps* seems most surely generated by the wont of standing shoulder to shoulder against a common foe. Even the shifty baron, "Lucanus an Apulus anceps," whose feudal allegiance dovetailed into both kingdoms, that professional warrior who "signed on," now with the northern, now with the southern team, might well grow keen on a side for which he had won a goal, and bitter against the ex-comrades who by fair or foul play had come best out of a hot scrimmage. Heartier would be the animosity of bonnet-lairds and yeomen, between whom lifting of cattle and harrying of homes were points in the game. Then even grooms and gillies, with nothing to lose, dutifully fell into the way of fighting for their salt, when fighting with somebody came almost as natural to men and boys as to collie dogs. So the generations beat one another into neighbourly hatred and national pride; till the Border clans half forgot their feuds in a larger sentiment of patriotism; and what was once an adventurous exercise, rose to be a fierce struggle for independence. The Borderers were the "forwards" of this international sport, on whose fields and strongholds became most hotly forged the differences in which they played the part of hammer and of anvil by turns. Here, it is said, between neighbours of the same blood, survive least faintly the national resentments that may still flash up between drunken hinds at a fair. Hardly a nook here has not been blackened and bloodstained, hardly a stream but has often run red in centuries of waxing and waning strife whose fiery gleams are long faded into pensive memories, and its ballad chronicles, that once "stirred the heart like a trumpet," can now be sung or said to general applause of the most refined audiences, whether in London or Edinburgh.

The most famous ground of those historic encounters lies about the East Coast Railway route, where England pushes an aggressive corner across the Cheviots, and the Tweed, that most Scottish of rivers, forms the frontier of the kingdoms now provoking each other to good works like its Royal Border Bridge. Beyond it, indeed, stands Berwick-upon-Tweed, long the football of either party, then put out of play as a neutral town, and at last recognised as a quasi-outpost of England, whose parsons wear the surplice, and whose chief magistrate is a mayor, while the townsfolk are said to pride themselves on a parish patriotism that has gone the length of calling Sandy and John Bull foreigners alike. This of course is not, as London journalists sometimes conceive, the truly North Berwick where a prime minister might be seen "driving" and "putting" away the cares of state. That sea-side resort is a mushroom beside Berwick of the Merse, standing on its dignity of many sieges. The Northumberland Artillery Militia now man the batteries on its much-battered wall, turned to a picturesque walk; and the North British and North Eastern Railways meet peacefully on the site of its castle, where at one time Edward I. caged the Countess of Buchan like a wild beast, for having dared to set the crown upon Bruce's head. At another, it was in the hands of Baliol to surrender to an Edward as pledge of his subservience; and again, its precincts made the scene of a friendly spearing match between English and Scottish knights, much courtesy and fair-play being shown on both sides, even if over their cups a perfervid Grahame bid his challenger "rise early in the morning, and make your peace with God, for you shall sup in Paradise!" who indeed supped no more on earth.

The North British Railway will carry us on near a stern coast-line to Dunbar, whose castle Black Agnes, Countess of March, defended so doughtily against Lord Salisbury, and here were delivered so signally into Cromwell's hands a later generation of Scots "left to themselves" and to their fanatical chaplains; then over a land now swept by volleys of golf balls, to Pinkie, the last great battlefield between the kingdoms, where also, almost for the last time, the onrush of Highland valour routed redcoat soldiery at Prestonpans. But tourists should do what they do too seldom, tarry at Berwick to visit the tragic scenes close at hand. In sight of the town is the slope of Halidon Hill, on which the English took their *revanche* for Bannockburn. Higher up the Tweed, by the first Suspension Bridge in the kingdom, by "Norham's castled steep," watch-tower of the passage, and by Ford Castle where the siren Lady Ford is said to have ensnared James IV., that unlucky "champion of the dames," a half-day's walk brings one to Flodden, English ground indeed, but the grave of many a Scot. Never was slaughter so much mourned and sung as that of the "Flowers of the Forest," cut down on these heights above the Tweed. The land watered with "that red rain" is now ploughed and fenced; but still can be traced the outlines of the scene about the arch of Twizel Bridge on which the English crossed the Till, as every schoolboy knew in Macaulay's day, if our schoolboys seem to be better up in cricket averages than in the great deeds of the past, unless prescribed for examinations.

NEIDPATH CASTLE, PEEBLESSHIRE

Battles, like books, have their fates of fame. Flodden long made a sore point in Scottish memory; yet, after all, it was a stunning rather than a maiming defeat. A far more momentous battlefield on the Tweed, not far off, was Carham, whose name hardly appears in school histories, though it was the beginning of the Scotland of seven centuries to come. It dates just before Macbeth, when Malcolm, king of a confused Scotia or Pictia, sallied forth from behind the Forth, and with his ally, Prince of Cumbria on the Clyde, decisively defeated the Northumbrians in 1018, adding to his dominions the Saxon land between Forth and Tweed, a leaven that would leaven the whole lump, as Mr. Lang aptly puts it. Thus Malcolm's kingdom came into touch with what was soon to become feudal England, along the frontier that set to a hard and fast line, so long and so doughtily defended after mediæval Scotland had welded on the western Cumbria, as its cousin Cambria fell into the destinies of a stronger realm. Had northern Northumberland gone to England, there would have been no Royal Scotland, only a Grampian Wales echoing bardic boasts of its Rob Roys and Roderick Dhus, whose claymores might have splintered against Norman mail long before they came to be beaten down by bayonets and police batons.

But we shall never get away from the Border if we stop to moralise on all its scenes of strife—most of them well forgotten. Border fighting was commonly on a small scale, with plunder rather than conquest or glory for its aim; like the Arabs of to-day, those fierce but canny neighbours were seldom in a spirit for needless slaughter, that would entail fresh blood-feuds on their own kin. The Border fortresses were many, but chiefly small, designed for sudden defence against an enemy who might be trusted not to keep the field long. On the northern side large castles were rare; and those that did rise, opposite the English donjon keeps, were let fall by the Scots themselves, after their early feudal kings had drawn back to Edinburgh. In the long struggle with a richer nation, they soon learned to take the "earth-born castles" of their hills as cheaper and not less serviceable strongholds.

The station for Flodden, a few miles off, is Coldstream, at that "dangerous ford and deep" over which Marmion led the way for his train, before and after his day passed by so many an army marching north or south. The Bridge of Coldstream has tenderer memories, pointed out by Mr. W. S. Crockett in his *Scott Country*. This carried one of the main roads from England, and the inn on the Scottish side made a temple of hasty Hymen, where for many a runaway couple were forged bonds like those more notoriously associated with the blacksmith of Gretna Green. Their marriage jaunts into the neighbour country were put a stop to only half a century ago, when the benefits of Scots law, such as they were, became restricted to its own inhabitants. English novelists and jesters have made wild work with the law, by which, as they misapprehend, a man can be wedded without meaning it; one American story-teller is so little up-to-date as to marry his eloping hero and heroine at Gretna in our time. The gist of the matter is that while England favoured the masculine deceiver, fixing the ceremony before noon, it is said, to make sure of the bridegroom's sobriety, the more chivalrous Scots law provided that any ceremony should be held valid by which a man persuaded a woman that he was taking her to wife. No ceremony indeed was needed, if the parties lived by habit and repute as man and wife. The plot of Colonel Lockhart's *Mine is Thine*, one of the most amusing novels of our time, turns on a noted case in which an entry in a family Bible was taken as a sufficient proof of marriage. It is only gay Lotharios who might find this easy coupling a fetter; though in the next generation, especially if it be careless to treasure family Bibles, there may arise work for lawyers, a work of charity when the average income of the Scottish Bar is perhaps five pounds *Scots* per annum.

Gretna Green, of course, lies on the western highroad from England, beside which the Caledonian Railway route from Carlisle enters Scotland, soon turning off into a part of it comparatively sheltered from invasion by the Solway Firth, whose rapid ebb and flow make a type of many a Gretna love story. This side too, has often rung with the passage of armed men. At Burgh-on-Sands, in sight of the Scottish Border, died Edward I., bidding his bones be wrapped in a bull's hide and carried as bugbear standard against those obstinate rebels. The rout of Solway Moss made James V. turn his face to the wall, his heart breaking with the cry, "It came with a lass and it will go with a lass!" And the Esk of the Solway was seldom "swollen sae red and sae deep" as to daunt hardy lads from the north who once and again

> Swam ower to fell English ground,
> And danced themselves dry to the pibroch's sound.

These immigrants, unless they found six feet of English ground for a grave, seldom failed to go "back again," perhaps with an English host at their heels. Prince Charlie's army passed this way on its retreat from Derby. But this side of the Borderland is less well illustrated by stricken fields and sturdy sieges. It has, indeed, no lack of misty romance of its own, such as an American writer dares to bring into the light of common day by adding a sequel to Lady Heron's ballad, in which the fair Ellen is made to nurse a secret grudge at last confessed: she could not get over, even on any plea of poetic license, that rash assertion:

> There are maidens in Scotland more lovely by far
> Who would gladly be bride to the young Lochinvar!

"Fosters, Fenwicks, and Musgraves," how they rode and they ran on those hills and leas in days unkind to "a laggard in love and a dastard in war"! These names belong to the English side, as does Grahame in part. Elliot and Armstrong, Pringle and Rutherford, Ker and Home, Douglas, Murray, and Scott, are Scottish Border clans, who kept much together as in the Highlands. "Is there nae kind Christian wull gie me a night's lodging?" begged a tramp on the Borders, and had for rough answer, "Nae Christians here; we're a' Hopes and Johnstones!" a jest transmuted farther north into the terms of a black Mackintosh and red Macgregors.

The first name of fame passed on the Caledonian line is Ecclefechan, birthplace of Thomas Carlyle, now a prophet even in his own country, but it is recorded how a devout American pilgrim of earlier days found no responsive warmth in the minds of old neighbours. "Tam Carlyle—ay, there was Tam!" admitted an interrogated native. "He went tae London; they tell me he writes books. But there's his brither Jeems—he was the mahn o' that family. He drove mair pigs into Ecclefechan market than ony ither farmer in the parish!" Tom had carried his pigs to a better than any Dumfriesshire market. If we turned west by the Glasgow and South-Western Railway, we should soon come among the shrines of Burns and the monuments of Wallace. But let us rather take the central route, on which flourishes a greener memory.

ABBOTSFORD, ROXBURGHSHIRE

The "Waverley" route from Carlisle, a central one between those East and West Coast lines, so distinguishes itself as passing through the cream of the country associated with Sir Walter Scott, its first stage being the wilds of Liddesdale, where he spent seven holiday seasons collecting the Border Minstrelsy. This district, where "every field has its battle and every rivulet its song," can boast of many singers. From the days of Thomas the Rhymer comes down its long succession of ballad-makers who "saved others' names but left their own unsung." At Ednam was born James Thomson, bard of *The Seasons* and of "Rule, Britannia," who surely deserves a less prosaic monument than here recalls him. From Ednam, too, came Henry Lyte, a name not so familiar, but how many millions know his hymn "Abide with me"! Some of Horatius Bonar's hymns were written during his ministry at Kelso. About Denholm were the "Scenes of Infancy" of John Leyden, poet and scholar, cut off untimely. Near his humble home, now turned into a public library, is the lordly house of Minto, one of whose daughters wrote the "Flowers of the Forest." Thomas Pringle, the South African poet, was born at Blakelaw, near Yetholm, the Border seat of gipsy kings. Home, the author of *Douglas*, is said to have come from Ancrum, which can more certainly claim Dr. William Buchan of *Domestic Medicine* renown. Riddell, author of "Scotland Yet," began life as a Teviot shepherd. If we may touch on living names, was not Mr. Andrew Lang born among the "Soutars of Selkirk," who has gone so far *ultra crepidam*? But indeed a whole page might be filled with a bare catalogue of the bards of Tweed and Teviot.

The *genius loci*, greatest of all, while born in Edinburgh, sprang from a Border family of "Scotland's gentler blood." The cradle of his race was in Upper Teviotdale, near Hawick, that thriving "Glasgow of the Borders," among whose busy mills the old Douglas Tower still stands as an hotel, and rites older than Christian Scotland are cherished at its time-honoured Common Riding. Not far off are Harden, home of Wat Scott the reiver, and Branxholme, that after being repeatedly burned by the English, bears an inscription of its rebuilding by a Sir Walter Scott of Reformation times, whose namesake and descendant would make its name known so widely. At Sandyknowe farm, between the Eden and the Leader Water, he lived as a sickly child in his grandparents' charge, and under the massive ruin of Smailholm Tower, drank in with reviving health the inspiration of Border lore and romance—

> Ever, by the winter hearth,
> Old tales I heard of woe or mirth,
> Of lover's sleights, of ladies' charms,
> Of witches' spells, of warriors' arms;
> Of patriot battles, won of old
> By Wallace wight and Bruce the bold;
> Of later fields of feud and fight,
> When, pouring from their Highland height,
> The Scottish clans, in headlong sway,
> Had swept the scarlet ranks away.
> While stretch'd at length upon the floor,
> Again I fought each combat o'er,

> Pebbles and shells, in order laid,
> The mimic ranks of war display'd;
> And onward still the Scottish Lion bore,
> And still the scatter'd Southron fled before.

Later on, the old folks being dead, his sanatorium quarters were shifted to his aunt's home at Kelso, where also an uncle bought a house, inherited by the lucky poet. For a time he attended the Grammar School, whose pupils had for playground the adjacent ruins of the Abbey, so roughly handled in Border wars and by iconoclastic zealots. This boy had other resources than play, who could forget his dinner in the charms of Percy's *Reliques*; and his lameness did not hinder him from roaming over the beautiful country in which Tweed and Teviot meet. Their confluence encloses the ruins of Roxburgh Castle, once a favourite royal residence and strong Border fortress, before whose walls James II., trying to wrest it back from the English, was killed by the bursting of one of those new-fangled "engines" that were to break down moated castles, replaced by such sumptuous mansions as Floors, the modern *château* of the Duke of Roxburghe. Roxburgh town has disappeared more completely than its castle, its name surviving in that of the picturesque Border shire where, off and on, Scott spent much of his youth, photographing on a sensitive mind the scenes he has made famous, and getting to know the flesh-and-blood models of Meg Merrilies, Edie Ochiltree, Old Mortality, Dandie Dinmont, Josiah Cargill, and other "characters" that but for him might now be forgotten.

Kelso stands almost on the site of Roxburgh, but its place as county town is taken by Jedburgh, guard of the "Middle March," farther to the south, yet not so near the crooked border line. It stands upon a tributary of the Teviot, among "Eden scenes of crystal Jed," flowing down from the Cheviots. Tourists do not know what they miss by grudging time to divagate on the branches connecting the two main lines of the North British Railway. Jedburgh, birthplace of scientific celebrities, Sir David Brewster and Mrs. Somerville, has another grand Abbey, that suffered much from early English tourists; and its jail occupies the site of a vanished royal castle. In this old seat of "Jeddart justice," Scott began his career at the Bar, by the defence of such a poacher and sheep-stealer as his own forebears had been on a bolder scale. Here a few years later, he met Wordsworth in the house recently marked by a memorial tablet; and other dwellings are pointed out as having housed Queen Mary and Prince Charlie, while Burns has left a warm record of his visit, so many of Scotland's idols has Jedburgh known, and may well reproach the hasty travellers who pass it by.

The young advocate did not waste much of his genius on defending sheep-stealers and the like; but in those halcyon days of patronage, through the influence of his chief, the Duke of Buccleuch, he soon got the snug berth of Sheriff of Selkirk. This brought him to live at Ashestiel on the Tweed, where he spent his happiest days, writing his best poems, and beginning *Waverley*, to be laid by and forgotten for years. Selkirk, too, has the misfortune of lying off the main line; but strangers would do well to turn aside here for the wild pastoral scenes of St. Mary's Loch and the "Dowie Dens of Yarrow." Too many, like Wordsworth, put off this trip to rheumatic years; yet it may be easily done by the coach routes from Selkirk and from Moffat on the Caledonian line, that meet at Tibbie Shiels' Inn, whose visitors' book enshrines such a collection of autographs; and its homely fame scorns the pretensions of the new "hotel." This is the heart of Ettrick Forest, where stands a monument of its shepherd, James Hogg, unfairly caricatured as the genial buffoon of the *Noctes*, but second only to Burns as a popular poet, and best known over the English-speaking world by his "Bird of the wilderness, blithesome and cumberless." All the schooling he had was a few months in early childhood; he taught himself to write on slate stones of the hillside where he herded cows, and this art he had to relearn when he first tried to sing of green Ettrick—

> In many a rustic lay,
> Her heroes, hills, and verdant groves;
> Her wilds and valleys fresh and gay,
> Her shepherds' and her maidens' loves.

The North British junction for Selkirk is at Galashiels, another thriving woollen town, whose mills may not have improved the physique of the "braw lads of Gala Water." Before reaching this, the main line, holding up the Tweed where it is looked down upon by a colossal statue of Wallace, passes two more of David I.'s quartet of Abbeys, so that the tourist has no excuse for not visiting Dryburgh and Melrose. Melrose, indeed, is a tourist shrine, that owns a somewhat sheltered climate, with natural charms enough to fill its adjacent Hydropathic and the hotels about the Abbey and the Cross, nucleus of a group of Tweedside hamlets, to which warm red stone, sometimes filched from the ruins, gives a snug and cheerful aspect; then the nakedness of the slopes, held by Scott a beauty, though he laboured to clothe it with plantations, hides nooks like that Rhymer's Glen, where True Thomas was spirited away by the Fairy Queen, and that Fairy Dean in which the White Lady of Avenel appeared to Halbert Glendinning. Above rise the triple Eildon Hills, in whose caverns Arthur and his knights lie sleeping, and from the top, as our Last Minstrel boasted, can be seen more than forty spots famed in history or song.

Of Melrose Abbey, the finest remains of Scottish ecclesiastical architecture in its golden age, and of its illustrious tombs, let the guide-books speak, and the romance that deals with this neighbourhood of "Kennaquhair," an *alias* plagiarised by Carlyle in his *Weissnichtwo*. Visiting it "by pale moonlight" or otherwise, few will not turn three miles up the river to that other showplace, Abbotsford, the Delilah of his imagination that bound Scott in withs of care and set him to toiling for Philistines. The baronial mansion, now overlooked by outlying villas of Galashiels, was all his own creation, and most of the trees were planted by himself, in the absorbing process that began with buying a hundred ill-famed acres, and ended with such unfortunate success in making, as he said, "a silk purse out of a sow's ear." When one thinks what it cost him, this exhibition of artificial feudalism has its painful side; yet another Sir Walter, a romancer of our own generation, declares that it "would make an oyster enthusiastic." But more moving is the pilgrimage from Melrose down the Tweed to where, in St. Mary's Aisle of Dryburgh Abbey, the most beautiful fragment of a noble fane, among the tombs of his kin lies at rest

Scotland's most illustrious son, he who best displayed the warp and woof that makes the chequered pattern of his country's nature.

MELROSE, ROXBURGHSHIRE

When will Cockney revilers learn that Scotland is not all thrift, caution, and kailyard prose, but a nation showing two main strains, which Mr. John Morley suggests as the explanation of Gladstone's complex character? One component may be hard, practical, frugal, in politics tending to democracy, in religion to logic; but this has been crossed by a spirit, better bred in the romantic Highlands, that is generous, proud, quick-tempered, reckless, reverent towards the past, rather than eager for progress. The painter of Scottish life must recognise how Fitz-James and Roderick Dhu are countrymen with Bailie Nicol Jarvie and Andrew Fairservice, how Flora MacIvor is not less a Scotswoman than Mause Headrigg or Jenny Dennison, and how the Jacobite and the Presbyterian enthusiasm smacked of the same soil. If one shut one's eye to half the case, it would be easy to make out that rash impetuosity flourished beyond the Tweed rather than the thistly prudence taken for a more congenial crop.

Scott comprehended both of these elements. By birth and training he belonged to the Saxon, by sympathy to the Celt. If his father was a douce Edinburgh "writer," one of his forebears had been that "Beardie" who bound himself never to shave till the Stuarts came back to their own. Brought up under the dry light of the Revolution Settlement, in his reminiscences of childhood he transforms a worthy parish minister into a "Venerable Priest," and in later life he came to be himself little better than an Episcopalian. It may be owned he had no more religion than became a Cavalier; even the romance of superstition did not take much hold on him, and that rhyming "White Lady" has not even a ghostly life on his page. His favourite heroes are the like of Montrose and Claverhouse, yet he can do justice to the stern virtues of the Covenanters. In the sober historian mood he duly warns his grandchild how life was galled and fettered in the good old days, which he was too willing to see *couleur de rose* when their picturesque incidents offered themselves to the romancer. He turns a blind eye, perhaps, too much on the faults of knights and princes, yet he knows the worth of ploughmen and fisherfolk, and into Halbert Glendinning's and Henry Morton's mouths he puts sentiments to which John Bright or Cobden might say amen. He is happiest, indeed, in the past, when "the wrath of our ancestors was coloured *gules*," whereas we have learned, like Mr. Trulliber's wife, to be Christians and take the law of our enemies. His appetite for imaginary bloodshed is a sore offence to writers like Mark Twain, who appear less scandalised that a pork-baron, a corn-lord, or a cotton-king should plot to be rich by starving children on the other side of the world. But Scott's very failings reflect the character of his countrymen, who, Highland and Lowland, have been mighty fighters before the Lord on a much wider field than from Berwick to John o' Groat's House. The pity is that this imaginative writer, who knew all characters better than his own, should have fancied himself a shrewd man of business, a part for which he was too generous and trustful. Of his personal merits, the most marked is that in a class of sedentary craftsmen notoriously apt to be irritable, bilious, jealous, and vainglorious, Walter Scott stands out by hearty, wholesome, human qualities which present him as the type of a Scottish gentleman.

> Whatever record leap to light,
> He never shall be shamed!

SCOTT'S FAVOURITE VIEW FROM BEMERSIDE HILL, ROXBURGHSHIRE

To have done with the "Scott Country," we should hold on westward up the Tweed to where its sources almost mingle with those of the Clyde, below the bold mass of Tinto and other hills that might claim a less modest title. This route would bring us by the renowned inn of Clovenfords, "howff" of Christopher North and many another choice spirit, by Ashestiel, then by Innerleithen, set up as a spa through its claim to represent St. Ronan's; and so to Peebles, a haunt of pleasure since the days when James I. wrote of "Peeblis to the play." For some reason or other, Peebles and Paisley have become butts of Gotham banter, their very names attracting the sly jests by which Scotsmen love to make fun of themselves. But neither of them is a town to be sneezed at. Peebles, for its part, after falling into a rather sleepy state, has been wakened up in our time through the Tontine "hottle," that so much excited Meg Dods' scorn; the huge Hydropathic that has introduced German bath practice into Scotland; and the Institution bestowed on the town by William Chambers, who hence set out to turn the proverbial half-crown into a goodly fortune. Was it not at this Institution that the local Mutual Improvement Society gravely debated the question, "*Shall* the material Universe be destroyed?" and decided, by a majority of one, in the negative! When Sir Cresswell Cresswell, from his peculiar bench, laid down the dictum that marriages between May and December often turned out ill, it must have been a Paisley statistician who wrote to him for the data on which he founded his assertion that "marriages contracted in the latter part of the year, etc." But Paisley has its manufacturing prosperity to fling in the teeth of calumny; and Peebles has romantic as well as comic associations, notably its Neidpath Castle and its Manor Water Glen, haunted by memories of the Black Dwarf.

The leisurely tourist might gain Edinburgh by a branch line through Peebles, and this route can be recommended to the hippogriffs of cycles and motors. Beyond the Catrail, ancient barrier of the Picts or the Britons of Strathclyde, our main railroad, as its way is, keeps on straight up the course of the Gala, leaving to its right the dreary Lammermoors; then between the Castles of Borthwick and Crichton, it enters on the more prosaic Lothian country. To the left is seen the Pentland ridge, and straight ahead springs up the cone of Arthur's Seat beaconing us to Edinburgh, goal of the race for which a Caledonian express will be speeding along the farther side of the Pentlands.

And not a kilt have we seen yet, since leaving London! Of this more anon; kilts are not at home on the Borders, though I have seen one on the Welsh Marches, worn in conjunction with a pith helmet by a retired Liverpool tradesman. Since "gloves of steel" and "helmets barred" went out of fashion on Tweedside, the local colour has been that modest shepherd's plaid displayed in Lord Brougham's trousers to the ribaldry of *Punch*, and even that goes out of homely wear. You may buy Scott and Douglas tartans in the shops, but they seem vain things, fondly invented, as indeed are some of the patterns now seen in the Highlands. But there will be a good show of kilts in Edinburgh Castle, where once they were like to be bestowed in the dungeon:—

> Wae worth the loons that made the laws
> To hang a man for gear—

> To reave o' life for sic a cause
> As *lifting* horse or mare!

And here our North British express, panting through the fat Lothians, comes to slacken under the castellated walls of that gaol which tourists are apt to take for the Castle—no true kilts to be looked for there nowadays, yet perhaps at the Police Court under the head of drunk and disorderly! So let us leave the Borderland behind with a quotation from an American writer (*Penelope in Scotland*) who knows what's what, and who at first sight fairly loses her heart to Edinburgh, *haars*, east winds, and all, that are its thorns in the flesh. "I hope," she very sensibly says, "that those in authority will never attempt to convene a Peace Congress in Edinburgh, lest the influence of the Castle be too strong for the delegates. They could not resist it nor turn their backs upon it, since, unlike other ancient fortresses, it is but a stone's-throw from the front windows of all the hotels. They might mean never so well, but they would end by buying dirk hat-pins and claymore brooches for their wives; their daughters would all run after the kilted regiment and marry as many of the pipers as asked them, and before night they would all be shouting with the noble Fitz-Eustace,

> Where's the coward that would not dare
> To fight for such a land?"

CHAPTER II
AULD REEKIE

"Auld Reekie," as it is fondly called, still raises its smokiest chimneys and most weathered walls along the "hoary ridge of ancient town" that culminates in the Castle Rock, looking across a long central line of gardens to the farther swell of land on which stands the New Town of Scott's day. But New Town now seems a misnomer, since the cramped site of the old city, itself much sweetened and aerated by innovations, is surrounded by newer towns expanding in other directions. Southwards, of late years, Edinburgh has grown more rapidly up to the foot of the hills that here edge the suburbs of Newington, Grange, and Morningside. Westwards she spreads out towards Corstorphine Hill and Craiglockhart. On the east her progress is barred by the mass of Arthur's Seat, but round the base of this creep rows of tall houses that will soon connect her with Portobello, that minor Margate of the capital, now comprised within her municipal boundaries. Northwards, she goes on "flinging her white arms to the sea," which she almost touches at Granton and Trinity; and a long unlovely street leads to the Piræus of this modern Athens, Leith, still stiffly standing aloof in civic independence. Including Leith, which refuses to be included, the Scottish metropolis began the century with a population not far short of 400,000.

On high in the midst of these modern settings, the charms of Old Edinburgh are thrown into becoming relief, as the medley smartness of Princes Street is enhanced by its facing the grim backs of the High Street "lands." Ruskin and other critics have said hard things of the New Town's architects; but their strictures do not go without question. What, at all events, must strike strangers is an imposing solidity of the modern buildings, whether tall "stairs"—*Anglicé* flats—or roomy private houses, nearly all built of a grey stone that seems in keeping with the atmosphere; and this not only in the central streets and squares, but in outer suburbs, innocent of brick and stucco. If a too classical regularity has been aimed at, this is tempered by the unevenness of the ground, breaking up the "draughty parallelograms," giving vistas into the open country, and at night such long panoramas of glittering lights displayed on slopes and crests. The place, says R. L. Stevenson, who has so well caught the picturesque points of his native city, "is full of theatre tricks in the way of scenery.... You turn a corner, and there is the sun going down into the Highland hills. You look down an alley, and see ships tacking for the Baltic." And if the city fathers have been ill advised in the past, its municipality may claim the credit of being first in the kingdom to take powers for disinfecting it against the plague of mendacious and hideous advertisements that are too much allowed to pock our highways and byways.

EDINBURGH FROM "REST AND BE THANKFUL"

A peculiar feature of the city is its "Bridges," by which certain streets span others at different levels, physically and socially. From the unique Dean Bridge, in the heart of the West End, one overlooks what might be taken for a Highland glen but for the lines of mansions that edge it above. When I came to Edinburgh as a homesick little schoolboy, appalled by the "boundless continuity" of street, I devoted my first Saturday freedom to an attempt at discovering the open country. This was happily before the days of schoolboys being driven and drilled to play. Striking the Water of Leith at Stockbridge, I turned along the path leading into this glen that might well satisfy desires for a green solitude. But on reaching the village of Dean, embedded below the bridge, I climbed up to find myself beside the dome of St. George's Church, lost deeper than ever in that bewildering city. Still, a little trimmed and tamed, an oasis of wooded bank shuts in the rushing stream, now purified and stocked with trout, where we were content to catch loaches and sticklebacks.

What a loss to this city was the classically-minded Gothicism or carelessness through which came to be rooted up so many noble trees that once dotted the parks of Drumsheugh and Bellevue! But Edinburgh has been well endowed afresh with open spaces and shrubberies, those that separate the blocks of the New Town mainly private joint-stock paradises, yet serving for public amenity. The Old Town is enclosed between the noble stretch of the Princes Street Gardens on the north, and on the south the open Meadows, with its "Philosopher's Walk" of Dugald Stewart's and Playfair's days, rising into the Bruntsfield Links. Then the city is almost ringed about by parks, more than one of them including grand features of natural scenery. Philadelphia is the only city I know which has such wild scenes at her very doors, in her case collected together in the Fairmount Park, where miles of hill and river landscape have been left almost untouched among the streets and suburbs, yet boasting no points so noble as the head of Arthur's Seat, with its girdle of crags, screes, and lakes.

This miniature Ben, imposing as it looks, is under 1000 feet high, and easily climbed. Those almost past their climbing days may seek Blackford Hill on the south side, where Scott tells us that he bird's-nested as a truant boy, and speaks of it as at a later day brought under cultivation; but it has relapsed again to its native wildness, laid out as a rough park and as site for the squat domes of the new Observatory. From this eminence one gets Marmion's view of the city, now grown up to its foot, shut in between Arthur's Seat and the wooded ridge of Corstorphine, and bounded to the north across the Firth by the heights of Fife, above which, in clear weather, stand up the blue bastions of the Highlands. Behind Blackford, one may keep up the wooded hollow of the Hermitage, by a public path following the stream, and thus gain the Braid Hills, overlooking the city a little farther back. Keeping along their edge, at some risk from flying golf balls, one can hold on to the hotel built between the old and the new south roads. Here, at the terminus of suburban trams, looking to the Pentlands up the valley of the Braid Burn, by which runs a field path towards Swanston, the country home of R. L. Stevenson, one might hardly guess oneself so near a great city, but for the lordly poorhouse and fever-hospital buildings to the back of Craiglockhart Hill.

EDINBURGH FROM SALISBURY CRAGS—EVENING

In the very heart of the city are view-points fine enough to content hasty travellers, from the battlements of the Castle, from the spire of Scott's Monument, from the slopes of the Calton Hill, with its array of ready-made ruins and monuments with which Edinburgh has sought to live up to her classical pretensions. This rises beyond the east end of Princes Street, opposite the battlemented gaol, and a little way past that Charing Cross of Auld Reekie, where its main ways meet between the Post Office, the Register House and the tower of a new North British Hotel looking down upon the glass roofs of the sunken Waverley Station. At the other end of Princes Street, an opening before the Caledonian Station may be called Edinburgh's Piccadilly Circus, radiating into its Mayfair quarter. This end is dom-inated by the Castle, suggesting to Algerian travellers a duodecimo edition of that wonderful rock-set city Constantine. It shows little of the modern fortress, rather a pile of ugly barracks which a Japanese cruiser could knock to pieces from the Firth; but one understands how in old days its site made it a Gibraltar citadel, that often could hold out when the town was overrun by foemen taking care to keep themselves beyond range of the Castle guns. Taylor, the Water Poet, who had seen something of war in his youth, judged it "so strongly grounded, bounded, and founded, that by force of man it can never be confounded." The King himself did not gain admittance on his recent visit without a ceremony of summons by the Lord Lyon King of Arms; but all and sundry, at reasonable hours, may stroll across its drawbridge to lounge on the ramparts, to be conducted over historic relics by veteran ciceroni, or to wait for the stunning report of the gun, which, fired from Greenwich at one o'clock, brings every watch within hearing to the test.

From this "Maiden Castle," safe refuge for princesses of the good old times, a conscientious tourist makes for Holyrood by the long line of High Street and Canongate, bringing him past most of the historic sites and monuments—the "Heart of Midlothian," the Parliament House, the swept and garnished Cathedral of St. Giles, beside which John Knox now lies literally buried in a highway, as was Dr. Johnson's pious wish for him; the restored Market Cross, the Tron Church, Knox's House, which counts rather among Edinburgh's Apocrypha, and many an-other ancient mansion, once alive with Scotland's proudest names, now degraded to an Alsatia of huge dingy tenements, swarming forth vice and misery at night-fall. The way narrows through an unsavoury slum as it approaches the deserted home of kings, beyond which opens a park such as no king has at his back door.

Holyrood was originally an abbey, founded by David I. "in gratitude," says the legend, "for his miraculous deliverance from a stag on Holy Rood Day, and prompted thereto by a dream." Similar stories are told of many another prince less disposed to ecclesiastical benefactions than David, that "sair saint to the crown"; even John of England founded one abbey, at Beaulieu, as an act of grace prompted by nightmare visions. Beside David's Abbey of the Holy Cross sprang up a pal-ace that, as well the sacred precincts, suffered much in the troubles of the Stuart reigns, being frequently burned or spoiled by English tourists of their period, on the last occasion "personally conducted" by one Oliver Cromwell, who had small respect either for palaces or abbeys. In Charles II.'s time it was rebuilt somewhat after the style of Hampton Court, while the Abbey, devastated by a Presbyterian mob, came to be refitted with a too heavy roof that crushed it into utter ruin. The present building is thus modern, but for the ruins behind, and the restored portion incorporating Queen Mary's apartments. The name of the Sanctuary opposite was no vain one up till about half a century ago, when impecunious debtors used to take asylum within its bounds, privileged to issue free on Sundays, else venturing forth to feast or sport only at the risk of thrilling adventures with bailiffs.

Everyone who has been to Edinburgh knows the sights of this show place: the portraits of Scottish kings, more or less mythical, "awful examples" as works of art, the whole gallery, it is said, done by a Dutch painter of the seventeenth century for a lump sum of £250; the tapestried rooms of Darnley; the Queen's bedchamber; and the dark stain on the flooring where Rizzio is believed to have gasped out his life, after being dragged from the side of his mistress. Every reader must know Scott's story of the traveller in some patent fluid for removing stains, who pressed the use of his nostrum on the horrified custodian. What every stranger does not know is how this "virtuous palace where no monarch dwells" is still used for functions of state. Annually, in May, the Lord High Commissioner takes up his quarters here as representative of the Crown in the General Assembly of the Church, when green peas ought to come into season to make their first appearance on the quasi-royal table. Ireland, that makes such loud boast of her grievances, basks in the smiles of a Lord-Lieutenant all the year, while poor patient Scotland has a blink of reflected royalty for one scrimp fortnight, during which the old palace wakes to the life of *levèes*, drawingrooms, and dinners, where black gowns and coats are more in evidence than in most courtly circles. The Commissioner's procession from the palace to open the Assembly lights up the old Canongate with a martial display; and more or less festivity is held within the walls according to the wealth or liberality of the Commissioner, who, like the Lord Mayor of London, should be a rich man to fill his office with due *éclat*. But when King Edward VII. recently visited Edinburgh, to the regret of the citizens, he did not take up his quarters in the palace, pronounced unsuitable by the prosaic reason of its drains being somewhat too Georgian, a matter that has now been amended.

A more occasional function fitly transacted here is the election of representative peers for Scotland in a new parliament. As every schoolboy ought to know, our Constitution admits only sixteen Scottish peers to sit in Parliament, most of them indeed having place there in virtue of British peerages—the Duke of Atholl as Lord Strange, for instance, the Duke of Montrose as Lord Graham, and so forth. Of those left out in the cold, sixteen are "elected" by a somewhat cut-and-dried process very free from the heat and excitement of popular voting. As I have seen it, the ceremony seemed to lack impressiveness. Some dozen gentlemen in pot hats and shooting jackets assembled in the Picture Gallery before an audience chiefly consisting of ladies, more than one of these legislators in mien and appearance suggesting what Fielding says about Joseph Andrews, that he might have been taken for a nobleman by one who had not seen many noblemen. Each of the privileged order, in turn, wrote and read out a list of the peers for whom he voted, usually ending "and myself." Certain practically-minded peers sent in their votes by post. The most moving incident was the expected one of an advocate in wig and gown rising to put in for a client some unrecognised claim to a title or protest as to precedency, duly listened to and noted down. The whole ceremony struck one as rather a waste of time; but perhaps the same might be said of most ceremonies. One thing has to be remembered about these unimposing lords, that they are a highly select body in point of blue blood, all representing old families, as the fount of their honour was dried up at the Union, and the king can make an honest man as soon as a Scottish peer.

The tourist who comes in for any of such functions will realise the truth of what R. L. Stevenson says for his native city:—

> "There is a spark among the embers; from time to time the old volcano smokes. Edinburgh has but partly abdicated, and still wears, in parody, her metropolitan trappings. Half a capital and half a country town, the whole city leads a double existence; it has long trances of the one and flashes of the other; like the king of the Black Isles, it is half alive and half a monumental marble. There are armed men and cannon in the citadel overhead; you may see the troops marshalled on the high parade; and at night after the early winter evenfall, and in the morning before the laggard winter dawn, the wind carries abroad over Edinburgh the sound of drums and bugles. Grave judges sit bewigged in what was once the scene of imperial deliberations. Close by in the High Street perhaps the trumpets may sound about the stroke of noon; and you see a troop of citizens in tawdry masquerade; tabard above, heather-mixture trowser below, and the men themselves trudging in the mud among unsympathetic bystanders. The grooms of a well-appointed circus tread the streets with a better presence. And yet these are the Heralds and Pursuivants of Scotland, who are about to proclaim a new law of the United Kingdom before two-score boys, and thieves, and hackney-coachmen."

Tourists are too much in the way of seeing no more of Edinburgh than its historic lions and rich museums, as indicated in the guide-books. I would invite them to pay more attention to the suburbs straggling on three sides into such fine hill scenery as is the environment of this city. Open cabs are easily to be had in the chief thoroughfares; and Edinburgh cabmen have the name of being rarely decent and civil, as if the Shorter Catechism made an antidote to the human demoralisation spread from that honest friend of man, the horse. Give a London Jehu something over his fare, and his first thought seems to be that you are a person to be imposed upon; but I, for one, never had the same experience here. I know of a stranger who took a cheaper mode of finding his way through Edinburgh; he had himself booked as an express parcel and put in charge of a telegraph messenger, who would not leave him without a receipt duly signed at his destination. But the wandering pedestrian is at great advantage where he seldom has out of sight such landmarks as the Castle and Arthur's Seat. There is no better way of seeing the city than from the top of the tramcars that run in all directions, the main line being a circular route from the Waverley Station round the west side of the Castle, then through the south suburbs, and back beneath Arthur's Seat to the Post Office. Public motor cars also ply their terror along the chief thoroughfares. The trams are on the cable system, invented for the steep ascents of San Francisco, but out of favour in most cities. The excuse for its adoption here was that bunches of over-head wires would spoil such amenities as are the city's stock in tourist trade. It has the objectionable habit of keeping up along the line a rattle disquieting to nervous people, while the car itself steals upon one like a thief in the night; but it appears that accidents to life and limb are not so common as hitches in the working.

CRAIGMILLAR CASTLE, NEAR EDINBURGH

The trams now run on Sunday, an innovation that shocks many good folk, brought up in days when the streets of a Scottish city were as stricken by the plague, unless at the hours when all the population came streaming on foot to and from their different places of worship. A few years ago, I felt it my duty to correct the late Max O'Rell, who had gathered some wonderful stories supposed to illustrate the manners of Scotland. As he related how, getting into an Edinburgh tramcar on Sunday, his companion insisted on their riding inside not to be seen of men, one was able to inform him that since the days of Moses no public vehicle had disturbed Edinburgh's Sabbath quiet. It is not so now; and all the old stories about "whustlin' on the Sabbath" and so forth will soon be legends, so fast is the peculiar observance of Scottish piety melting away.

R. L. Stevenson humorously called himself "a countryman of the Sabbath," but this institution is not so clearly a native of Scotland as has been taken for granted. John Knox played bowls on Sunday; and the rigidity that came in later was due as much to English Puritanism as to the thrawnness of Scottish revolt against Catholic practices. Whatever its origin, Sabbatarianism once weighed heavily on human nature north of the Tweed. "Is this a day to be talking of days!" was the rebuke of the Highlander to a tourist who ventured to remark that it was a fine Sunday. Not so many years ago, I have known a Highland farmer refuse the loan of a girdle to bake scones for a breadless family, "not on the Sabbath"; yet this orthodox worthy and his sons, living as far from a church as from a baker's shop, seemed to spend most of the day of rest lying by the roadside smoking their pipes and reading the newspaper. An exiled Scot, in far distant lands, has told me how the shadow of the coming Sabbath began to fall on his youth as early as Wednesday night. The holy day was a term of imprisonment for juvenile spirits, its treadmill two long services, chiefly sermon, sometimes run into one, or separated by only a few minutes' interval, to economise short winter light in which worshippers might have to trudge miles to church. It is in the Highlands and other out-of-the-way parts, of course, that such austerities linger, while the urban populations more readily adopt English compromises on this head.

In Edinburgh one generation has seen a great thawing of the Sabbath spirit. I can remember the excitement caused all over Scotland by a sermon in which Dr. Norman Macleod proclaimed that there was no harm in taking a walk on Sunday. The *Scotsman*, a paper that has never much flattered its readers' prejudices, came out with a sly humorous article headed "Murder of Moses' Law by Dr. Norman Macleod," and it is said that some good people read this in the sense that the "broad" divine had actually committed homicide. Even earlier, Edinburgh people had tacitly sanctioned a walk to a cemetery, as echoing the teachings of the pulpit. The story went that the present King, when at Edinburgh University, was sternly denied admission to the Botanic Gardens on Sunday; but he might unblamed have taken a stroll through the adjacent tombs of Warriston. From the Dean Cemetery, the West End ventured on extending its Sunday ramble as far as "Rest and be Thankful" on Corstorphine Hill; then it was a fresh scandal when a very Lord of Session came to show himself on this road in tweeds, instead of the full phylacteries that might attest previous church-going. Of another judge living at Corstorphine it is told that he once sought to mend the morals of a cobbler helplessly drunk at his gate on Sunday afternoon, but was met by the hiccoughed repartee, "Wha's you, without your Sabbath blacks?"

LINLITHGOW PALACE

In my youth the police would put a stop to skating or such like diversions on Sabbath; but now Sunday bicycles flit over the country; the iniquity of a Sunday band is tolerated in the parks; while a society is suffered to promote Sunday concerts and lectures indoors. Another sign of the times is that Christmas in Edinburgh begins to be almost as much observed as the national festival of New Year's Day, whereas orthodox Presbyterianism once made a point of ignoring fasts and feasts sanctioned by prelacy or popery. As for its own fasts, they have long been transmuted into junketings; and the sacramental "preachings" of large towns are now frankly abolished in favour of public holidays answering to the English saturnalia of St. Lubbock, observed only by banks across the Tweed. The Communion, in old days administered but once or twice a year, and regarded in some parts with such awe that few ventured to put themselves forward as participants, is now a frequent rite in Presbyterian Churches, whose congregations are throwing off their horror of ornament and ceremony, as may be seen in St. Giles. Old-fashioned English rectors of the Simeon school have been known to shake their heads at the services now read in the ears of descendants of that Jenny Geddes who so forcibly testified against a prayer-book declared by ribald jesters hateful to Scotland through its too frequent mention of "Collect."

The honest stranger, then, has nothing to fear from the austerity of Scottish morals, not even the supposed risk of being married by mistake. It will be his own fault if he fail to find a welcome across the Tweed. Effusive manners are not the Scot's strong point, and he may be accused of a certain suspicion of offence, kept sharp by the careless and not ill-natured insolence of southrons who are so free with their jovial jests about "bawbees" and such like, well-worn and rusty pleasantries coined in the days of Bute's unpopularity and Johnson's bearish dogmatism. Among the baser sorts of Scots are still current inverse sarcasms against English "pock-puddings," conceived as fat and greedy; but they would have to be fished up from a low social stratum by the travelling gent who cannot understand that, however little disposed Sandy may have been to hang his head for honest poverty, he ill relishes its being flung in his face. "A sooth bourd is nae bourd," says the old proverb; but now, what with tourists, and trade, and Scotsmen who come back again, bringing the spoils of the world with them, the reproach of poverty ceases to be so sore a one.

Though in the eyes of busy Glasgow Edinburgh may pass as a retired capital, living on its means of attraction, it has in fact several industries from which to earn a livelihood. Along with the lodging and amusing of strangers, it must do a good business in the tartans, pebbles, silver-work, and other showy wares displayed in Princes Street shop windows. "Edinbury Rock," done up in tartan wrappers, is much pressed upon the notice of tourists; the same indeed being sold in other towns under their own name. As for shortbread, scones, biscuits, and other manufactures of the "Land of Cakes," these have invaded London, where every baker not a German is like to be a Scot. It will be noted by Cockney revilers as a proof of Scotch thriftiness, which might bear another interpretation, that what costs a penny in a London baker's shop is here sold for a halfpenny. Well known to strangers are the Princes Street confectioners' shops, several of them extensive restaurants like that one which, crowning its storeys of accommodation, has a roof garden looking upon the Castle opposite.

THE BASS ROCK—A TRANQUIL EVENING

The staple trades of Edinburgh have come to be printing and publishing, and, as the nettle grows near the dock, brewing and distilling. The great Scottish publishing firms have of late years shown a tendency to gravitate towards London; but more than one still keeps its headquarters here, beside some of the largest and best printing establishments in the kingdom. It must be confessed that what is spoken of as "*the* trade," is whisky, too much consumed about the premises, as visitors are apt to note. The worst shame a Scotsman need take for Scotland is on account of what Englishmen specially distinguish as "Scotch." I never heard sadder jest than the laughing comment of a group of Dundee lasses, as they passed a braw lad wallowing in the gutter at mid-day—"He's having his holidays!" Yet as to this reproach, something might be said in plea for mitigation of judgment. Something to the purpose was said by that experienced toper who explained how "whusky makes ye drunk before ye are fu', but yill makes ye fu' before ye are drunk." The whisky drunk by the lower classes here is a demon that takes no disguise. It seems that, while there is more brutal intoxication in Scotland, there may be less toping sottishness than in England. Men seen so helplessly overcome at the ninth hour of a holiday are perhaps of ordinarily sober habits, all the more readily affected by occasional indulgence in fiery spirit. A woman frequenting public-houses implies a lower depth of degradation. In the north, a larger proportion of the population are abstainers; young people and the class of domestic servants for instance, drink water where in English families they would expect beer. In all classes, there are still too many Scotsmen religious in the worship of their native Bacchus, vulgar and violent deity as he is; but every year adds to the number of Protestants against this perverted fanaticism. By the Forbes Mackenzie Act, all public-houses are closed on Sunday, when, however, if all stories be true, a good deal of *shebeening* or illicit drinking goes on in the cities. It is not unreasonable to suppose that the austerity of Scottish Sabbatarianism has driven many into vicious indulgence; and much is to be hoped from the churches taking an interest in honest amusement as a help and not a hindrance to religion. But a sneer often thrown out by strangers against the supposed hypocrisy of Scotsmen, only shows ignorance of a country where those most concerned about Sabbath observance have long been the deadliest enemies of drinking habits.

Whisky, as well as golf, has now so masterfully invaded England, that this can no longer be called "Scottish Drink," as it was not by Burns. In his day, home-brewed beer was the Lowland beverage, of which a Cromwellian soldier complained as more like brose for its thickness. Up to our day "Edinburgh Ale" made the capital's chief contribution to the heady gaiety of nations. Whisky came in from the Highlands, its name a contraction of *uisgebeatha*, "water of life," which Burns and Scott write *usquebaugh*, the Celtic word for water being the same that appears in so many river names *Esk, Usk, Exe, Axe*, and so forth. Even in the Highlands, this mountain dew would seem to have supplanted beer within historic times; and old writers admire the temperance as much as the honesty and courage of Highlanders. Both Highland and Lowland gentlemen preferred brandy, in the days when, as Lord Cockburn tells us, claret was hawked about the Edinburgh streets in a cart, a jug of any reasonable size being filled for sixpence.

> Firm and erect the Caledonian stood,
> Old was his mutton, and his claret good.
> Let him drink port! a beef-fed statesman cried.
> He drank the poison and his spirit died.

The preference for French wine and spirits before the days of Hanoverian fiscalities, relates to the old alliance with France, which has left its mark also on Scottish speech. That warning cry "Gardy-loo" (*gardez l'eau*), which gave such scandal to early English tourists, was of course a survival of a far-spread practice in cities before the days of drainage or even of ash-backets (*baquets*). Many French household words are used in Scotland at this day, as "caraff" (*carafe*), "ashet" (*assiette*), a "jiggot" of mutton (*gigot*) a "haggis" (*hachis*); and Burns's "silver tassie" was of course a *tasse*. A "cummer" (*commère*) "canna be fashed" (*se fâcher*) to step out to the "merchant's," who may be "douce" or "dour" and an "honest" man (*honnête*), though sharp in his bargains. "Ma certie (*certes*), that's a braw (*brave*) vest!" quoth a lass to her lad, a word here used like the French *garçon* or *gars*, while *gosse* will be distinguished as a "laddie," who grows to be a "young lad" in spite of orgies on sour "grozers" or "grozets" and "gheans," which in France are *groseilles* and *guignes*, but in England gooseberries and wild cherries. French names too have taken root in Scotland, Janet (Jeannette) being very common with one sex, as Louis or Ludovic is not unknown in the other. For the matter of that, one might string together instances of how the well of Old English flows undefiled by time in the north.

> Then brought to him that maiden meek
> *Hose* and *shoon* and *sark* and *breek*.

These words are used to this day in every Scottish cottage, as once in the stately style of an early southron minstrel. Shakespeare and the Bible show many picked phrases which are now wild flowers in the north; and high example might be found for the *shalls* and *wills* that here run loose from the enclosures of modern grammarians. But as Mr. David MacRitchie suggests in an interesting pamphlet, "to *doubt* that one is *colded* and can't go to *the* church," seem rather specimens of French idioms transplanted during the three centuries or so that Capets and Stuarts stood together against the Plantagenets.

Protestantism availed to draw Scotland from the arms of France into those of England; then Prelacy and Presbytery set the near neighbours again at odds. For some generations, the young Scotsmen who had once sought the Catholic schools of the Continent, were more in the way of finishing their education at Dutch or German Universities. Scotland had also an old connection, chiefly in the way of trade, with Scandinavia and Poland, in both of which countries Scottish family names are naturalised, as Swedish Dicksons and Polish Gordons. Scots students of our day still look to Germany, under whose professors they are apt to forget the Shorter Catechism for the categories of Kant and the secret of Hegel. The Union was not fully consummated till Macs began to make themselves at home in Oxford and Cambridge, while for a time the renown of Scottish philosophy drew some of the promising English youth to Edinburgh, whose medical school kept up the attraction. In the last generation or two, Scotsmen have been only too ready to go south for education, seeking a stamp of Anglified gentility as well as better qualities which were perhaps not to be had from those rude old dominies under whom the young laird and the barefoot loon once sat together in friendly hatred of "carritch" and rudiments.

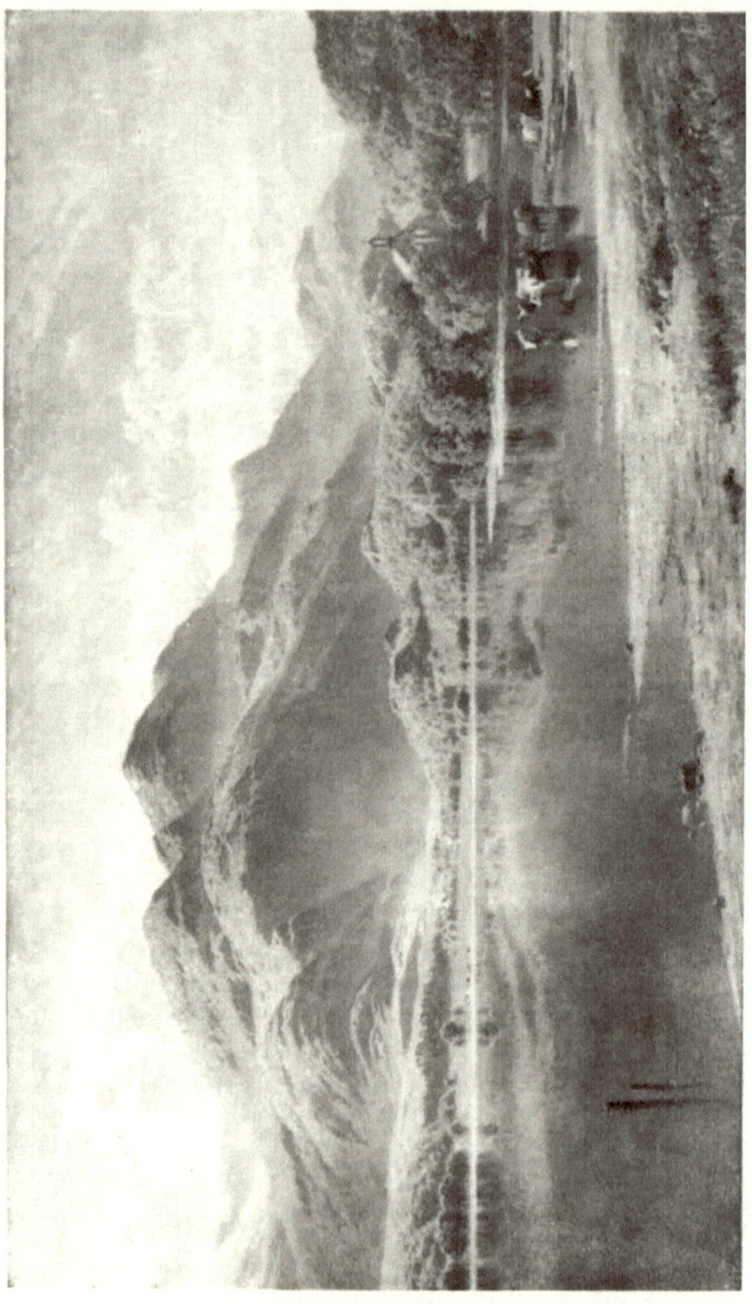

LOCH ACHRAY, THE TROSSACHS, PERTHSHIRE

Such foreign communications cannot but help young Scotsmen to put their native prejudices in due proportion, and to doubt if the sun of truth has always shown most clearly in the sky of one small people much beset by mists and east winds. Yet Scottish parents seem much "left to themselves" in sending their sons and daughters beyond Edinburgh for schooling. One of the most important industries of this city has come to be education. It abounds in teaching of all kinds, from its venerable University to spick and span board schools. Those who believe the fable of Scotch niggardliness should consider that no place in the United Kingdom, unless it be Bedford, is so rich in educational endowments, and palatial charity schools, which have long ceased to be charities. Edinburgh, indeed, suffered from such an embarrassment of benefactions of this kind, that in our time, several of them have been turned into day-schools, giving a complete education to thousands of boys and girls of the better class. The latest large endowment, that of Sir William Fettes for the children of necessitous families, was applied to building a sumptuous pile, handed over *per saltum* to the upper class as a seminary on the model of English public schools, which only in the course of generations came so far from the intention of their pious founders. This competition has but set on their mettle the once "New" Academy, for the best part of a century the chief school in Scotland, and the old High School that nursed so many generations of distinguished Scotsmen.

So, as at Bedford, where marriageable damsels complain of the *hims* as being either too ancient or too modern, the population of the Scottish capital is increased by a selection of retired family-fathers, and a swarm of youngsters who appear to thrive on the easterly winds and haars. This hint about the weather is let slip unhappily, since I am about to put forward a bold pretension for "mine own romantic town," in a character not obviously associated with it. In case of seeming too presumptuous on its behalf, I will quote from Black's *Guide to Edinburgh*, which ought to be well informed on such matters:—

> "In the holiday season, when Edinburgh is deserted by the upper class of its inhabitants, why should it not be sought as a pleasant change by the inhabitants of more grimy cities or less inspiring scenes? It may seem strange to mention the capital of Scotland as a health resort; yet, when one comes to think of it, 'Auld Reekie' has more claim to this extra title than many less famous places which flourish in full reputation for gay and picturesque salubrity. The fact is, that had Edinburgh not been a great city, it might well be a Clifton or a Scarborough, and its ancient dignity need not be allowed to overshadow its other merits. To begin with, the climate is airy and bracing, notoriously rather too much so at most seasons, but the sea-breezes cool the heat of summer, and the moderate rainfall is soon carried off on the sloping streets. Practically it stands on the sea, the shore being hardly farther from the centre of Edinburgh than from some parts of Brighton. By train or tram one can run down at any hour to Portobello, where are sands, donkeys, crowds, bathing-machines,

pleasure-boats, and ornamental pier to satisfy the most fastidious Margateer. At Craiglockhart, a mile or so from the outskirts of the town, there is a first-class hydropathic establishment, nestling under the wild scenery of the Pentland Hills. Nor is mineral water wanting, if that be desired. In the valley of the Water of Leith, below the stately mansions of Moray Place, a sulphurous spring may be found dispensed in a little classical temple that elsewhere would pass for a creditable pump-room, though many citizens of Edinburgh, perhaps, know nothing about it. Bands play almost daily in one or other of the parks; and even nigger minstrels, no doubt, might be found, if that feature seemed indispensable to the character of a holiday resort. There is no want of theatrical and other performances. Then, as we have shown, few cities are so well off for coach, steamboat, and railway excursions which would bring one back in a day from a round through half of Scotland."

CHAPTER III

THE TROSSACHS ROUND

Beyond Edinburgh, perhaps the best known town in Scotland is Stirling, which hordes of pilgrims pass in the round trip of a single day through the famous Trossachs District, displaying such a finely mixed assortment of Scottish scenery, lochs, woods, and mountains

> that like giants stand
> To sentinel enchanted land.

Stirling, on the edge of the Highlands, played a central part, even long after the Scottish kings had been drawn down to the rich fields of Lothian and the Merse. From the rock on which the Castle stands, only less boldly than that of Edinburgh, one looks over the Links of Forth, making such sinuous meanderings upon its Carse, and across to the Ochil Hills that border Fife; then from another point of view appear the rugged Bens among which Roderick Dhu had his strongholds. Not fair prospects alone are tourists' attraction to Stirling. The palace of James V., the houses of great nobles like Argyll and Mar, the execution place of the last Roman Catholic Archbishop of Scotland, the memorials of Protestant martyrs, the proud monuments of Bruce and Wallace, the ruins of Cambuskenneth Abbey, with its royal sepulchre, all show this region the heart of mediæval Scottish history. While Edinburgh grew to be recognised as the capital, Stirling Castle was the birthplace and the favourite residence of several among the James Stuarts that came to such an uneasy crown in boyhood; sometimes it was their prison or their school of sanguinary politics, when possession of the royal person counted as ace in the game played by truculently treacherous nobles. It has the distinction of being the last British castle to stand a siege, raised in 1746 by the Duke of Cumberland, when, as his panegyrical historian says, "in the Space of one single Week, his Royal Highness quitted the Court of the King his Father, put himself at the head of his Troops in *Scotland*, and saw the Enemy flying with Precipitation before him, so that it may be said that his progress was like Lightning, the rebels fled at the flash, fearing the Thunder that was to follow." Its ramparts look down on Scotland's dearest battlefields, that where Wallace ensnared the invader at the Old Bridge, and that of Bannockburn, when Bruce turned the flower of English chivalry to dust and to gold, for, as the latest historian says, "it rained ransoms" in Scotland after this profitable victory.

STIRLING CASTLE FROM THE KING'S KNOT

One may speculate what might have been the fate of the United Kingdom had Bannockburn ended otherwise. Would the barons of the north have found a master in Edward III.? Would the Plantagenets, with Scotland to back them, have made good their conquest of France? Would the stern reformers across the Tweed have suffered the Tudors to shape and re-shape the Church as they did? Would the Scottish adventurers who once kept their swords sharp as soldiers of fortune all over Europe, have sooner found a career in forcing themselves to the front of British society? This much seems clear, that there has been a woeful waste of ill-blood before a union that came about after all, in the way of peace. Yet are we so made that the most philosophic Scot, even fresh from a course of John Stuart Mill or Herbert Spencer, cannot look down upon these battle-grounds without a throb in his heart. It was Bannockburn that made us a nation, poor but free to be ourselves. Then, since we did not always come off so well in our battles with England, naturally we make much of the points won in a doubtful game. When I was at school there came among us perfervid young Scots an English boy, before whom, we agreed, it would be courteous and kind not to mention Bannockburn. Yet in the end some itching tongue let slip this moving name, but without ruffling our new comrade's pride. It turned out that he complacently took Bannockburn to have been an English victory; at all events, one more or less made no great matter to his thinking. Englishmen take their own national trophies so much for granted, that they are apt to forget the susceptibilities of other peoples. Such a one was re-buked by a coachman driving him over the field of Bannockburn. "You Scotch are always boasting of your country, but when you come south you are in no hurry to get back again." With thumb pointed to the ground, the Scot made stern answer: "There was thirty thousand o' you cam north, and no mahny o' them went back again!" There are other battlefields about Stirling, of which Scotland has no such title to be proud, as that of Falkirk, where Wallace brought his renown to a falling market and Prince Charles Edward had but half a victory; that of Sauchieburn, where James III. was foully slain; and that of Sheriffmuir, the Culloden of 1715.

Let us hang a little longer upon the Castle ramparts to take a bird's-eye view of the stirring story that often came to centre round this rock. Over Highland mountain and Lowland strath the clouds lift away, giving here and there a doubtful glimpse of Scots from Ireland, Celts from who knows how far, Britons of Strathclyde, and dim Picts of the east, each such a wild race as "slew the slayer and shall himself be slain," among whom intrude Roman legions and Norse pirates, the former falling back from their thistly conquest, the latter settling themselves firmly on the coasts. Out of this welter, as out of the Heptarchy in the south, emerges a more or less dominant kingdom seated on the Tay. While the power of the Scots seems to have gone under, their name floats at the top, so as to christen the new nation, that on the south side, from the wide bounds of Northumbria, takes in a stable element destined to be the cement of the whole.

The next act shows the struggle of a partly Saxonised people against the An-glo-Norman kings and their claims to feudal superiority. The curtain rises on a sensational melodrama of confused alarms and excursions, where the ill-drilled Celtic supernumeraries at the back of the stage often fall to fighting like wild cats among themselves, while the mail-clad barons prance now on one side and now on the other, as the scenes shift about a border-line almost rubbed out by the cross-ing and recrossing of armies. The heroes of the most thrilling tableaux are Wallace and Bruce; and the loudest applause hails the culminating blaze of lime-light on Bannockburn.

THE OUTFLOW OF LOCH KATRINE, PERTHSHIRE

The wars of Independence are not yet at an end, but the Scots people have learned more or less firmly to stand together, and their chiefs, when not led astray by feud and treachery, begin to enter into the spirit of the piece, in which France now takes a leading part. But Banquo's ill-fortune dogs the line not yet fully consecrated by misfortune. Over the stage passes that woeful procession of boy kings, most of them cut off before they had learned to rule, each leaving his son to be in turn kidnapped and tutored by fierce nobles to whom John Knox might well have preached on the text "Woe to thee, O land, when thy king is a child!" more profitably than he denounced that "monstrous regiment of women." This act culminates in the Reformation, when for a generation Scotland is not clear whether to cry "Unhand me, villain!" to France, or to England, the two powers that at her side play Codlin and Short in a tragic mask.

When James VI. had posted off to his richer inheritance, we might expect an idyllic transformation scene of peace out of pain. But the Scot has no turn for peace. Is it the mists and east winds that set such a keen edge on his temper? When not at loyal war, he is robbing and raiding his neighbours, as if to keep his hand in; and if no strife be stirring at home, he hires himself out as a professional fighter or football player over foreign countries and counties, for pelf indeed, but also for the zest of the game. And now that Scotland has no longer its wonted national exercise of defending itself against England, it developed at home that notable taste for spiritual combat; so the next act has for its main interest a controversy as to what things were Cæsar's, throughout which the hard-headed and hot-hearted theologians of the north made fitful efforts to be loyal to Cæsar, who, on his part, gave them little cause for loyalty.

With the Revolution Settlement and the Act of Union the stage appears cleared for a happy denouement, which, indeed, but for episodes of rebellion and vulgar grudges on both sides, comes on at length as the two rivals learn how after all they are not hero and villain, but long-lost brothers, the one rich and proud but generous, the other poor and honest. Already, before the world's footlights, we see them fallen into each other's arms, blessed by nature and fortune, to the music of "Rule, Britannia," amid the cheers of a crowd of colonies, though foreign spectators may shrug their shoulders and twirl their moustaches when invited to applaud.

But may there not be an epilogue to the sensational acts of Scottish history? As Saxondom overcame the plaided and kilted clans, is not Scotland in turn destined to overlie the rest of the island? Here we approach a delicate subject of consideration. In this enlightened age when, as a great Scotsman says, "the Torch of Science has now been brandished and borne about with more or less effect for five thousand years and upwards," the truly philosophic mind should be capable of rising above the pettiness of national prejudice. Only foolish and uninstructed persons can cling to the belief that their peculiar community, large or small, is necessarily identified with the highest excellences of creation. Wise men agree to recognise that as a poor vanity which winks fondly at the halo consecrating its own faults, while blind to the plainest merits of its neighbours. Excesses, defects, and compensations must be everywhere recognised and allowed for, then at last we can take a calm and exact account of human nature in its different manifestations regarded by the light of impartial candour. And when in such a judicious spirit we come to survey mankind from China to Peru, there can surely be little doubt as to the due place of Scots in the broken clan of McAdam.

IN THE HEART OF THE TROSSACHS, PERTHSHIRE

BRIG O' TURK AND BEN VENUE, PERTHSHIRE

The above edifying principles were earnestly enforced upon me by a French
savant with whom I once travelled in the Desert of Sahara, who yet almost foamed

at the mouth if one pointed the moral with a Prussian helmet-spike. Hitherto, alas!
international characterisations have been coarse work, usually touched with a
spice of malice. Every parish flatters itself by locating Gotham just over its boundary, as any county may have some unkind reproach against its neighbours, Wilt-
shire moon-rakers, Hampshire hogs, or what not; and nations, too, bandy satirical
epithets, like those of a certain poet—

> France is the land of sober common-sense,
> And Spain of intellectual eminence.
> In Russia there are no such things as chains;
> Supreme at Rome enlightened reason reigns.
> Unbounded liberty is Austria's boast,
> And iron Prussia is as free—almost.
> America, that stationary clime,
> Boasts of tradition and the olden time.
> England, the versatile and gay,
> Rejoices in theatrical display.
> The sons of Scotia are impulsive, rash,
> Infirm of purpose, prodigal of cash.
> But Paddy— —

But, indeed, the rest is too scandalous for publication.

The most marked feature of the Scottish national character is perhaps an en-
gaging modesty that forbids me to dwell on the achievements of a small country's
thin population, who have written so many names so widely over the world. But
it must be admitted how the King of Great Britain sits on his throne in virtue of
the Scottish blood that exalted a "wee bit German lairdie." Our men of light and
leading are naturally Scotsmen, the leaders of both parties in the House of Commons, for instance. Since Disraeli—himself sprung from the Chosen People of the
old Dispensation—Lord Salisbury was our only Premier not a Scotsman. Both the
present Archbishops of the Anglican Church come from Presbyterian Scotland.
The heads of other professions in England usually are or ought to be Scotsmen.
The United States Constitution seems to require an amendment permitting the
President to be a born Scot; but such names as Adams, Polk, Scott, Grant, McClel-
lan, and McKinley have their significance in the history of that country, while in
Canada, of course, Mac has come to mean much what Pharaoh did in Egypt. It
is believed that no Scotsman has as yet been Pope; but there appears a sad falling away in the Catholic Church since its earliest Fathers were well known as
sound Presbyterians. The first man mentioned in the Bible was certainly a Scot,
though English jealousy seeks to disguise him as James I. Your "beggarly Scot"
has the Apostles as accomplices in what Englishmen look on as his worst sin, a
vice of poverty which, in the fulness of time, he begins to live down. Both Major
and Minor Prophets deal with their Ahabs and Jezebels much in the tone of John
Knox. A legend, not lightly to be despised, makes our ancestress Scota, Pharaoh's
daughter; but I do not insist on a possible descent from the lost Tribes of Israel.
Noah is recorded as the first Covenanter. Cain and Abel appear to have started the
feud of Highlander and Lowlander. Father Adam is certainly understood to have

worn the kilt. The Royal Scots claim to have furnished the guard over the Garden of Eden, in which case unpleasing questions are suggested as to the duties of the Black Watch at that epoch. The name of Eden was at one time held to fix the site of Paradise in the East Neuk of Fife; but the higher criticism inclines to Glasgow Green. In the south of Lanark, indeed, are four streams that have yielded gold; but they compass a country more abounding in lead, and the climate seems not congenial to fruit trees. "I confess, my brethren," said the controversial divine, "that there is a difficulty here; but let us look it boldly in the face, and pass on."

The antiquities of Stirling contrast with the modern trimness of its neighbour, the Bridge of Allan, lying at the foot of the Ochils two or three miles off, a Leamington to the Scottish Warwick, the tramway between them passing the hill on which, to humble southron tourists, Professor Blackie and other ardent patriots reared that tall Wallace Monument whose interior makes a Walhalla of memorials to eminent Scotsmen like Carlyle and Gladstone. Bridge of Allan is a place of mills and bleach works, and of resort for its Spa of saline water, recommended, too, by its repute for a mild spring climate, rare in the north. The "Bridge," which we have so often in Scottish place-names, points to a time when bridges were not matters of course; as in the Highlands we shall find "Boats" recording a more backward stage of ferries. This bridge spans the wooded "banks of Allan Water," up which a pleasant path leads one to Dunblane, with the Ochil moorlands for its background.

Dunblane is notable for one of the few Gothic cathedrals still used in Scotland as a parish church. Sympathetically restored, it has even become the scene of forms of worship which scandalised true-blue Presbyterians, while on the other hand I once came across an Anglican lady much shocked to find how "actually there was a Presbyterian service going on!" Carved screen, stalls, and communion table make ornaments seldom seen in the bareness of a northern kirk, this one admirable in its proportions and mouldings, if without the elaborate decoration of Melrose. It has a valuable legacy in the library of a divine well known in both countries, the tolerant Archbishop Leighton.

Among Scotsmen, Dunblane enjoys a modest repute as a place of *villeggiatura*; to tourists it is perhaps best known as junction of the Caledonian line to Oban, which brings them to Callander, a few miles from the Trossachs. This line at first follows the course of the Teith, "daughter of three mighty lakes," past Doune Castle, not Burns's "Bonnie Doon," but an imposing monument of feudal struggles and crimes, that has housed many a royal guest, if not, as one of its parish ministers gravely declares for unquestionable, Fitz-James himself on the night before his adventurous chase. So late as 1745, Home, the author of *Douglas*, had an adventure here, confined as prisoner of war in a Jacobite dungeon, from which he escaped, with five fellow-captives, in quite romantic style; and this, we know, was one of the stages of Captain Edward Waverley's journey. Farther up the river, another place of note is Cambusmore, where Scott spent the youthful holidays that made him familiar with the Trossachs country. Callander he does not mention, its name not fitting into his metre, whereas its neighbour Dunblane's amenity to rhyme brought to be planted there a flower of song at the hands of a writer who perhaps knew it only by name. But Callander has grown into a snug little town of hotels and lodging-houses below most lovely scenery, little spoiled by the chain of lakes above being harnessed as water-works for thirsty Glasgow, whose Bailie Nicol Jarvies now lord it over the country of Rob Roy and Roderick Dhu.

BIRCHES BY LOCH ACHRAY, PERTHSHIRE

Another way to the Trossachs is by "the varied realms of fair Menteith," through which a railway joins the banks of the Forth and the Clyde. The name of Menteith has an ugly association to Scottish ears through Sir John Menteith, a son of its earl, who betrayed Wallace to the English; the signal for these Philistines' onrush was given by his turning a loaf upside down, and so to handle bread was long an insult to any man of the execrated name. Sir John afterwards fought under Bruce; but however Scottish nobles might change sides in the game of feudal allegiance, the Commons were always true to patriotic resentment; and no services of that house have quite wiped out the memory of a traitor remembered as Gan among the peers of Charlemagne or Simon Girty on the backwoods frontier of America. And fortune seems to have concurred in the popular verdict, for till even the shadow of it died out in a wandering beggar, little luck went with the title of Menteith, least of all in a claim to legitimate heirship of the Crown; then this earldom seemed doubly cursed when transferred to the Grahams, one of whom was ringleader in the murder of James I.

Menteith, one of the chief provinces of old Scotland, has shrunk to the name of a district described in a witty booklet by a son of the soil, far travelled in other lands.[1] "A kind of sea of moss and heath, a bristly country (Trossachs is said to mean the bristled land) shut in by hills on every side," in which "nearly every hill and strath has had its battles between the Grahams and the Macgregors"; but now "over the Fingalian path, where once the red-shank trotted on his Highland garron, the bicyclist, the incarnation of the age, looks to a sign-post and sees *This hill is dangerous*." Its stony fields and lochans lying between hummocks are horizoned by grand mountains, among which Ben Lomond, to the west, is the dominating feature, "in winter, a vast white sugar-loaf; in summer, a prismatic cone of yellow and amethyst and opal lights; in spring, a grey, gloomy, stony pile of rocks; in autumn, a weather indicator; for when the mist curls down its sides, and hangs in heavy wreaths from its double summit 'it has to rain,' as the Spaniards say."

Menteith became a resort before Callander, when, early in the eighteenth century, we find Clerk of Penicuik taking his family there on a "goat's whey campaign," for which remedy the Highland borders were often visited in his day. At an earlier day, canny Lowlanders would be shy of trusting themselves, on business or pleasure, beyond the Forth; and, even later, we know how Bailie Nicol Jarvie thought twice before venturing into the haunts of that "honest" kinsman of his. As Ben Lomond dominates this landscape, so looms out the memory of Rob Roy Macgregor, that doughty outlaw who, like Robin Hood, has taken such hold on popular imagination. Graham as he is, one suspects the above-quoted representative of the old earls to have his heart with an ancestral enemy who practised a kind of wild socialism—

>To spoil the spoiler as he may,
>And from the robber rend the prey.

---

[1] *Notes on the District of Menteith*, by R. B. Cunninghame Graham.

HEAD OF LOCH LOMOND, LOOKING UP GLEN FALLOCH, PERTHSHIRE

It appears that Scott had Rob Roy in his eye as a model for Roderick Dhu, and it is the Macgregor country which he has given to his fictitious Vich Alpines. Mr. Cunninghame Graham points out how the Highland borders were always more troubled than the interior clandom, and how here especially the vicinity of a rich lowland offered constant temptation for followers of the "good old rule, the simple plan" recorded by Wordsworth. The Forth made a boundary against these predatory excursions, yet sometimes a Roderick Dhu would harry fields and farms as far as the home of "poor Blanche of Devon," beyond Stirling. The "red soldiers" in turn came to pass the Highland line. On Ellen's Isle women and children took refuge from Cromwell's men; Monk marched by Aberfoyle, noting for destruction its woods that harboured rebels; and not to speak of Captain Thornton's unlucky expedition, no less authentic a hero than Wolfe once commanded the fortress which the Georges placed at Inversnaid, near Rob Roy's home, to bridle that broken clan of Ishmaelites.

The railway, from Glasgow or from Stirling, passes to the south of the Loch of Menteith, with its islands, to which a short divagation might be made. Here, on the "Isle of Rest," shaded by giant chestnuts which tradition brings from Rome, are the ruins of a cloister whither the child Queen Mary was carried for refuge after the battle of Pinkie, before setting out for France with her playmate maids of honour.

> Last night the Queen had four Marys,
> To-night she'll have but three;
> There was Mary Beaton and Mary Seaton
> And Mary Carmichael and me.

Mary Livingston was the authentic fourth of the quartette in those days, and Mary Fleming held the place of Mary Carmichael. The luckless heroine of this touching ballad was a Mary Hamilton supposed by Scott to have been one of the Queen's attendants later on, but her identity is somewhat dubious; and one writer shows reason to believe that the story of her crime and punishment has been strangely shifted from the Russian Court of Peter the Great, where she might well exclaim—

> Ah! little did my minnie think,
> The night she cradled me
> The lands that I should travel in,
> The death that I should dee!

Beyond this lake a railway branch brings us to Aberfoyle, on the banks of the "infant Forth," its nursery name the Avon Dhu, "Blackwater," haunted like a child's dreams by fairies of whom prudent Bailie Nicol Jarvie spoke under his breath, though he professed to hold them as "deceits of Satan." Here the change-house of Lucky M'Alpine has been replaced by an hotel offering all the comforts of the Saltmarket, along with golf links and fishing at Loch Ard. As Ipswich shows the very room in the White Hart occupied by Mr. Pickwick and the green gate at which Sam Weller met Job Trotter, so among the lions here are the ploughshare valiantly handled by Bailie Nicol Jarvie, nay, even the identical bough from which he swung suspended by his coat tails. Such relics let one guess why that worthy citizen would not give "the finest sight in the Hielands for the first keek o' the Gorbals of Glasgow!" But he might have taken another view had he seen the great slate quarries that now scar the braes of Aberfoyle, or that pleasure-house on Loch Katrine set apart for Glasgow magistrates to disport themselves at the source of their city's water supply.

GOLDEN AUTUMN, THE TROSSACHS, PERTHSHIRE

From Aberfoyle or from Callander, the rest of the journey is by road to the Trossachs Hotel, which seems to represent Fitz-James's imagination of "lordly tower" or "cloister grey"; then on through the mile of bristling pass to the foot of Loch Katrine. How many a peaceful stranger has passed this way since the Knight of Snowdoun's steed here "stretched his stiff limbs to rise no more"! What "cost thy life, my gallant grey" would be the fact that even in the poet's day, the path to Ellen's Isle was more like a ladder than a road. Now the danger most to be feared is from Sassenach cycling, which caused a coach accident in the vicinity a few years ago. Umbrellas had replaced claymores so far back as Wordsworth's time; and waterproofs are the armour most displayed, where once

> Refluent through the pass of fear
> The battle's tide was pour'd;
> Vanish'd the Saxon's struggling spear,
> Vanish'd the mountain-sword.
> As Bracklinn's chasm, so black and steep,
> Receives her roaring linn,
> As the dark caverns of the deep
> Suck the wild whirlpool in,
> So did the deep and darksome pass
> Devour the battle's mingled mass:
> None linger now upon the plain,
> Save those who ne'er shall fight again.

Macaulay, in his slap-dash style, has explained the want of taste for the picturesque in a bailie or such like of more romantic times. "He is not likely to be thrown into ecstasies by the abruptness of a precipice from which he is in imminent danger of falling two thousand feet perpendicular; by the boiling waves of a torrent which suddenly whirls away his baggage and forces him to run for his life; by the gloomy grandeur of a pass where he finds a corpse which marauders have just stripped and mangled; or by the screams of those eagles whose next meal may probably be on his own eyes." But Dr. Hume Brown (*Early Travellers in Scotland*) shows how there were bold and not unappreciative tourists in the Highlands before the era of return tickets. Whatever the guide-books say, it is certainly not the case that the Trossachs were discovered by Scott. In Dr. T. Garnett's *Tour through the Highlands*, published 1800, he relates a visit to the "Drosacks," and speaks of the place as sought out by foreigners. Several years before the publication of the *Lady of the Lake*, Wordsworth, with Coleridge and his sister, on a Scottish tour, turned aside to this beauty-spot, which they duly admired in spite of the rain; and there they met a drawing-master from Edinburgh on the same picturesque-hunting errand. Dorothy Wordsworth's *Journal* tells us how the cottars were amused to hear of their secluded home being known in England; how two huts had been erected by Lady Perth for the accommodation of visitors; and how a dozen years before the minister of Callander had published an account of the Trossachs as a scene "that beggars all description."

THE RIVER TEITH,
WITH LOCHS ACHRAY AND VENNACHAR, PERTHSHIRE

The bad weather proved too much for Coleridge, who turned back from the tour here; and his muse seems not to have been inspired by this land of the mountain which he found also a land of the flood. Wordsworth, however, made several attempts to annex Scotland to his native domain. Truth to tell, the lake poet's harp sounds sometimes out of tune across the Border, as witness his woeful travesty of the "Helen of Kirkconnel" story, and the philosophic considerations which he attributes to Rob Roy over what may have been that bold outlaw's grave. There is one verse in his "Highland Reaper" which seems a perfect epitome of the future Laureate's qualities, who, if he "uttered nothing base," could come too near being commonplace. *"Will no one tell me what she sings?"* is surely in the flat tone which one irreverent critic describes as a "bleat." *"Perhaps the plaintive numbers flow"* —is not this the false gallop of eighteenth-century verse, out of which Wordsworth vainly believed that he had broken his Pegasus? But in such pinchbeck setting, what a pearl of price—

> For old, unhappy, far-off things,
> And battles long ago!

Thus to him, too, "Caledonia stern and wild" could breathe her secret, while to put life into the raids and combats of long ago was for another bard who plays drum and trumpet in the orchestra of British poetry. I am not going to string vain epithets on the Trossachs, familiar to all readers if only from the pages of their great advertiser. But let me hint to tourists who come duly furnished with the *Lady of the Lake*, that Black's *Guide to the Trossachs* includes an excellent commentary on the poem from what may seem an unpoetical source, the pen of an Astronomer-Royal, Sir G. B. Airey, whose topographical analysis will be found most instructive. These scenes appear somewhat trimmed since an old writer described the Highlands "as a part of the creation left undrest." The lake edges have been smoothed off, as the "unfathomable glades" of the Trossachs are opened up by a road, below the line of the old pass and the hill tracks by which the Fiery Cross was sped towards Strath-Ire.

For an account of this country as it is in our day, we may refer to a French story by a writer named, of all names, André Laurie, whose native heath ought to be the bonny braes of Maxwelton. This book has the serious purpose of giving a view of English school athletics, and pointing the moral that Frenchmen so trained would be all the fitter for *la revanche*. The hero, sent to school in England, is, as part of his educational course, taken by the schoolmaster on a shooting excursion in the Highlands. They put up at the *White Heart*, one of the principal hotels of *Glascow*, and the landlord is so interested in their bold enterprise that he personally conducts them on the *chasse aux grouses*. Nay more, he equips them with a pack of piebald pointers, well trained to retrieve in water, which he had come by in a remarkable manner: a certain Lord Stilton, breakfasting at the hotel, with true British generosity made his host a present of these matchless hounds by way of *largesse* for an excellent dish of trout—a rare treat, it seems, in this part of the world.

VEILED SUNSHINE, THE TROSSACHS, PERTHSHIRE

NEAR ARDLUI, LOCH LOMOND, DUMBARTONSHIRE

The first day's proceedings of the sporting troop are most notable. They "leave
the civilised country" at Renfrew. How they get across the Clyde does not appear;

but there are no doubt stepping-stones in all Highland streams. Having thus invaded the Lennox, they forthwith stalk its desolate moors from Loch Lomond to Loch Katrine, where as a touch of local colour the author is careful to point out that one must not use the word lakes. Nine or ten strong, the company is thrown out in skirmishing order, those who have guns marching in front behind the dogs, while the unarmed members are invited to bring up the rear "as simple spectators." Scotland being such a proverbially hospitable country, they do not judge it necessary to provide themselves with leave or license, but their hotel-keeper for two or three shillings hires a bare-legged shepherd in "a short petticoat" to show them where the game lies. In spite of this liberality, towards the end of the day the bag amounts only to three or four head, including one hare, explained to be a *rara avis* hereabouts, and one fierce bull which has given a spice of danger to their sport. In the evening, however, the grouse begin to "rise," spring up "every instant under their feet," and nearly two dozen are brought down, enough to serve for supper. The question of lodging presents more difficulty, the Trossachs being an "absolutely desert" country without a village for six leagues round; but the whole party are comfortably accommodated in a fisherman's hut, fifteen to twenty feet square, which must have been a tight fit for ten, even though there was no furniture beyond a table, two benches and a sheepskin. With genuine Scottish pride the fisherman refuses to accept a bawbee from his guests; though rather too much given to "bird's eye tobacco" and "that abominable product of civilisation Scotch whisky," he is a superior person, by his parents designed for the national church, but the honour of "wearing a surplice," it is explained, had not seemed to him worth the frequent birching which makes the discipline of parish schools in the north.

Next day, for a change, the strangers give themselves up to the kindred sport of angling; and two of them undertake the Alpine ascent of one of the peaks above Loch Katrine, but, without a guide, come to sore grief, and have to be rescued by a search party led by those sagacious pointers in true Ben St. Bernard style. In such cases, our author points out "the superiority of the savage over the civilised man, at least in the desert." Only to the Highland fisherman had it occurred that those luckless adventurers might want something to eat; but he, taught by experience, produces in the nick of time a bottle of whisky, a biscuit and a slice of bacon; and thus the perishing hero's life is saved to "dance a Scottish *gigue*" — O M. Laurie, M. Laurie, O!

The dancing comes through a luxurious experience of Highland high-life, when this band of youths fall in with an old schoolfellow, a Scottish nobleman who bears what seems the exotic title of Lord Camember, but his family name is that well-known aristocratic one of Orton. He welcomes them to his castle, where his coming of age is being celebrated by crowds strangely enormous for such a "desert country," who are entertained under tents "vast as cathedrals," with splendid hospitality open to all comers, fountains flowing with beer, speeches, music, dancing, and fireworks. As *bouquet* of the festivities, he invites the strangers to a review of his stags, driven together "in full trot" till their gigantic antlers "gave the illusion of the marching forest in the Macbeth legend." The drive past lasts more than an hour, in the course of which are enumerated 5947 horns, so that, allowing for absentees, the young lord estimates a round number of seven thousand as the stock of his deer forest. There could have been no such head of game in the district when Fitz-James galloped all the way from the Earn to Loch Katrine after one stag, losing it as well as his way. One can't help feeling that our author's excursion through the scenes of his story must have been an equally rapid one.

The Trossachs pass leads us to that lake that gets a fair-seeming name not from any saint, but from the Highland *Caterans* who once infested its banks; and it is hinted that "Ellen's Isle" may have come to be christened through Scott's mistaking the Gaelic word *Eilean* (island). There was, indeed, a certain Helen Stuart who played a grimly fierce part in defending this place of refuge, as related in the poem, but her exploit was performed against Cromwell's soldiers. In sight of the "Silver Strand," tourists are wont to take steamboat as far as Stronachlachar, and there cross by coach to the "bonny, bonny banks of Loch Lomond." They whose "free course" moves not by "such fixed cause," might well hold on to the head of Loch Katrine, crossing to Loch Lomond over the wild heights of Glengyle; or they would not find it amiss to turn back to Aberfoyle, thence past Loch Ard and the Falls of Ledard, following the track round Ben Lomond on which Rob Roy led Osbaldistone and the Bailie out of his country. But one knows not how to direct strangers to that wild region vaguely outlined by the above-mentioned French author, where our generation may shoot grouse and bulls as they go, and find quarters in any convenient hut or castle, when the Trossachs hotel happens to have "not a bed for love or money." His story, one fears, must be counted with the mediæval wonders of Loch Lomond, fish without fins, waves without wind, and such a floating island as still emerges after hot summers in Derwentwater.

Dorothy Wordsworth, for one, rather belittles Loch Katrine as an "Ulswater dismantled of its grandeur and cropped of its lesser beauties," though she compliments the upper part as "very pleasing, resembling Thirlmere below Armboth." But no critic can carp at the fame of Loch Lomond as the most beautiful lake in Scotland; and one author who, as a native of the Lennox, is not indeed unprejudiced, Smollett to wit, gives it the palm over all the lakes he has seen in Italy or Switzerland. Dr. Chalmers wondered if there would not be a Loch Lomond in heaven. "A little Mediterranean" is the style given by a seventeenth-century English tourist, Franck, to what Scott boldly pronounces "one of the most surprising, beautiful, and sublime spectacles in nature," its narrow upper fiord "lost among dusky and retreating mountains," at the foot opening into an archipelago of wooded islands, threaded by steamboats, while up the western shore runs one of the best cycling roads in the kingdom, past memorials of Stuarts and Buchanans, Colquhouns and wild Macfarlanes. On the other side are caves associated with the adventures of Rob Roy, and spots sung by Wordsworth. And all this wonderland is overshadowed by Ben Lomond, its ascent easily made on foot or pony-back by a traveller not bound to do this whole round in one day. But let him beware of getting lost in the mist and having to spend all night on the mountain, as was the lot of that New England Sibyl, Margaret Fuller. Also he should not imitate a facetious friend of mine who left his card in the cairn at the top, and two or three days later received it enclosed in this note: "Mr. Ben Lomond presents his compliments to Mr. — — and begs to say that not only does his position prevent him from returning visits, but he has no desire for Mr. — —'s further acquaintance."

THE SILVER STRAND, LOCH KATRINE, PERTHSHIRE

LOCH ACHRAY AND BEN VENUE, PERTHSHIRE

At the foot of Loch Lomond we regain the rails that will carry us to Edinburgh, to Glasgow, to Stirling, or to the western Highlands. The first stage is down the Vale of Leven to Dumbarton, *arx inexpugnabilis* of old Scotland, its name *Dunbritton* recording the older days when it was the stronghold of a Cumbrian kingdom. Here the literary *genius loci* is that not very ethereal shade Tobias Smollett, who, born on the banks of Leven, has nothing to say of the Trossachs, but looked back on the scene of Roderick Random's pranks as an eighteenth-century Arcadia, that could move him to a rare strain of sentiment in his "Ode to Leven Water."

> Devolving from thy parent lake,
> A charming maze thy waters make,
> By bowers of birch, and groves of pine,
> And hedges flower'd with eglantine.
> Still on thy banks, so gaily green,
> May numerous herds and flocks be seen,
> And lasses chanting o'er the pail,
> And shepherds piping in the dale,
> And ancient faith that knows no guile,
> And industry embrown'd with toil,
> And hearts resolved, and hands prepared,
> The blessings they enjoy to guard.

CHAPTER IV

THE KINGDOM OF FIFE

LIKE Somerset, claiming to be something more than a mere shire, the county half fondly, half jestingly entitled a kingdom, lies islanded between two firths, cut off from the world by the sea and from the rest of Scotland by the Ochil ridges. The "Fifers" are thus supposed to be a race apart; but it would be more like the truth to take Fifeishness as the essence of Saxon Scotland. Fife is, in fact, an epitome of the Lowlands, showing great stretches of practically prosaic farming, others of grimy coal-field, with patches of moor, bog, and wind-blown firs, here and there swelling into hill features, that in the abrupt Lomonds attain almost mountain dignity in face of their Highland namesake, sixty miles away. Open to cold sea winds, it nurses the hardy frames of "buirdly chiels and clever hizzies"; and all the invigorating discipline of the northern climate is understood to be concentrated in the East Neuk of Fife, where a weakling like R. L. Stevenson might well sigh over the "flaws of fine weather that we call our northern summer." It is in the late autumn that this eastern coast is at its best of halcyon days. As we have seen, the poet lived a little farther south who still laid himself open to Tom Hood's reproach—

> 'Come, gentle spring, ethereal mildness come!'
> O Thomson, void of rhyme as well as reason,
> How could'st thou thus poor human nature *hum*—
> There's no such season!

In the *Antiquary's* period, we know how Fife was reached from Edinburgh by crossing the Firth at Queensferry, as old as Malcolm Canmore's English consort, or by the longer sail from Leith to Kinghorn, where Alexander III. broke his neck to Scotland's woe. A more roundabout land route was *via* Stirling, chosen by prudent souls like the old wife who, being advised to put her trust in Providence for the passage, replied, "Na, na, sae lang as there's a brig at Stirling I'll no fash Providence!" Lord Cockburn records how that conscientious divine, Dr John Erskine, feeling it his duty to vote in a Fife election, when too infirm to bear the motion of boat or carriage, arranged to walk all the way by Stirling, but was saved this fortnight's pilgrimage by the contest being given up. Till the building of its Firth bridges, the North British Railway's passengers had to tranship both in entering and leaving Fife, a mild taste of adventure for small schoolboys. Now, as all the world knows, the shores of Lothian are joined to Fife by that monumental Forth Bridge that humps itself into view miles away. Then all the world has heard of the unlucky Tay Bridge, graceful but treacherous serpent as it proved in its first form, when one stormy Sabbath night it let a train be blown into the sea. By these constructions the line has now a clear course on which to race its Caledonian rival, either for Perth or Aberdeen. But there is no racing done on the cobweb of North British branches woven to catch Fife-farers, at whose junctions, as a local statistician has calculated, the average Fifer wastes one-seventh of his life or thereabouts. Ladybank Junction, stranded on its moor, used to have the name of a specially penitential waiting-place, which yet lent itself to romantic account in one of those *Tales from Blackwood*.

THE CASTLE OF ST. ANDREWS, FIFESHIRE

The towns of Fife are many rather than much. Cupar, the county seat, is still a quiet little place, whose Academy stands on the site of a Macduff stronghold, recalling that Thane of Fife with whom the Dukedom of our generation is connected only in title. "He that maun to Cupar, maun to Cupar," says the proverb, but few strangers seem to risk this vague condemnation. When James Ray passed through the town on his way to Culloden, he has little to tell of it unless that he put up at the "Cooper's Arms" which, more by token, was kept by the Widow Cooper. The above proverb, by the way, seems to belong to Coupar-Angus, usually so distinguished in spelling, and is transferred to its namesake by "Cupar-justice," a Fife version of the code honoured at Jedburgh. A Scotch cooper or couper may not have to do with barrels, unless indirectly in the way of business, but is also a chaffer or chapman, *par excellence*, of horses; and one would like to believe, if philologists did not shake their heads, that these towns got their name as markets, like English Chippings and Cheaps.

In an out-of-the-way edge of the county, below the Lomonds, lies Falkland, whose royal palace, restored by the late Marquis of Bute, was the scene of that dubious tragedy enacted in the *Fair Maid of Perth*, where the dissolute Duke of Rothesay is a little white-washed to heighten the dramatic atrocity of his death. A few miles behind Queensferry is Dunfermline, another place where kings once sat "drinking the blood-red wine," now a thriving seat of linen manufacture, among its mills and bleachfields containing choice fragments of royal and ecclesiastical architecture, as well as modern adornments given by its bounteous son Mr. Andrew Carnegie, native of the town where Charles I. was born, and Robert Bruce buried beside Malcolm Canmore and his queen. There are some fine modern monuments in the new church, which adjoins the monastic old one, testifying stiffly to Presbyterian distrust of Popish arts; and altogether Dunfermline is one of those places that might well "delay the tourist."

But the largest congregation in Fife is that "long town" of Kirkcaldy, flourishing on jute and linoleum since the days when Carlyle and Irving were dominies here, the former a humane pedagogue, though he scourged grown-up dunces so unmercifully, while the bygone peace of the place was often broken by the wailing of Irving's pupils under the tawse with which he sought to drive them into unknown tongues. Kirkcaldy has older historic memories; but somehow it is one of those Scottish towns that, like Peebles and Paisley, lend their names to vulgar or comic associations. Was it not a bailie of Kirkcaldy who said, "What wi' a' thae schules and railways, ye canna' tell the dufference atween a Scotchman and an Englishman noo-a-days!"

Let the above words be text for a sermon, to which I invite seriously-minded readers, while the otherwise-minded may amuse themselves by taking a daunder among the lions of Kirkcaldy. The subject is Scottish Humour, which Englishmen are apt to rank with the snakes of Iceland or the breeks of a Highlander. Foreigners do not make the same mistake, as how can they when the best known English humorists are so often Scotsmen or Irishmen? It is the pure John Bull whose notions of the humorous are apt to be rather childish; so when he gets hold of a joke like that about the surgical instrument, he runs about squibbing it in everybody's face, and never seems to grow tired of such a smart saying, nor cares to ask if there be any truth in it beyond the fact that one people may not readily relish another's wit or wisdom.

The vulgar of all nations have a very rudimentary sense of the comic, coarse enough in many Scotsmen who can appreciate no more pointed repartee than—

> The never a word had Dickie to say,
> Sae he ran the lance through his fause bodie!

The characteristic form of English humour is more or less good-natured chaff, bearing the same relation to keen raillery as a bludgeon does to a rapier. A master of this fence was Dr. Johnson, who, if his pistol missed fire, knocked you down with the butt end of it. Sydney Smith's residence in Edinburgh should have given him a finer style, which he turned to so unworthy use in mocking at Scottish "wut." As to the distinction between wit and humour, I know of no better than that which defines the one as a flash, the other as an atmosphere. It may be granted that the Scottish nature does not coruscate in flashes. But what your Sydney Smiths do not observe is that it develops a very high quality of humour, which has self-criticism as its essence. Know thyself, has been styled the acme of wisdom; and when the Scotsman's best stories come to be analysed, the point of them appears to be a more or less conscious making fun of his own faults and shortcomings, which is a wholesomer form of intellectual exercise than that parrot-trick of nicknaming one's neighbours. The bailie's boast above quoted is a characteristic instance over which an Englishman may chuckle without seeing the true force of it. All those hoary *Punch* jests as to "bang went saxpence," and so forth, are good old home-made Scottish stories, which the southron brings back with him from their native heath, and dresses them up for his own taste with a spice of malice, then rejoices over the savoury dish which he has prepared by seething poached kids in their mother's milk. Yet often print fails to bring out the true gust that needs a Doric tongue for sauce; and the Englishman who attempts any Scottish accent is apt to merit their fate who ventured to meddle with the ark, not being of the tribe of Judah. The effect of such a story depends as much on the actor as on the words. To mention but one of many noted masters of this art, who that ever spent an evening with the late Sir Daniel Macnee, President of the Scottish Academy, could hold the legendary view of his countrymen's want of fun? He had to be heard to be appreciated; but, at the risk of misrepresenting his gift, here is one of his anecdotes. He was travelling with a talkative oil merchant who, after much boast of his own business, began to rally the other on his want of communicativeness—"Come now, what line are you in?"—"I'm in the oil trade too," confessed the painter, whereupon his companion fell to pressing him for an order.—"We'll do cheaper for you than any house in the trade!" At last, to get rid of his persistency, Sir Daniel said, "I don't mind taking a gallon from you."—"A gallon! Man, ye're in a sma' way!"

Perhaps this humour is a modern production, like certain fruits cultivated in Scotland "with deeficulty." There were times, indeed, when life here was no laughing matter. But even the sun-loving vine is all the better for a touch of frost at its roots, and the best wines are not those the most easily made. In contrast with other home-brewed fun that soon goes flat, and with such cheap brands as "Joe

Miller," the vintage of Scottish humour, if not distinguished by effervescing spurts of fancy, has body and character which only improve by age, keeping well even when decanted, and giving a marked flavour when mixed with less potent materials, into *Punch*, let us say. There is also a dry quality thrown away on palates used to the public-house tap; Ally Sloper, for instance, might not taste the womanthropy, as he would call it, of that bachelor divine who began his discourse on the Ten Virgins with "What strikes us here, my brethren, is the unusually large proportion of *wise* Virgins." A good Scotch story, with the real smack upon the tongue, bears to be told again, like an aphorism distilled from the wisdom of generations. Sound humour is but the seamy side of common-sense, for a sense of the incongruous degenerates into nonsense if not shaped by a clear eye for the relation and proportion of things. If the reader will consider the many specimens of Scottish humour now current in England, or to be drawn from such treasuries as Dean Ramsay's; and if he will reflect on their weight and minting, he may understand the value of this coinage in the national life.

The northern Attic salt abounds in one savour that appears in a hundred stories like that of the preacher who, at Kirkcaldy or elsewhere, apologised for his want of preparation: "I have been obliged to say what the Lord put into my mouth, but next Sabbath I hope to come better provided!" If there is any subject which the Scot takes seriously it is religion, that yet makes the favourite theme of his jests. Revilers have gone so far as to state that the incongruous elements of Scottish humour are usually supplied by a minister and a whisky bottle. It is certainly the case that a Scotsman relishes playing upon the edge of sacred things, and that the pillars of his church will shake their sides over stories which strike Englishmen as irreverent. But has not vigorous faith often shown a tendency to overflow into backwaters of comicality, as in the gargoyles of our cathedrals, the mediæval parodies of church rites, and the homely wit of Puritan preachers? There are some believers who can afford a laugh now and then at their sturdy solemnities, others who must keep hush lest a titter bring down their fane like a house of cards. Familiarity with the language of the Bible counts for a good deal in what seems the too free handling of it in the north. But note how the irreverence of the Scot's humour is usefully directed against his own tendency to fanaticism. It is only of late years, I think, that he has taken to joking on the religious practices of his neighbours, whose shortcomings once seemed too serious for joking. That "one" of the servant girl who described the services at Westminster Abbey as "an awful way of spending the Sabbath" may be taken as a sign of growing charity. Yet, in the past, too, a Scotsman seldom chuckled so heartily as over any rebuke to priestly pretension within his own borders. Jenny Geddes's rough form of remonstrance with the dignitary who would have read the mass in her lug was a practical form of Scotch humour, that on such subjects is apt to have a good deal of hard earnest in it. As for the Kirk's own ministers, the tyranny ascribed to them by Buckle has long been tempered by stories at their expense. Buckle's famous comparison of Spain and Scotland is vitiated by his leaving out of account that natural sense of humour that has aided popular instruction in counteracting superstition. Dean Ramsay ekes out Carlyle and other weighty authors who explain how Irving found no depth of earth in Scotland for the seeds of his wild enthusiasm, and why the tourist seeks in vain for winking Madonnas at Kirkcaldy, long ago done with all relics and images but the battered figureheads of her whalers.

LOCH LUBNAIG, PERTHSHIRE

Kirkcaldy's whalers now grow legendary, and strangers beholding her shipping to-day, may take for a northern joke that this ranks as the third Scottish port of entry; but the fact is that a whole string of Fife harbours are officially knotted together under its name, as all North America was once tacked on to the manor of Greenwich, and every British child born at sea belongs to the parish of Stepney. The coast-line here is thick-set with little towns of business and pleasure, grimy coal ports and odorous fishing havens, alternating with bathing beaches and golf-links in the openings of the low cliffs. At the western edge has now been taken in the old burgh Culross, pronounced in a manner that may strike strangers as curious. Not far from the Forth Bridge is the prettiest of Edinburgh seaside resorts, Aberdour, with its own ruins to show, and the remains of an abbey on Inchcolm that shuts in its bay, and behind it Lord Moray's mansion of Donibristle, part of which stands a charred shell, burned down and rebuilt three times till its owner accepted what seemed a decree of fate. Opposite Edinburgh, Burntisland's prosaic features make a setting for the castle of Rossend, with its romantic scandal about Queen Mary and Chastelard. Beyond Kirkcaldy come Leven and Largo, trying to grow together about the statue of Alexander Selkirk; and Largo House was home of a more ancient Fifeshire mariner, Andrew Wood, his "Yellow Frigate" a sore thorn in England's side, as commemorated by a novel of James Grant, who wrote so many once-so-popular romances of war. Fife coast towns have a way of sorting themselves in couples. At the corner of the bay overlooked by Largo Law, Elie and Earlsferry flourish together as a family bathing place, behind which, at the pronunciation of Kilconquhar the uninitiated may take a thousand guesses in vain. Then we have Anstruther and Crail on Fifeness, that sharp point of the East Neuk of Fife. Round this, at the mouth of the Eden, we come to St. Andrews, "gem of the province."

Everybody has heard of St. Andrews, but only those who have seen it understand its peculiar rank among seaside resorts. It is distinguished by a certain quiet air, like some high-born spinster's, accustomed to command respect, whose heirlooms of lace and jewellery put her above any need of following the fashions. Her parvenu rivals must lay themselves out to attract, must make the best of their advantages, must ogle and flirt, and strain themselves to profit by the vogue of public favour. St. Andrews does not display so much as an esplanade, standing secure upon her sober dignity, a little dashed, indeed, of Saturday afternoons by excursions from Dundee. Other sea-side places may be said to flourish, but the word seems inappropriate in the case of this resort, that yet thrives sedately, as how should she not with so many strings to her bow? First of all she is a venerable University city, whose Mrs. Bouncers ought to make a good thing of it with the students and the sea-bathing visitors playing "Box and Cox" for them through the winter session and the summer season. Then she is a Scottish Clifton or Brighton of schools, recommended by the singular healthiness of the place. Unless in the smart new quarter near the railway station, the dignified bearing of an ancient town carries it over the flighty manners of a watering-place. The only pier is a thing of use, where the wholesome smell of seaweed mingles with a strong fishy flavour. No gilded pagoda of a bandstand profanes the "Scores," that cliff road which your Margates would have made into a formal promenade. A few bathing machines on the sands alone hint at one side of the town's character. In one of the rocky coves of the cliff is a Ladies' bathing place, which I can praise only by report. But the Step Rock, with its recent enclosure to catch the tide, is now more than ever the best swimming place on the East Coast.

IN GLENFINLAS, PERTHSHIRE

What first strikes one in St. Andrews is its union of regularity and picturesqueness, and of a cheerful well-to-do present with relics of a romantic past. Its airy thoroughfares, with their plain solidity of modern Scottish architecture, form an effective setting for bits of antiquity, such as the ivy-clad fragment of Blackfriars' Chapel, and the Abbey wall, beneath which no professor cares to walk, lest then should be fulfilled a prophecy that it is one day to fall upon the wisest head in St. Andrews. The architectural treasures of this historic cathedral city would alone be enough to make it a place of pilgrimage. "You have here," says Carlyle, "the essence of all the antiquity of Scotland in good and clean condition." Southron strangers will hardly understand how these fragments of ecclesiasticism have become a nursery of Protestant sentiment. A generation ago it was stated that but one solitary Romanist could be found in the little city. Generations of Scottish children, like myself, have been shown that gloomy dungeon at the bottom of which once pined the victims of Giant Pope, a sight to fill us with shuddering horror and hate of persecuting times; but we were not told how Protestants could persecute, too, while they knew not yet of what spirit they were. What shades of grim romance haunt these crumbling walls, what memories of Knox and Beaton, what dreams of the old Stuart days! I never realised the power of their associations till one evening, on the Scores, there sat down beside me two French tourists who had somehow strayed into St. Andrews, and their light talk of boulevards, theatres, and such like, seemed sacrilegious under the shadow of the Martyrs' Memorial.

I have an acquaintance with St. Andrews going back more than half a century. My introduction to club life was at *the* club here, then a cottage of two or three rooms, into which I was invited under charge of my nurse, and treated to the refreshment of gingerbread snaps by a member who seemed to me little short of a patriarch. In the scenery of my childhood, nothing stands out more clearly and cheerfully than those sandy green links dotted with red jackets and red flags, not to speak of the red balls with which enthusiasts bid defiance to snow and ice. Nay, another among my earliest reminiscences is of seeing the multitudinous seas themselves incarnadined, when, for once, the golfers allowed their attention to be drawn from their own hazards. A cry had been raised that a lady was drowning; then every group of red jackets within hearing forgot their balls, flung down their clubs, raced across the links, dashed into the waves, and struggled emulously to the rescue. I think a caddie, after all, was the fortunate youth who had the glory of achieving such an adventure.

Since those days, when feather balls cost half-a-crown and few profane foreigners had penetrated its mysteries, the Golf Club has been transformed in a style becoming the chief temple of this Benares, hard by a more modest "howff" for the "professionals" who are its Brahmins, where little "caddies" swarm like the monkeys of an Indian sanctuary. For golf is the idol of a cult that draws here many pilgrims from far lands, now that, in the international commerce of amusement, while barelegged little Macs take kindly to cricket, the time-honoured Caledonian game spreads fast and far over England, over the world, indeed, for on dusty Indian *maidans* good Scotsmen can be seen trying to play the rounds of Zion in that strange land, and under the very Pyramids a golf course is laid out, where the dust of Pharaohs may serve as a tee, or a mummy pit prove the most provoking of bunkers. In the home of its birth this pastime flourishes more than ever. Parties are given for golf along with tea and tennis; schools begin to lay out their golf ground as well as their football field; and at St. Andrews we have the Ladies' Links, where many a masculine heart has been gently spooned or putted into the hole of matrimony. Fair damsels may even be seen lifting and driving in a "foursome," an innovation frowned at by some old stagers, who hardly care to talk about the game till it is ended, and then can talk of nothing else. "*Tee*, veniente die, *tee*, decedente—!" is the song of St. Andrews, which asks for no more absorbing joy than a round in the morning and a round in the evening. In the eyes of inveterate golfers, all prospects are poor beside those links that make the Mecca, the Monte Carlo, the Epsom of the royal game, so one is free to give up the surrounding country as not much contributing to the attractions of the place, many of whose visitors hardly care to stir beyond their beloved arena, unless for a Sunday afternoon walk along the shore as far as that curious freak of the elements known as the Spindle Rock.

Besides its devotion to the game where clubs are always trumps, St. Andrews has in the last generation had an attraction for celebrities in literature and science. The University staff, of course, makes a permanent depot of intellect. The facile essayist A.K.H.B. was long parish minister here, when the Episcopal bishop was a nephew of Wordsworth, himself an author too well known to schoolboys. Here Robert Chambers spent the evening of his days. Blackwood the publisher had a house close at hand, where many famous authors have been guests. In the vicinity, too, is Mount Melville, seat of Whyte-Melville, the novelist. Not to mention living names, the late Mrs. Lynn Linton was a warm lover of St. Andrews. It must have been well known to Mrs. Oliphant, more than one of whose novels take this country for their scene.

Is it impertinent to say a word in praise of a writer, too soon forgotten at circulating libraries, where she was but too voluminously in evidence for the best part of her lifetime? Had she been content with a flat in Grub Street, Mrs. Oliphant might now be better remembered than by the mass of often hasty work for which her way of life gave hostages to fortune and to publishers. Her novels often smell too much of an Aladdin's lamp that had to be rubbed hard for copy; there is awful example to money-making authorship in a middle period of them that scared off readers for whom again she would rise to her early charm. Defects she had, notably a curious warp of sympathy that led her to do less than poetic justice to prodigal ne'er-do-weels; but her chief fault was in writing too much, when at her best she was very good. Her best known stories are those which deal with English life; yet she was not less happy in describing her native Scotland, having an extraordinary insight that set her at home in very varied scenes and classes of society. Few writers are found in touch with so many phases of life. Even George Eliot, sure as she is in portraying her Midland middle-class life, seems a little *depaysé* when she strays among fine folk; and many a skilful novelist might be mentioned who falls into convention or caricature as soon as he gets out of his own familiar environment. But, after Sir Walter, I doubt if there be any author who has given us such a varied gallery of Scottish characters, high and low, divined with Scott's sympathy and often drawn with Jane Austen's minute skill. Her servants and farmers seem as natural as her baronets and ministers, all of them indeed ordinary human beings, not the freaks and monsters of the overcharged art that for the moment has thrown such work as hers into the shade.

ON THE DOCHART, KILLIN, PERTHSHIRE

Of her tales dealing with Fife, perhaps the best, at least the longest, is "The Primrose Path," a beautiful idyll of this East Neuk, its scene laid within a few miles of St. Andrews, evidently at Leuchars, where such a noble Norman chancel is disgraced by the modern meeting-house built on to it, and the old shell of Earl's Hall offered itself as a fit setting for the drama of an innocent girl's heart, that at the end shifts its stage to England. The hero, he that is to be made happy after all, plays a somewhat colourless part in the background; but heroes have license to be lay figures. The real protagonist, the imperfectly villainous Rob Glen, seems to walk out of the canvas; and all the other characters, from the high-bred, scholarly father to the love-sick servant lass, are alive with humour and kindliness. As for the scenery, it is thus that Mrs. Oliphant puts the East Neuk in its best point of view:—

"There does not seem much beauty to spare in the east of Fife. Low hills, great breadths of level fields: the sea a great expanse of blue or leaden grey, fringed with low reefs of dark rocks like the teeth of some hungry monster, dangerous and grim without being picturesque, without a ship to break its monotony. But yet with those limitless breadths of sky and cloud, the wistful clearness and golden after-glow, and all the varying blueness of the hills, it would have been difficult to surpass the effect of the great amphitheatre of sea and land of which this solitary grey old house formed the centre. The hill, behind which the sun had set, is scarcely considerable enough to have a name; but it threw up its outline against the wonderful greenness, blueness, goldenness of the sky with a grandeur which would not have misbecome an Alp. Underneath its shelter, grey and sweet, lay the soft levels of Stratheden in all their varying hues of colour, green corn, and brown earth, and red fields of clover, and dark belts of wood. Behind were the two paps of the Lomonds, rising green against the clear serene: and on the other side entwining lines of hills, with gleams of golden light breaking through the mists, clearing here and there as far as the mysterious Grampians, far off under Highland skies. This was one side of the circle; and the other was the sea, a sea still blue under the faint evening skies, in which the young moon was rising; the yellow sands of Forfarshire on one hand, stretching downwards from the mouth of the Tay, the low brown cliffs and green headlands bending away on the other towards Fifeness—and the great bow of water reaching to the horizon between. Nearer the eye, showing half against the slope of the coast, and half against the water, rose St. Andrews on its cliff, the fine dark tower of the college church poised over the little city, the jagged ruins of the castle marking the outline, the cathedral rising majestically in naked pathos; and old St. Rule, homely and weather-beaten, oldest venerable pilgrim of all, standing strong and steady, at watch upon the younger centuries."

From the flattest part of Fife, let us turn to its inland Highland side. The main North British line to Perth, after passing a dreary coal-field, brings us suddenly beneath the bold swell of Benarty, round which we come in view of the Lomonds with Loch Leven sparkling at their foot. Here indeed we soon get into the small shire of Kinross; but this may be taken as a dependency of the kingdom of Fife, its lowlands also running on the west side into a miniature Highland region, reached by the railway branch that from Loch Leven goes off to Stirling by the Devon Valley and the Ochils, at the end of which Clackmannan vies with Kinross as the Rutland of Scottish counties.

Loch Leven is celebrated for its breed of trout, and for that grey tower half hidden by trees on an islet, which was poor Mary Stuart's prison. The dourest Scotsman's heart has three soft spots, the memory of Robert Burns, the romance of Prince Charlie, and the misfortunes that seem to wash out the errors of that girl queen. This is dubious ground, into which tons of paper and barrels of ink have been thrown without filling up a quaking bog of controversy. I myself have heard a distinguished scholar hissed off the most philosophic platform in Scotland for throwing a doubt on Queen Mary's innocence, so I will say no more than that her harshest historian, if shut up with her in Loch Leven as page or squire, might have been tempted to steal the keys and take an oar in the boat that bore her over those dark waters to brief freedom and safety. Had Charles Edward only had the luck to get his head cut off in solemn state, how much more gloriously dear might now be his memory!

As Scott points out, Fife was noted for a thick crop of gentry, who were apt to be found on the side of the Queen Marys and Prince Charlies, whereas its sturdy common folk rather favoured Whig principles. Not far from Kinross, the grey homespun of Scottish life is proclaimed by one of those ugly obelisks that have so much commended themselves for the expression of Protestant sentiment. At Gairney Bridge, on the Fife and Kinross border, in 1733, four suspended ministers formed themselves into the first Presbytery of the Original Secession Church, a most fissiparous body which brought forth a brood of sects not yet altogether swallowed up in the recent union of the Free and United Presbyterian churches. I am bound to special interest in that foundation, for as a forebear of mine appears riding away from the shores of Loch Leven in Queen Mary's train, so one of those four seceders was my great-great-great-great (or thereabouts) grandfather, Moncrieff of Culfargie, himself grandson of a still remembered Covenanter. His spiritual descendants make a point of the fact that being a small laird, he yet testified against the unpopular system of patronage, and thus is taken to have been before his time. But *Plato amicus*, etc., or as Sterne translates, "Dinah is my aunt, but truth is my sister," and a closer examination reveals among the heads of my forefather's testimony against the Church of Scotland a conscientious protest in favour of executing witches and persecuting Roman Catholics, so perhaps the less said about his views the better. A few years before, a poor old wife, rubbing her hands in crazy delight at the blaze, had been burned as a witch for the last time in Scotland; and the "moderate" ministers were now content to ignore an imaginary crime which a few years later became wiped out of the statute-book.

The ancestral shade should know how filial piety urged me, perhaps alone in this generation, to perform the rite of reading his works, which indeed want such "go" and "snap" as are admired by congregations who "have lost the art of listening to two hours' sermons." He was truly a painful and earnest preacher, in one volume of whose discourses I note this mark of wide-mindedness, that it is entitled "*England's* Alarm," whereas other old Scottish divines seem rather to treat the neighbour country as beyond hope of alarming. His brother-in-law, Clerk of Penicuik, characterises Culfargie as "a very sober, good man, except he should carry his very religious whims so far as to be very uneasy to everybody about him." It is recorded of him that he prayed from his pulpit for the Hanoverian King in face of the Pretender's bristling soldiery, like that other stout Whig divine whose petition ran, "As for this young man who has come among us seeking an earthly crown, may it please Thee to bestow upon him a heavenly one!"

Loyalty to the same line was less frankly shown by a very different member of our clan, Margaret Moncrieff, a name little renowned on this side the Atlantic, while she figures in more than one American book as the "Beautiful Spy." Being shut up among rebels in New York, when the besieging Engineers were commanded by her father Colonel Moncrieff, she got leave to send him little presents, among them flower-paintings on velvet, beneath which were traced plans of the American works. The device being discovered, it might have gone hard with her but for Yankee chivalry, that expelled that artful hussy unhurt, in the end to bring no honour upon her name, if all tales of her be true.

The ancestral worthy whose memory has led me into a digression, lived and laboured in Strathearn, to which from Kinross we pass by Glenfarg, no Highland glen but a fine gulf of greenery with stream, road, and railway winding side by side through its banks and knolls, that called forth Queen Victoria's warm admiration on her first visit to Scotland. At the other end of this Ochil gorge we are welcomed to Perthshire by the wooded crags of Moncrieff Hill, round which the Earn bends to the Tay; then some dozen miles behind, rises the edge of the true Highlands, where "to the north-west a sea of mountains rolls away to Cape Wrath in wave after wave of gneiss, schist, quartzite, granite, and other crystalline masses."

CHAPTER V

THE FAIR CITY

PERTH, the central city of Scotland, whose name has been so flourishingly transplanted to the antipodes, is a very ancient place. Not to insist on fond derivation from a Roman *Bertha*, there seems to have been a Roman station on the Tay, probably at the confluence of the Almond; and curious antiquarians have found cause for confessing to Pontius Pilate as perhaps born in the county, a reproach softened by the consideration of his father being little better than a Roman exciseman. The *alias* of St. Johnston Perth got from its patron saint, who came to be so scurvily handled at the Reformation. At this date it was the only walled city of Scotland. Before this, it had been intermittently the Stuart capital in such a sense as the residence of its Negus is for Abyssinia; and farther back Tayside was the seat of the Alpine kingdom that succeeded a Pictish power. Now sunk in relative importance, Perth makes the central knot of Scottish railway travelling; so on the Eve of St. Grouse its palatial station becomes one of the busiest spots in the kingdom, though the main platform is a third of a mile long. To the stay-at-home public it may perhaps be best known by an industry that has given rise to the proverb "See Perth and *dye*," one which might have darker significance in days when this low site depended for drainage on the floods of the Tay flushing its cellars and cesspools. But its own citizens are brought up to believe that no Naples of them all has so much right to the title of the "Fair City."

Legend tells how Roman soldiers gaining a prospect of the Tay from the heights south of Perth, exclaimed on its North Inch as another Campus Martius; but later visitors have not always shared the local admiration. One modern Italian traveller, Signor Piovanelli, after wandering two or three hours about the Perth streets, took away an impression of dull melancholy; but then he began with an unsatisfactory experience at the Refreshment Room. An else conscientious French tourist explains the bustle of Perth station as its being the rendezvous of the inhabitants seeking distraction from their *triste* life. These be ignorant calumnies. At least our northern York is a typical Scottish town, well displaying the strata of its development. In quite recent years it has been much transmogrified by a new thoroughfare, fittingly named Scott Street, which, running from near the station right through the city, has altered its centre of gravity. The old High Street and South Street, with their "vennels" and "closes," lead transversely from Scott Street to the river, cut at the other end by George Street and John Street, which had supplanted them as main lines of business. "Where are the shops?" I was once asked by a bewildered party of country excursionists, wandering unedified about the vicinity of the station. In those days one had to send them across the city to the streets parallel with the river; but now Scott Street has attracted the Post Office, the Theatre and the Free Library, and bids fair to become the Strand or the Regent Street of the Fair City, fringed by such a display of latter-day villas as attests the prosperity of its business quarters.

PERTH FROM THE SLOPES OF KINNOUL HILL

Fragments of mediæval antiquity also must be sought for towards the river. Off John Street stands the old Cathedral, in the practical Scottish manner shared into three places of worship, once containing dozens of altars, among which an impudent schoolboy threw the first image-breaking stone that spread such a ripple of iconoclasm through the shrines of Scotland. Close by, on the river bank, the Gaol occupies the site of Gowrie House, where James VI. had his mysterious or mythical escape from treason. The Parliament House, too, has vanished, its memory preserved by the name of a "close," the Scottish equivalent for alley. The citizens have lately adopted a traditional "Fair Maid's" house as their official lion, to which indicators point the way from all over the city. This, whatever the higher criticism may say of its claims, has been well restored as a specimen of a solid burgher's home in those days when Simon the Glover was so vexed by the vagaries of his Highland apprentice and by the roistering suitors of his daughter. Since then, Perth has not wanted Fair Maids; but in our time the title has sometimes had a satiric tang as implying what the French stigmatise as *une rosse.*

Simon, as we know, lived close to the royal lodging, which, after the destruction of the castle, was wont to be thriftily taken in the great monastery of Blackfriars, now represented only by the names of a house and a street. In it were enacted stirring scenes of history as well as of fiction, its darkest tragedy the murder of James I. on a February night of 1437. Handsome, brave, a scholar and poet, with the advantage of an involuntary English education, in quieter times this king might have shown himself the best of the Stuarts. He had the welfare of the people at heart, and on his return from the captivity in which he spent his boyhood, tried to bring some degree of order among the lawless feuds of his barons, using against them indeed high-handed and crooked means that were the statecraft of the age. Thus he roused fell enemies who were able to take him unawares, though the story goes that, like Alexander and Cæsar, he had warning from an uncredited seer. Betrayed by false courtiers, he was retiring to bed when the monastery rang with the tramp and cries of the fierce Highlandmen seeking his blood. While the queen and her ladies tried to defend the door, Catherine Douglas giving her broken arm, says the legend, as a bar, James tore up the flooring and let himself down into a drain which he had, unluckily, blocked up a few days before, since in it his tennis balls got lost. There he was discovered by the conspirators, and after a desperate struggle their leader, Sir Thomas Graham, stabbed him to death. Not a minute too soon, for already the good burghers were roused to the rescue, and the regicides had some ado to spur off to the Highlands, safe only for a time, the principal criminals being taken for tortures that horrified even their cruel contemporaries.

From the windings of the Blackfriars quarter, one emerges by what was the North Port, upon Perth's famous Inch, bordered by erections that a generation ago were the modest West End of the city—Athole Place, the Crescent, Rose Terrace, and Barossa Place. At the foot of the Inch, by the river, stands a tall obelisk in honour of the 90th Regiment, the "Perthshire Volunteers," now amalgamated with the Cameronians; and near it the customary statue of Prince Albert, one of the first inaugurated by Queen Victoria, who then insisted on knighting the Lord Provost of the city, a worthy grocer, much to his discontent, and, if all tales be true, to his loss in business. Perth, as becomes the ex-capital, has a Lord Provost, who cannot meet the Lord Provost of Glasgow without raising sore points of precedence. Invested with special powers when Perth was a royal residence, its magistrates were not persons to be trifled with, as an English officer found early in the eighteenth century. This mettlesome spark, quartered here, had fatally stabbed a dancing-master who stood in the way of troublesome attentions to one of his pupils. The same day, tradition has it, the slaughterer was seized, tried, and hanged under the old law of "red-hand," then put in force for the last time. An ornament to the story is that the criminal's brother commanded a ship of war in the Firth of Forth, over which was the way to Edinburgh, and that he long kept watch for a chance of capturing some Perth bailie on whom to take revenge. These were the good old times.

By the bridge at the foot of the North Inch, a pretentious classical structure, marking the era of Provost Marshall whom it commemorates, rears its dome above a Museum of Antiquities such as becomes an ancient city. This faces the end of Tay Street, the pleasant river-side boulevard between the North and South Inches, towards the farther end of which a newer Museum contains a remarkable natural history collection. At its corner of South Street are the County Buildings, adorned with portraits of local worthies, and at the end of High Street, the City Buildings with windows illustrating Perth's history. Perth has now two bridges and everything handsome about it—besides the Dundee railway bridge with its footway from the South Inch. The central bridge is only three or four years old, but here stood one washed away in 1621, since when the citizens had long to depend on what is now the old bridge below the North Inch.

This bridge leads over into the transpontine suburb, above which, on the slopes of Kinnoul Hill, the rank and fashion of the city have inclined to seek "eligible building sites," *Scotticè*, "feuing plots." The banks of the river, too, on this side have long been bordered by villas and cottages of gentility; but about "Bridge End" there is still a fragment of the humbler suburb that has had more than one famous sojourner in our time. Here, in a house now distinguished by a tablet, and afterwards in Rose Terrace opposite, John Ruskin spent bits of his childhood with an aunt, wife of the tanner whose unsavoury business had the credit of keeping the cholera away from Bridge End. That amateur of beauty, for his part, has nothing but good to say of Perth: he remembers with pleasure the precipices of Kinnoul, the swirling pools of the "Goddess-river," even the humble "Lead," in which other less gifted children have found "a treasure of flowing diamond," now covered up to belie his vision of its defilement; and his lifelong impression was that "Scottish sheaves are more golden than are bound in other lands, and that no harvests elsewhere visible to human eyes are so like the 'corn of heaven' as those of Strath Tay and Strath-Earn." Yet youthful gladness turned to pain, when through his connection with Perth Ruskin came to make that ill-matched marriage with its fairest maid, afterwards known as Lady Millais. Their brief union he passes over in silence in his else most communicative reminiscences; and the writer were indiscreet indeed who should revive rumours spun round a case of hopeless incompatibility. One misty legend, probably untrue, declares him, for certain reasons, to have vowed never to enter the house in which her family lived, that Bowerswell mansion, a little up the hill, where a crystal spring had often arrested his childish attention. He did enter the house once, to be married, according to the custom of the bride's Presbyterian Church: *hinc illae lacrimae*, according to the legend.

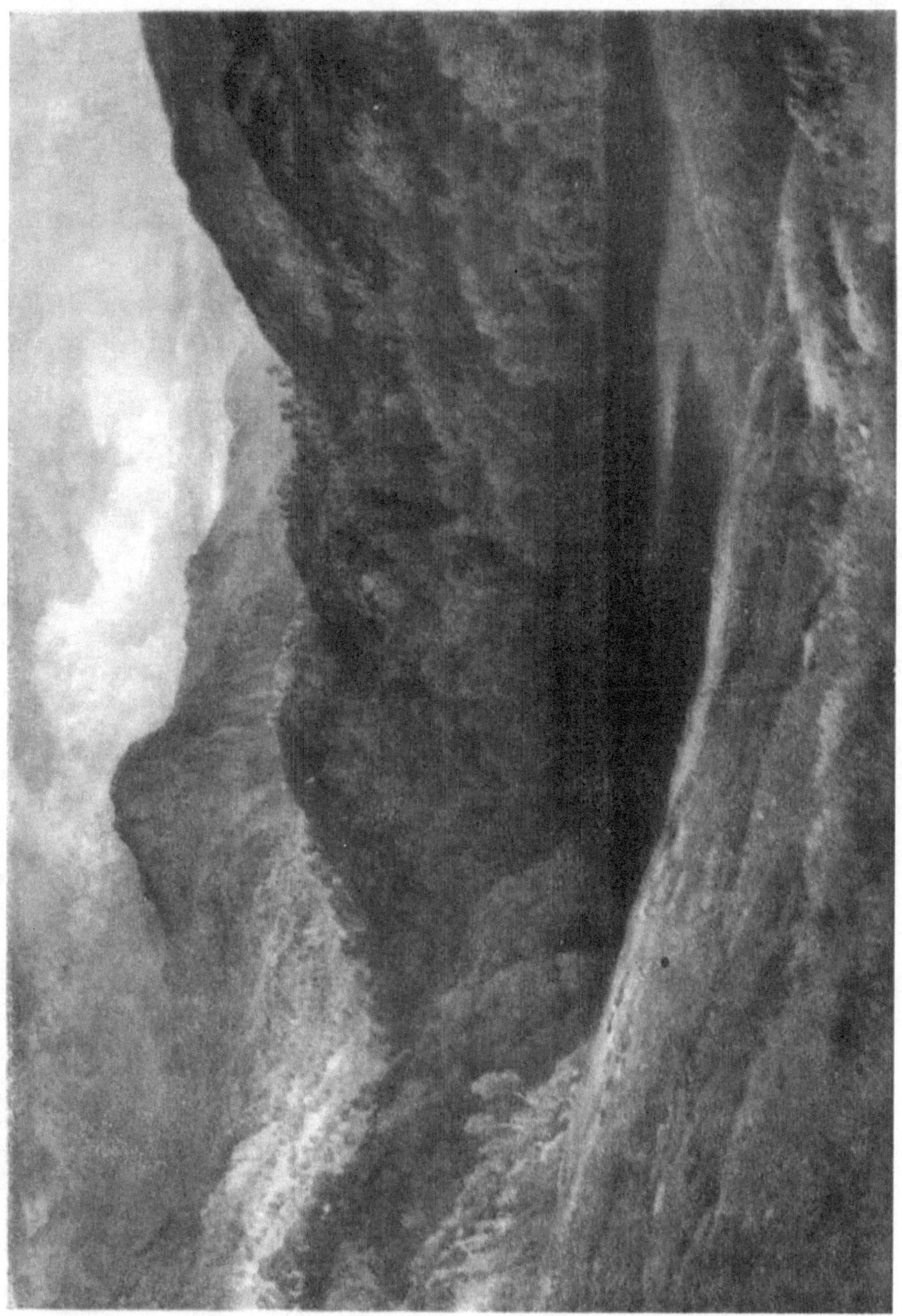

BEN A'AN, CORNER OF LOCH KATRINE, PERTHSHIRE

LOCH VENNACHAR, PERTHSHIRE

Like that great prose-poet, the reader's humble servant, without being able to boast himself a native of Perth, spent part of his youth here and has pleasant memories that tempt him, too, to be garrulous. I have no recollection of seeing Ruskin at Perth, but I well remember Millais in the prime of manly beauty. In the early days of his fame he lived much with his wife's family at Bowerswell; and several of the children he then painted so charmingly were playmates of mine, who would come to our Christmas parties in the picturesque costumes he had been putting on canvas. For some reason or other, he never proposed to immortalise my features; but I have boyish memories of him that seem to hint at the two sides of his art. My sister sat for one of his most famous pictures, on which, in the capacity of escort to his child model, I had the unappreciated privilege of seeing him at work. What struck a little Philistine like me was how the painter paid no attention to a call to lunch, working away in such a *furor* of industry as I could sympathise with only if mischief were in question. Someone brought him a plate of soup and a glass of wine, which he hastily swallowed on his knees, and again flung himself into his absorbing task. My internal reflection was that in thus despising his meals this man showed such sense as Macfarlane's geese who, as Scott records, loved their play better than their meat. But a quite different behaviour on another occasion excited stronger disapproval of the future P.R.A. in my schoolboy mind. When out shooting with my father one hot day, I took him to a little moorland farm where the people would offer us a glass of milk. Millais rather scornfully asked if they had no cream. They brought him a tumblerful, the whole yield for the day probably, and he tossed if off with a "Das ist kleine Gabe!" air that set me criticising the artistic temperament. It was a fixed notion with young Scots that all English people were greedy: "Set roasted beef and pudding on the opposite side o' the pit o' Tophet, and an Englishman will make a spang at it!" exclaimed the goodwife of Aberfoyle. Thus we give back the southron's sneer for our frugal poverty. Our old Adam might welcome the good things of life that fairly came our way; but we schooled each other in a Spartan point of honour that forbade too frank enjoyment. Millais was born very far south; and there are those who say that he might have been a still greater painter, had he shown less taste for the cream of life.

From Bowerswell, an artist had not far to go for scenes of beauty. The road past the house, winding up to a Roman Catholic monastery built since those days, leads on into the woods of Kinnoul Hill, which is to Perth what Arthur's Seat is to Edinburgh. No tourist should, as many do, neglect to take the shady climb through those woods, suggesting the scenes of a tamed German "Wald." At the farther side one comes out on the edge of a grand crag, the view from which has been compared to the Rhine valley, and to carry out this similitude, a mock ruin crowns the adjacent cliff. We have here turned our backs on the Grampians so finely seen from the Perth slope of the hill, and are looking down upon the Tay as it bends eastward between this spur of the Sidlaws and the wooded outposts of the Ochils opposite, then, swollen by the Earn, opens out into its Firth in the Carse of Gowrie, dotted with snug villages and noble seats such as the Castle of Kinfauns among the woods at our feet, a scene most lovely when

> The sun was setting on the Tay,
> The blue hills melting into grey;
> The mavis and the blackbird's lay
> Were sweetly heard in Gowrie.

The Gowrie earldom, once so powerful in Perth, has disappeared from its life; but the title is still familiar as covering one of those districts of a Scottish county that bear enduring by-names, like the Devonshire South Hams or the Welsh Vale of Glamorgan. To a native ear, the scene is half suggested by the word *Carse*, implying a stretch of rich lowland along a river-side, whereas Strath is the more broken and extensive valley of a river that has its upper course in some wilder Glen or tiny Den, the *Dean* of so many southern villages. The course of the Tay from Perth to Dundee, below Kinnoul, ceases to be romantic while remaining beautiful in a more sedate and stately fashion as it flows between its receding walls of wooded heights, underneath which the "Carles of the Carse" had once such an ill name as Goldsmith's rude Carinthian boor, but so many a "Lass of Gowrie" has shown a softer heart—

> She whiles did smile and whiles did greet;
> The blush and tear were on her cheek.

There are various versions of this ballad, whose tune makes the Perth local anthem; but they all tell the same old tale and often told, with that most hackneyed of ends—

> The old folks syne gave their consent;
> And then unto Mass-John we went;
> Who tied us to our hearts' content,
> Me and the Lass o' Gowrie.

Many a stranger comes and goes at Perth without guessing what charming prospects may be sought out on its environing heights. But half an hour's stroll through the streets must make him aware of those Inches that prompt a hoary jest concerning the size of the Fair City. The North and South Inches, between which it lies, properly islands, green flats beside the Tay, are in their humble way its Hyde Park and Regent's Park. The South Inch, close below the station, is the less extensive, once the grounds of a great Carthusian monastery, then site of a strong fort built by Cromwell, now notable mainly for the avenue through which the road from Edinburgh comes in over it, and for the wharf at its side that forms a port for small vessels and excursion steamers plying by leave of the tide. On the landward side, beyond the station, Perth is spreading itself up the broomy slopes of Craigie Hill, which still offers pleasant rambles. Beyond the farther end stands a gloomy building once well known to evil-doers as the General Prison for Scotland; but of late years its character has undergone some change; and I am not sure how far the old story may still keep its point that represents an inmate set loose from these walls, when hailed by a friendly wayfarer as "honest man," giving back glumly "None of your dry remarks!"

A more cheerful sight is the golf links on Moncrieff Island, above which crosses the railway to Dundee. This neighbour has long surpassed Perth, grown on jute and linen to be the third city of Scotland, its name perhaps most familiar through the marmalade which used to be manufactured, I understand, in the Channel Islands, when wicked wit declared its maker to have a contract for sweeping out the Dundee theatre. Northern undergraduates at Oxford and Cambridge are believed to have spread to southern breakfasts the use of this confection in the form so well known now that its materials are so cheap. The name has a Greek ancestry, and the thing seems to have come to us as quince-preserve, through the Portuguese *marmelo*, in time transferred and restricted to another fruit. Oranges, indeed, could not have been as plentiful as blackberries in Britain, when the Euphuist Lyly compared life without love to a meal without marmalade.

A CROFT NEAR DALMALLY, ARGYLLSHIRE

Such a twenty-miles digression from the South Inch implies how little there is to say about it. Now let us take a dander up the larger North Inch, Perth's Campus Martius, at once promenade, race-course, review ground, grazing common, washing green, golf links, cricket-field, and area for unfenced football games in which, summer and winter, young Scots learn betimes to earn gate-money for English clubs. Opposite the Perth Academy appears to have been the arena where that early professional, Hal o' the Wynd, played up so well in the deadly match by which the Clan Kay and the Clan Chattan enacted the less authentic tragedy of the Kilkenny cats. This spacious playground is now edged by a neat walk, which makes the constitutional round of sedate citizens, who on the safe riverside have the spectacle of pleasure boating against the difficulties of a strong stream and shallow rapids, and of the pulling of salmon nets in the season. Here a barelegged laddie, with the rudest tackle, has been known to hook a 30-lb. fish, holding on to the monster for two hours till some men helped him out with his fortune. The salmon of the Tay, reared in the Stormontfield Ponds above Perth, are famous for size, a weight of over 70 lbs. being not unknown; and cavillers on other streams cannot belittle its bigger fish by the sneer of "bigger liars there!" The keeping of fish in ice, and railway communications, have much enhanced the price, to the astonishment of a Highland laird who in a London tavern ordered a steak for himself and a "salmon for Donald" without guessing that his henchman's meal must be paid for in gold as his own in silver. The old story of masters contracting not to feed their servants on salmon more than twice a week, is told, by Ruskin for one, of Tayside as of other river-lands. But so masterful are the demands of London now, that salmon may sometimes be dearer on the banks of the Tay than in the glutted metropolitan market. The Tay has another treasure, for now and then valuable pearls have been fished out of it by boys who, in a dry summer, can wade across its shallows just above the old bridge. A very different sight might be seen here when the river was frozen across and roughened by a jam of miniature icebergs.

Half-way up the town side of the Inch, where a few trees dotted across it mark its old limits, extended more than a century ago, stands the now restored mansion of Balhousie, which used to be known as *Bushy* by that curious trick of contraction, more common in Scottish than in English names, that drove a bewildered foreigner to complain of our pronouncing as *Marchbanks* what we spelt as *Cholmondeley*. But one notes how in Scotland as in England, the tendency is to restore such words to their full sound, as in this case. Near the station in Perth is Pomarium Street, marking the orchard of the old Carthusian monastery, or, as some have held, the outskirt of the Roman City. *Consule Planco*, I knew it only as the *Pow*; but out of curiosity I lately tried this abbreviation in vain on a postman and on a telegraph boy of the present generation. Methven, near Perth, was always pronounced *Meffen*; Henry VIII. spells it *Muffyn*; as Ruthven was and perhaps still is *Riven*. The station of Milngavie is no longer proclaimed by railway porters as *Millguy*, and the place Claverhouse—no hero indeed at spelling—spells *Ruglen*, tends to assume its full dignity of Rutherglen, as Cirencester or Abergavenny lose their old contractions in this generation's mouth. Many other examples might be given of a change, with which, I fancy, railway porters have much to do; but one of the best authorities on such matters, Dr. H. Bradley, puts it down to what he calls half-education, setting up spelling as an idol. As for the altered pronunciation of Scottish family names, that seems often to come from English blundering, modestly adopted by their owners. Bálfour, to take a distinguished example, was Balfoúr, till the trick of southern speech shifted back the accent. Forbes is still vernacularly a dissyllable in the Forbes country, as in *Marmion*, and in the old schoolboy saw about General 4 B's, who marched his 4 C's, etc. Dalziels and Menzies must have long given up in despair the attempt to get their names properly pronounced in the south as *Déél* and *Meengus*. The family known at home as *Jimmyson* become now content to have made a noise in the world as Jameson. But some such changes have been long in progress. It was "bloody *Mackengie*" whom audacious boys dared to come out of his grave in Greyfriars' Churchyard; and if we go far enough back we find the name of this persecutor written Mackennich. In the good old times every gentleman had his own spelling, as what for no? There is a deed, and not a very ancient one, drawn up by certain forebears of mine, in which, among them, they spell their name five different ways. In general, it may be remembered, the z that makes such a stumbling-block to strangers in so many Scottish names, is to be taken as a *y*. When we have such real enigmas as Colquhoun and Kirkcudbright to boggle over, the wonder is that Milton should make any ado at Gordon or "Galasp," by which he probably meant Gillespie.

Nearly opposite Balhousie, which has suggested this digression, across the Tay, peeps out the house of Springlands, which reminds me how Perth has been the cradle of a sect. The Sandemans of Springlands in my youth exhibited some marked religious leanings, but none of them, I think, followed the doctrine of their ancestor. The sect in question was founded in the days of early methodism by John Glass, a Scottish clergyman; but his son-in-law, Robert Sandeman, proved so much the Paul of the new faith by preaching it as far as America, that there, as in England, the body is known as Sandemanians, while in Scotland they still sometimes bear the original name Glassites. Their most famous member was Michael Faraday, who preached in the London meeting-house. Its doctrine had, like Plymouth Brethrenism, a strange attraction for old Indian officers, who, cut off from home influences, repelled by surrounding heathenism, and their brains perhaps a little addled by the sun, have often been led to read odd meanings into revelations and prophecies, studied late in life. There used to be a detachment of retired veterans encamped about Perth as headquarters of their Bethel, whose wives and children, in some cases, attended the Episcopal Chapel. A peculiarity of their belief was an absolute horror of being present at any alien worship, even family prayers, as I could show from some striking instances. This must have borne hard on soldier converts, who, in the army, are allowed a choice of only three forms of worship. "No fancy religions in the service," growled the sergeant to a recruit who professed himself a Seventh Day Baptist: "fall in with the Roman Catholics!" Another note of the Sandemanians was an unwillingness to communicate their views, what even seemed a resentfulness of inquiry by outsiders. Disraeli excused a similar trait in the Jews by the dry remark, "The House of Lords does not seek converts." I once in the innocent confidence of youth asked a Glassite leader to enlighten me as to their faith, and was snubbed with a short "The doors are open." But I never heard of any stranger trusting himself within the doors of that meeting-house.

Report gave out a love-feast as a main function, from which the sect got "kailites" as a nickname. The kiss of peace, it was understood, went round; and ribald jesters represented the presiding official as obliged to exhort, "Dinna pass over the auld wife!" This much one can truly say of the congregation, that they were kind and helpful to each other, a Glassite in distress being unknown in the Fair City, where they had adherents in all classes. As for their spiritual exclusiveness, against that reproach may be set the old story of the "burgher" lass who, having once attended an "anti-burgher" service with her lad, was rebuked by her own kirk-session for the sin of "promiscuous hearing."

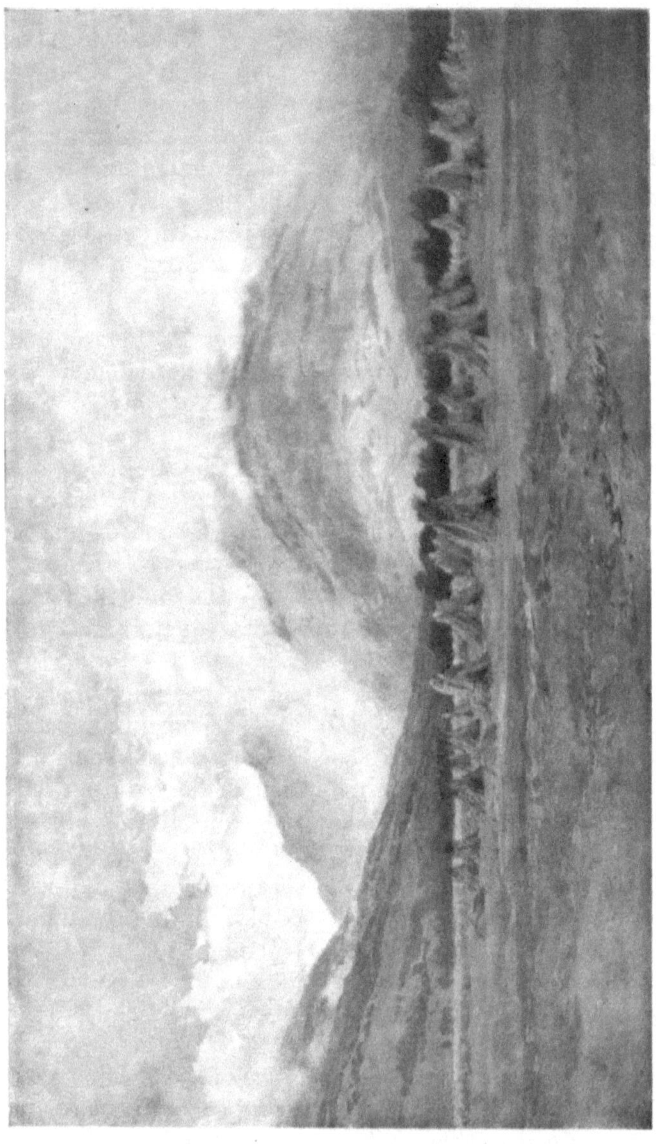

WET HARVEST TIME NEAR DALMALLY, ARGYLLSHIRE

Above the Inch comes the less trim space called the "Whins," where lucky caddies glean lost golf balls in its patches of scrub and in pools formed by the highest flowing of the tide from the Firth. With this ends the public pleasure-ground; but the walk may be prolonged along the elevated bank of the river, above the sward that makes the town bathing-place, and brown pools that Ruskin might have found perilous as well as picturesque, but as he speaks of himself as keeping company with his girl cousin, not to speak of the fear of his careful mother, we may suppose that he made no rash excursions into the water. One deep swirl within a miniature promontory is aptly known as the "Pen and Ink"; then higher up a shallow creek encloses the "Woody Island," no island to bare-legged laddies who here play Robinson Crusoe.

The opposite bank shows a lordly park with timber that should bring a blush to the cheek of Dr. Johnson's ghost, concealing the castellated Scone Palace, seat of its Hereditary Keeper, Lord Mansfield, who has another enviable home beside Hampstead Heath. Little remains of the old royal Castle and Abbey of Scone; the Stone of Destiny, that ancient palladium, fabled pillow of Jacob's vision of the angels, on which the Scottish kings were crowned, has been in Westminster Abbey since Edward I.'s invasion. The modern mansion contains some relics of Queen Mary and her son, but its owners do not encourage visitors. An eminence near at hand is known by the curious name of the Boot Hill, tradition making it formed by the earth which nobles after a coronation emptied out of their boots, so stuffed that each proud baron might feel the satisfaction of standing on his own ground!

Half-a-dozen miles farther up the river, on this side, one is free to seek the top of Dunsinnan Hill for what is believed to have been the site of Macbeth's Castle, and for a fine prospect of the Grampians with Birnam Wood in the foreground. Shakespeare, and the legend he followed, make no account of the fact that a considerable river guarded Dunsinnan from hostile advance of its distant neighbour. Yet a parish minister of these parts has convinced himself that the author of *Macbeth* must have known the neighbourhood. One conjecture is that he visited Perth with a far-strolling troop of actors. "You will say next that Shakespeare was Scotch!" exclaimed a scornful southron to a Scot who seemed too patriotic; and the cautious answer was, "Weel, his abeelity would warrant the supposeetion." As for Macbeth and his good lady, it is time that some serious attempt were made to whitewash their characters, as Renan has done for Jezebel, and Froude for Henry VIII. No doubt these two worthies represented the good old Scottish party, strong on Disruption principles and sternly set against the Anglican influences introduced through Malcolm Canmore, in favour of whose family the southern poet shows a natural bias. Did we know the whole truth, that gracious Duncan may have had a scheme to serve the Macbeths as the Macdonalds of Glencoe were served by their guests. The one thing clear in early Scottish history is that the dagger played a greater part than the ballot box, and that scandals in high life might sometimes be obscured by an eloquent advocate on one side or other. Sir Walter does give some hints for a brief in Macbeth's case, though in his *Tales of a Grandfather* he sets the orthodox legend strutting with its "cocked hat and stick." Macbeth, as he says, probably met Duncan in fair fight near Elgin; and the scene of his own discomfiture appears to have been the Mar country rather than the Tay valley.

But we are still strolling on the right bank of the Tay, to be followed for a mile or two up to the mouth of the Almond, a pretty walk, which few strangers find out for themselves. There is in Scotland a want of the field paths which Hawthorne so much admired in England, "wandering from stile to stile, along hedges and across broad fields, and through wooded parks leading you to little hamlets of thatched cottages, ancient, solitary farmhouses, picturesque old mills, streamlets, pools, and all those quiet, secret, unexpected, yet strangely-familiar features of English scenery that Tennyson shows us in his idylls and eclogues." Every inch of tillable land is in the north more economically dealt with; the farmer, struggling against a harsher climate, cannot afford to leave shady hedges and winding paths; his fields are fenced by uncompromising stone walls against a looser law of trespass. Embowered lanes, too, "for whispering lovers made," are rarer in this land of practical farming. Here it is rather on wild "banks and braes" of streams, unless where their waters can be coined into silver as salmon-fishings, that lovers and poets may ramble at will, shut out from the work-a-day world by thickets of hawthorn, brier, woodbine, and other "weeds of glorious feature":—

> The Muse, nae poet ever fand her
> Till by himsel' he learned to wander
> Adown some trotting burn's meander,
> An' no think lang.

If any ill-advised stranger find the streets of the Fair City dull, as would hardly be his lot on market-day, let him turn to Kinnoul Hill for a noble scene, and to the Tay banks for a characteristic one of broad fields and stately woods, backed by the ridge of the Grampians a dozen miles away. For another sample of Scottish aspects he might take the Edinburgh road across the South Inch, and over by Moncrieff Hill to the Bridge of Earn, where he comes into the lower flats of Strathearn, on which a tamed Highland stream winds sinuously to the Tay between its craggy rim and the rounded ridge of the Ochils. The village has a well-built air, due to the neighbourhood of Pitkaithly spa, that in Scott's day was a local St. Ronan's, whose patrons lodged at the Bridge of Earn, or even walked out from Perth, to take the waters, which before breakfast, on the top of this exercise, must have had a notable effect in certain cases. The original Spa in Belgium owed much of its credit to the fact of its springs being a mile or two out of the town. Our forefathers' ignorance of microbes seems to have been tempered by active habits: it was more than a dozen miles Piscator and his friends had to trudge from Tottenham before reaching their morning draught at Hoddesdon. As for Pitkaithly, there is at present an attempt to resuscitate the use of its waters, still dispensed near Kilgraston, a house founded by a Jamaica planter, who had two such sons as General Sir Hope Grant and Sir Francis Grant, P.R.A.

This part of Strathearn is a flat lowland plain, on which, once in a way, I have seen a pack of foxhounds, whereas, in the ruggeder mass of the county, as English squires must be scandalised to learn—

> Though space and law the stag we lend,
> Ere hound we slip or bow we bend,
> Whoever recked where, how, and when,
> The treacherous fox is trapped or slain.

Where foxes are sometimes like wolves for size and destructiveness, a Highland fox-hunter ranks with a rat-catcher. But Fife, at hand over the Ochils, is a civilised region in which Reynard claims his due observance. Near its border, still in Perthshire, is the sadly-decayed town of Abernethy, whose Round Tower makes the only monument of the days when it was a Pictish capital. Another seat of Pictish princes, not far away, was at Forteviot, near the Kinnoul Earls' Dupplin Castle, where Edward Balliol defeated the Regent Mar in a hot fight, before marching on to Perth to be crowned for a time, when Scotland, like Brentford, had two kings. If only for their natural amenities, these spots might well be visited; yet to tourists they are unknown unless as way-stations respectively on the rival North British and Caledonian railways from Edinburgh to Perth. But to me each of their now obscure names is dearly familiar, since the days when they were landmarks on my way back from school, from which in those days one came back more gladly; and *Auchterarder*, Forteviot, FORGANDENNY, made a *crescendo* of joyful sounds, each hailing a stage nearer home.

CHAPTER VI

THE HIGHLAND LINE

From Perth to Inverness runs the Highand Railway, that pierces through the heart of the Grampians. Giving off a branch to Loch Tay and coach routes to other choice nooks of the noblest northern county, this line mounts among the wilds of Atholl, and near its highest level brings us into Inverness-shire; then it descends to the old Badenoch Forest, down the upper course of the Spey, past Kingussie to Aviemore, where its main track turns over the Findhorn, and by Culloden to the capital of the Highlands. There is not a finer railway ride in the kingdom, as the tourist knows well enough from his programmes, so the Highland line needs no advertisement here.

But there is an older use of this name, for the irregular line along which the Highlands fall in a broken wave upon the richer country, a zone pointed out by Scott and other writers as the most charming part of Scotland. The austere spirit of mountain solitudes is not so easily caught as the varied charms of a debateable land, where "the rivers find their way out of the mountainous region by the wildest leaps, and through the most romantic passes," and Nature's rugged features straggle down among good roads and inns, the practical and the picturesque throwing each other into alternate relief. This is the special loveliness of southern and eastern Perthshire, across which the Grampians make an oblique border, once too often marked with fire and sword, while its straths and lake basins repeat in miniature the same mingling of Highland and Lowland scenery, and of homes thus contrasted by "Ian Maclaren": —

> "The lowland farm stands amid its neighbours along the highway, with square fields, trim fences, slated houses, cultivated after the most scientific method, and to the last inch, a very type of a shrewd, thrifty, utilitarian people. The Highland farm is half-a-dozen patches of as many shapes scattered along the hillside, wherever there are fewest stones and deepest soil and no bog, and those the crofter tills as best he can — sometimes getting a harvest, and sometimes seeing the first snow cover his oats in the sheaf, sometimes building a rude dyke to keep off the big, brown, hairy cattle that come down to have a taste of the sweet green corn, but often finding it best to let his barefooted children be a fence by day, and at certain seasons to sit up all night himself to guard his scanty harvest from the forays of the red deer. Somewhere among the patches he builds his low-roofed house, and thatches

it over with straw, on which by and by, grass with heather and wild flowers begins to grow, till it is not easy to tell his home from the hill. His farm is but a group of tiny islands amid a sea of heather that is ever threatening to overwhelm them with purple spray. Anyone can understand that this man will be unpractical, dreamy, enthusiastic, the child of the past, the hero of hopeless causes, the seer of visions."

THE GRAMPIANS FROM BOAT OF GARTEN, INVERNESS-SHIRE

We have already crossed the Highland line to the Trossachs. Now, in a few hours' walk by less famous scenes, let me lead the reader right up into the Highlands from the North Inch of Perth. Our way shall be the green banks of the Almond, with only now and then a turning aside on the roads which are seldom the most pleasing features of a Scottish countryside. The name, properly *Almaine*, as Wordsworth has it, seems of the same origin as the Irish Bog of Allen, *Moine Almhaine* in Celtic. There is more than one Almond in Scotland, which has countless streams of which this is a type, a true Highland water, now gathering into creamy pools, now rushing over pebbly shallows, here pent in a leafy glen, there rippling by open fields and works of man, everywhere wilful, cheerful, and eager.

At the Almond mouth, over which it straggles thinly in summer to join the swirls of the Tay, is believed to have stood the Roman station that may or may not have been the original Perth. The tributary's right bank is edged by a wide sward, up which anglers and other idlers can stroll freely for miles, unless barred by the red flag of a rifle range that has sent not a few marksmen to Wimbledon and Bisley. On this side stands a fragment of Huntingtower, a castle of the Gowries, widely known by the song founded on an obscure ballad, with the same motive as the English "Nut-brown Maid," in which a high-born lover—supposed to have been a Duke of Atholl—puts his sweetheart to the test by pretending to take leave, to be poor, to be already married; then, when nothing can shake her fidelity, rewards her with full avowal—

> Blair in Atholl's mine, Jeanie!
> Little Dunkeld is mine, lassie!
> St. Johnston's bower and Huntingtower—
> And a' that's mine is thine, lassie!

Here the idle stream is harnessed to service in bleachworks, whose white ware spread on green slopes makes a feature of the scenery about Perth. Above the villages of Almondbank and Pitcairn Green, the stream, like Simon Glover's apprentice, throws off its industrial disguise to put on a Highland garb of rocks and dells and bosky braes. A beautiful spot is the Glen of Lynedoch, famed by a touching tradition which the graves of Bessie Bell and Mary Gray attest as no mere legend. These "bonny lasses," as their song styles them, were bosom friends who beside the Almond built themselves a bower as refuge from the Great Plague, raging in Perth as in London. According to the story, they were visited by a lover who brought them food, and with it the fatal infection. Prosaic critics point out that such bowers were used as isolation huts for suspected cases. At all events, the girls died in their hermitage, and were brought to be buried at Methven Church, but the Methven folk stoned back the bearers of contagion from the ford; then in death, as in life, the bodies found a home by the Almond. Their fate was so well though vaguely remembered, that both Burns and Scott came to make inquiries about the grave, which had already been enclosed by the owner of the property, and is now marked by a railing, beneath a clump of yews, and by the inscription "They lived—they loved—they died."

KILLIN, PERTHSHIRE

A MOOR NEAR KILLIN, PERTHSHIRE

A more modern romance haunts this glen. Here stands in ruin the deserted mansion of a laird driven by grief into renown. This was Thomas Graham, who in the latter part of the eighteenth century devoted himself to such "improvements" as were then the fashion with cultured landowners, and planted exotic growths now running wild among the native greenery. The death of his beautiful wife, painted by Gainsborough, struck him so deeply to heart, that, when over forty years of age, he went to the wars, and rose to be the Lord Lynedoch who won the battle of Barossa. He had two other Peninsular veterans as neighbours, all three of them eyewitnesses of Sir John Moore's burial at dead of night, Sir George Murray, Wellington's Quartermaster-General, and Sir David Baird, of whom it is told that, when his mother heard how he was among Hyder Ali's prisoners, chained two and two, her first remark was, "Lord pity the chiel that's chained to oor Davie!" On either side are scenes of battles long ago: to the south, Methven, a disaster for Bruce, and its neighbour Ruthven, a victory for Montrose; to the north, Luncarty, where the founder of the Hay family is said to have turned the tide of battle against the Danes, by rushing in with his plough coulter like a legendary Nicol Jarvie.

Glenalmond, little sought as it is by strangers, is better known to many of Mudie's subscribers than they may be aware, being clearly the chief scene of "Ian Maclaren's" popular tales, in which, while dwelling so much on the character of the inhabitants, the author seems strangely reticent as to natural charms, well hinted at indeed in the title *Bonnie Brier Bush*. Drumtochty—the real name of a farm—is Logie Almond with its Heriotsfield village; Kildrummie is Methven; and Muirton, of course, is Perth. Some of his personages, also, appear taken from real prototypes, touched up into very much of fancy pictures, if neighbours are to be believed.

A little higher comes Trinity College, Glenalmond, founded as a buttress to the Scottish Episcopal Church, on the model of English public schools. Its first head was Dr. Charles Wordsworth, nephew of the poet, formerly second master at Winchester, and once tutor to Mr. Gladstone, with whom his conscientious disagreement in politics barred the ecclesiastical promotion which he deserved as well as his brother, Christopher of Lincoln. He never rose farther than the elective bishopric of the diocese which it pleases Scottish Episcopalians to style that "of St. Andrews, Dunkeld, and Dunblane"; and of late years their prelates have taken to sign themselves by such territorial designations, assumed by men whose legal status in the country is that of dissenting ministers. When Dr. Wordsworth became bishop, the whole income of himself and his score of clergy was some £2000 a year; but he had a private endowment in "Wordsworth's Greek Grammar," which enabled him without shame to give out from the pulpit, as I have heard, "It is my dooty to announce to you that a collection will be made in this chapel, next Sunday, for the purpose of increasing the income of the Bishop of the diocese." He was a learned and amiable man, but without much knowledge of human nature, as shown by his earnest effort to preach an Eirenicon between his exotic prelacy and Scotch Presbyterianism. In his memoirs he states that his Glenalmond pupils were the most Christian and gentlemanly boys he ever knew, on which let me comment that I have reason for calling some of them arrant poachers, whom the discipline of early days did not restrain from going fishing in the "wee short hours ayont the twal'." He cherishes the recollection that he had to expel only three of them, and that these were all "schismatics." I take him to have been deficient in sense of humour, to judge by the gusto with which he read aloud his great-uncle's most droning effusions. He would probably not have relished a story a friend of mine used to tell of North-Western Canada. Those wilds, in early days, were the charge of an Archbishop, who, visiting an unsophisticated part of his diocese, put up with a Scotch Presbyterian farmer as owner of the best house in the settlement. This hospitably entertained prelate, remarking how a newly born baby made part of the family, delicately inquired as to whether it had been yet baptized, and hinted that the parents might like to take advantage of such an occasion. But the good man seemed not duly pleased by the honour thus proffered. "I'll just step ben, and see what the mistress thinks," he said awkwardly; then presently returning: "We're both much obliged to ye, sir—we take it kindly; we know ye mean well; but if ye'll no mind, the mistress would rather wait till a regular meenister comes round."

The attempt to root a Winchester on the Highland border did not for a time find much deepness of earth, but the school has since flourished under other masters. Its lordly building had the fate of being set on fire by an unworthy pupil, son of an ex-Minister, whose connections could not save him from being brought to justice. A more tragic scandal, now a generation old, was when the owner of the neighbouring mansion, the second legal dignitary of Scotland, having been convicted of parliamentary bribery on the previous step of his career, both cut his throat and threw himself into the Almond. This points the moral of an abuse that has flourished more rankly in Scotland than in England, whereby legal posts go as spoils of party victory, though indeed a better era seems inaugurated by a Conservative Government which recently honoured itself by giving the highest judicial office to a political opponent as the most worthy. But we should not get far, if we are to stop for all the stories of fire and blood that haunt the Highland line.

Glenalmond now leads us fairly into the Highlands, and by the river we hold up through the Sma' Glen, or as Wordsworth calls it, the Narrow Glen, whose lion is the legendary grave of Ossian, man or myth, that had a more congenial birthplace in the "tremendous wilds" of Glencoe declared by Dickens "fearful in their grandeur and amazing solitude."

> In this still place, where murmurs on
> But one meek streamlet, only one,
> He sang of battles, and the breath
> Of stormy war, and violent death;
> And should, methinks, when all was past,
> Have rightfully been laid at last
> Where rocks were rudely heaped, and rent
> As by a spirit turbulent;
> Where sights were rough and sounds were wild,
> And every thing unreconciled,
> In some complaining, dim retreat
> For fear and melancholy meet;

But this is calm; there cannot be
A more entire tranquillity.

IN GLENFINLAS, PERTHSHIRE

Our half-day's walk may be prolonged to a whole one by path up the Almond and across to Loch Tay; but if one seek pleasant quarters not so far off, at Newton Bridge he may turn south by Foulford and Monzie to Crieff. This cheerful little border town ranks as favourite *sommerfrische* of Scots folk, apart from those places that are more sought by tourists. Well situated, looking south from the lowest slope of the hills, almost in the centre of the country, it is unusually dry as well as airy and genial, not pent in like Callander, nor too bracing for cold-blooded folk like Braemar. So Crieff has now two railways and everything handsome about it. Its spacious market-place proclaims it an old borough, with tolbooth, cross, and iron "jougs" for the terror of offenders; and here once the "kind gallows of Crieff" gave Lowlanders' answer to that high-flown boast—

> Aye, by my soul, while on yon plain
> The Saxon rears one shock of grain;
> While of ten thousand herds there strays,
> But one along yon river's maze,
> The Gael, of plain and river heir,
> Shall with strong hand redeem his share!

Why the *kind* gallows? not even Scott can say, but he suggests the idea of this seeming a kindred or natural doom to the Highlanders, who, it is said, used to doff their bonnets on passing a shrine fatal to so many of their blood. The gallows have now been well replaced by an endowed public school on the Scottish pattern; and perhaps the most important institution of modern Crieff is the Hydropathic, which, under the shelter of the Knock Woods, gathers Saxon and Celt together in sober amity. There are other such hostelries about the Highland line; but that of Crieff, one of the earliest, is still one of the most popular.

"Hydropathics" in Scotland—nobody thinks of calling them Establishments— do not much depend on hydropathy, which, in summer at least, falls to the background of their sociable life. They are more concerned with the administration of water internally. Where whisky is devoutly worshipped, there arises a strong nonconformist party leagued against the devil's sacrament, hence the vogue of these big temperance hotels, in which unhappy moral weaklings will be sometimes kept by their families, while others, conscious of feeble will, are glad to be out of the way of temptation. In the holiday season, the better class of townsfolk much affect the wholesome amusements of such *pensions*, most of them palatial and some expensive. And if strong drink be necessary for human happiness, it is whispered how that can be enjoyed, *sub rosa*, even within the walls of a hydropathic, with all the added zest of a "fearful joy." As the rigour of Maine laws does not always hinder an American hotel guest from "seeing the striped pig" or "giving ten cents to the baby," so here there has been observed such a demand for "shaving water" at various hours of the day, that one conscientious manager made a practice of putting a piece of soap into each jug so required. Several hydropathics, indeed, have so far relaxed their original rules as to connive at the appearance of bottles upon the well-spread table. Certain large ones tend to become too gay and worldly, patronised by young swells from Glasgow and Dundee, who take every opportunity of putting on company manners and evening dress. But those haunts of ephemeral gaiety find their business slack off with the holiday season; and their prosperity has not always answered to that of others which stick to quiet ways and moderate charges.

LOOKING UP GLEN LOCHAY NEAR KILLIN, PERTHSHIRE

BENEATH THE SLOPES OF BEN LEDI, NEAR CALLANDER, PERTHSHIRE

The Crieff Hydropathic has all along taken a stand among the latter class, has even had a name for special austerity, due perhaps to the fact that it is frequented by Presbyterian ministers, as one at Harrogate is by Roman Catholic priests. But the Scottish clergy, however formidable in the pulpit, are by no means reluctant to unbend out of it, within the limits of becoming mirth, as we should know from Dean Ramsay; and I don't think I ever made one of such a jovial and friendly congregation as was gathered in this house in the days when not only strong drink but cards and dancing were under an interdict. One scandal shocked the proprieties of the place. The doctor, its guiding genius and strict censor, had gone to be married. The cat being thus engaged, the mice took advantage of the occasion. Returning unexpectedly from his honeymoon, our moral and medical director found the kids of his abandoned flock capering in the drawing-room. I shall never forget the face with which he stood at the doorway like the statue in Don Juan, then turned away speechless from sorrow or from anger. His helpless indignation reminded me of a carter, noted for bad language, on whom certain graceless loons are said to have played a trick by stealthily letting down the tilt of his cart as it tugged up a load of sand; then they took a short cut to the hill top and disposed themselves for listening to his remarks at a safe distance; but all he could gasp out on discovering his loss, was, "Rin awa' hame, laddies: I'm no equal to the occasion!" Perhaps that new character as a bridegroom softened the doctor's severe rule. It is said that even Crieff has to some extent conformed to the world, yet I doubt if its frequenters have a happier time of it than in those Saturnian days.

One meets queer characters at such a place, "gorgons and *hydros* and chimæras dire," as a humorist of the neighbourhood used to call them. A few real invalids and some imaginary ones crop up among the crowd of ruddy and buxom pleasure-seekers. There was one gentleman, I remember, who gorged himself at every meal and spent most of the day in snoring about the public rooms; but at idle intervals buttonholed all and sundry to expatiate on his woeful lot of having lost both sleep and appetite. A rarer hydropathic case, and a purple patch on the general tone of honest *bourgeoisie,* was a still young ne'er-do-weel bearing more than one of Scotland's honoured names, who had been in, and out of, two crack regiments, had run through two fortunes, so he boasted, and looked on himself as heir to two or three more. Crippled by a drunken fall, his friends kept him practically imprisoned in this uncongenial retreat. His sole luxury was a daily carriage airing; and he liked to drive round the grounds of a certain castle near Crieff, within which the owner, his uncle, would not let him set foot. It was painful to hear him talk of what he would do when he came in for the property. He died before the uncle and the other kinsfolk from whom he had hoped to inherit, a victim of that plague through which this country has hardly a house where there is not one dead, soul or body.

One of the great attractions of Crieff is its being environed by noble and famous mansions, some of their parks thrown liberally open to visitors. Close at hand on the Lowland side is Drummond Castle with its grand woods and gardens, seat of the old family of Perth, that has had strange vicissitudes: its representative now unites several titles in that of the Lincolnshire Earl of Ancaster, while the direct line of the Perth Earls was ruined by its Jacobite loyalty. On the hills behind are the grounds of Ochtertyre, which inspired Burns's muse; and the often-visited Falls of Turret are, among several cascades, within a short walk. Behind the Knock lie Ferntower, once home of Sir David Baird, and Monzie Castle, which strangers must remember to pronounce with its z silent. Southrons will have some difficulty also in getting their tongues round the name of Cultoquhey, famed by the Laird of Cultoquhey's prayer: "From the greed of the Campbells, from the pride of the Grahams, from the ire of the Drummonds, and the wind of the Murrays, Good Lord deliver us!" This laird's name was Maxtone, which hints at his having emigrated from the Borders among such uncongenial neighbours; but in the whirligig of time his descendant has taken on "the pride of the Grahams," being now Maxtone-Graham, with Murrays and Drummonds still around him. The old laird's familiarity with the Litany may be explained by the fact of Muthill, a village near at hand, having kept for itself an Episcopal chapel through all adversities, as well as a parish church with rare relics of Catholic antiquity. The church and castle of Innerpeffray are other points of interest in a neighbourhood whose old families seem to have held their own against English and American invasion; but the Grahams themselves, Highland clan as they pass for and duly equipped with a tartan, seem to have come from the south, where Scott puts Roland Græme's kin in the Border "Debateable Land."

Of all the lairdly homes about Crieff, the best known in the world should be Gask, through the several authors whom the Oliphant family has produced. One daughter of this house was Lady Nairne, christened Carolina after the unfortunate prince for whom it had suffered poverty and exile. There was a Charles also, and George III. is said to have been tickled to hear how, every day after dinner, the old laird would turn to his son with "*Charles*, the king's health!" More than any other writer, by her Jacobite ballads and her *remaniements* of popular songs, "the White Rose of Gask" has inspired a tender sentiment of the lost cause to thrill so many hearts and piano strings, long after Scottish royalists had transferred their worship to such clay idols as George IV. In my youth, indeed, there were still Perthshire men who spoke more or less heartily of the Hanoverian "usurpers." I myself was brought up in a touch of the same sentiment, though that my father's Jacobitism went not very deep appeared from the gusto with which he used to tell the tale of his translating to a lady the inscription on the monument at St. Peter's dedicated by King George to the "last of the Stuarts," whereupon a Yankee standing by put in the remark, "I guess George was right smart to say it was the *last* of them!" Lady Nairne's hereditary feeling for the Stuarts might not perhaps have endured the test of experience; she was a devout Protestant, and in her old age showed sympathy with the Free Church movement, which is the antipodes of Jacobitism. So modest was she, that for the greater part of her life, her neighbours, and her own husband, were not aware of her hand in the songs which had crept into wide popularity. It was taken for granted that Burns must be the author of her noblest strain, the "Land o' the Leal," better known than understood, as we remember from Mr. Gladstone's blunder in confusing heaven and Scotland. "The Laird o' Cockpen," "Caller Herrin'," "Will ye no come back again?" are other favourites among her songs, grave and gay; but her most recurrent theme was that glorified memory that, like Queen Mary's, can wing a sentiment to pierce the joints of Scotland's logical armour,—

> Charlie is my darling,
> The young Chevalier!

A WILD SPOT, KILLIN, PERTHSHIRE

Most charming are the walks by the Highland streams that at Crieff fall into the Earn; and tempting the longer excursions on which brakes carry off sociable parties from the Hydropathic. The railway takes us on up Strathearn to Comrie, a still more beautiful resort lying on a rich plain between the wooded heights of Glen Lednock and "lone Glenartney's hazel shade," by which one might tramp across to Callander, from the basin of the Tay into that of the Forth. A prosaic critic observes that there is no hazel shade in this glen; but the poet always declined to "swear to the truth of a song." There is no spot in Scotland that so well unites lush Lowland charms with rugged features as Comrie; and it prides itself on being the only spot in Britain troubled by earthquakes, several slight shocks sometimes being felt in a year, which may bring a stone wall tumbling down, while scaring wild fowl, making the trout leap in the burns, fluttering the poultry yard and rattling the plates in the goodwife's kitchen.

A few miles higher up, the Earn debouches from its Loch at St. Fillans, near which "the stag at eve had drunk his fill" before being roused by Fitz-James's hounds. I once made his day's course mainly on foot, but by a more arduous line over the top of Ben Voirlich, and moreover without any breakfast till I came upon a shepherd's shanty in the afternoon; then instead of being welcomed at eve by any Lady of the Lake, I found every bed full at the Trossachs Hotel, as may often be the lot of weary wight in this much-toured district. Loch Earn, hitherto a quiet backwater in the stream of travel, has lately been thrown open by a railway, at its head bringing one to the Oban line from Callander, whose lights are now the fiery cross that "glance like lightning up Strath-Ire."

In the other direction, a road from Crieff goes by the Sma' Glen to Dunkeld, the gate of the mountains for the Highland Railway. This resort, as tourists know, is a kind of Perthshire Buda-Pesth, the old town of Dunkeld being on the left bank of the Tay, while the station is at Birnam on the other side. Village seems a fitter title for Dunkeld than town, yet it might claim to be a city in right of its Cathedral, whose choir is still the parish church. This is an ancient sanctuary to which in part was transplanted the influence of ruined Iona. Gavin Douglas, the translator of Virgil, was bishop here, but came to die of the plague in London. With Dunkeld also is connected the memory of Neil Gow, first of three generations of fiddlers who for Scotland's artless tunes did what Burns, Lady Nairne, and other writers did for its songs.

The Cathedral, as well as the Falls of Braan, the Rumbling Bridge and other lions are in the grounds of the Duke of Atholl, *the* Duke of this part of the world. The Duke of fifty years ago was a "character" who might be styled the last of the great Highland chiefs. This generation may have forgotten the sensation caused by his trying to shut the way through Glen Tilt, and his personal encounter with two Cambridge undergraduates, who got the best of the scrimmage. Among Leech's most effective sketches in *Punch* were that "Ducal Dog in the Manger" and the cartoon in which His Grace appeared playing the part of Roderick Dhu to the young Sassenachs. It was said that the Duke took his revenge on the artist by inviting him to shoot, the highest honour that can be hoped for in that part of the world; and in the end the pass was opened by a chieftain "so late dishonoured and defied."

THE FALLS OF TUMMEL, PERTHSHIRE

Since his day the champion obstructionist of this district was the veteran Sir Robert Menzies, who lately died much respected in the Rannoch country, in spite of an extraordinary itch for litigation, with his own family as well as with strangers. His most famous "ganging law plea" perhaps was with a railway company that, by the hands of half-a-dozen porters, had dragged the chieftain out of a carriage in which his ticket did not entitle him to ride. The fate of a reverend English tourist who landed from Loch Rannoch on his grounds was told with a shudder; and I must be thankful for my own escape when caught in the act of more than barefaced trespass in bounds where stranger was not always "a holy name." With a friend of mine, in our hot youth, I had gone in to swim, when on the lake bank we heard a stern voice and looked back to see Sir Robert's tartans waving over our clothes. Thus "at advantage ta'en,"

> I dare not say that now *our* blood
> Kept on its wont and tempered flood

But the "dangerous chief," seeing nothing in our Arcadian innocence to chafe his mood or cloud his brow, turned off with a courteous salutation—"Doubt not aught from mine array!"—and the sun's next glance shone "on bracken green and cold grey stone."

Across the Tay from Dunkeld, in the old duke's time, reigned an eccentric laird, to whose taste for building are due the baronial Birnam Hotel and other costly structures in the neighbourhood. Mrs. Oliphant hangs the scenes of a novel about his own empty and unfinished mansion; and the chief building among the woods of Murthly is now an Asylum. As for Birnam Wood, that has long marched off the face of the earth, to bear out the truth of Shakespeare's legend; but one or two ancient trees are pointed out as stragglers. Birnam was a favourite haunt of Millais, a keen sportsman as well as lover of the scenery which forms oases in the later stage of his art, when he seemed too much concerned to boil that large pot in Palace Gate.

From Dunkeld it is easy to reach the heart of the Highlands. A dozen miles of the high road takes us up to hill-girdled Pitlochrie, and through that pass where Dundee was shot, as pious souls whispered, with a silver bullet, while his claymores sheared down the Lowland soldiers, whose prudent leader, himself from the farthest north, gained in defeat the lesson to invent a more adaptable bayonet. So terrifying seemed long this Pass of Killiecrankie that a body of Hessian soldiers, brought over in the '45, are said to have flatly refused to march through it. But as usual, the victorious onrush at Killiecrankie did not carry the tartans far. They were checked at Dunkeld, dourly defended against them by troops of sternest temper, that Cameronian regiment raised among the most stubborn Whigs, who here had their baptism of fire and their chance of wreaking vengeance for bitter memories of Claverhouse. Their colonel, Cleland, fell in this fight with the barelegged foes he had satirised in verse bristling with scornful hatred of the "Highland host" brought down as a scourge for the west-country Covenanters. "They need not strip them when they whip them!" the Presbyterian poet exclaims like any ribald Cockney, and goes on to hint how the upper garments of such gallows-birds would not be worth the hangman's fees. So little love was lost between kindly Scots of those days, on opposite sides of the Highland line!

DUNKELD AND BIRNAM FROM CRAIGIEBARNS, PERTHSHIRE

A WOODED GORGE, KILLIN, PERTHSHIRE

Cleland is buried in Dunkeld Cathedral, where Sir John Steell's modern monument to officers of the 42nd reminds us how this Perthshire regiment was first embodied in the Dunkeld district about half a century after the Revolution, having its origin as the Black Watch, so called from their dark tartans as distinguished from the *sidier roy*, red soldier. They were originally raised to keep the peace on the Highland line, much as Parfidio Diaz has in our day put down the brigands of Mexico by enlisting the survivors as Rural Guards; but it would be too much to say that such a loyal and brave corps was made out of the leavings of that kind gallows of Crieff. Some of the private soldiers held themselves so proudly, that when a party was brought to show their exercise before George II. and the king ordered them to be tipped with a guinea apiece, each man, it is told, re-bestowed this donation upon the palace porter. Their tartan is a neutral one, forming the groundwork of several others, for time was when no Macpherson would don the hated trappings of the MacTavish. War Office arrangements have played havoc with this sentiment by sometimes redistributing the territorial corps in red-tape bundles; some years ago a Ross-shire militia battalion tacked on to the Cameron Highlanders—not to be confused with the west-country Cameronian regiment—was said not to have a single Cameron in the ranks, a change from days when Sandy MacDonalds or John Campbells had to be numbered in the kindred ranks like a long line of kings. The good discipline as well as the prowess of Highland soldiers was remarkable in early days, men of the same name and birthplace keeping up each other's *esprit de corps*, and no praise or punishment being more effectual than the thought of what might be posted as to a man's conduct on the door of his parish church.

The raising of Highland regiments, indeed, was sometimes carried on after the methods of the press-gang, or by landlords putting pressure on tenants who might be fathers of stout sons. There is a story of half-a-dozen brawny Celts tied neck and heels in a cart as recruits for the Laird of Macnab's "Volunteers"; and clansmen have been hunted down in the mountains when they refused to follow the modern fiery cross. There would be many a tragic tale of desertion like that of the "Highland Widow," especially when English martinets added pipe-clay to Highland accoutrements. But active lads were seldom backward to follow chief or laird leading them to war; then

> Bring a Scotsman frae his hill,
> Clap in his cheek a Highland gill,
> Say, "Such is royal George's will,
> And there's the foe!"
> He has nae thought but how to kill
> Twa at a blow.

As in the instance of the Cameronians, all Scottish regiments do not wear the kilt; and of those who do, but few men are to this manner born in our generation. Alphonse Daudet puts his little hero "Jack" into a kilt under the title of *costume anglaise*, which is no more absurd than the way in which English writers speak of this as the "Scottish dress." There are even Highland Celts whose ancestors never wore it; and in its palmy days the kilt was the "servile dress" of clansmen, whose chiefs as a rule went in trews. Now it is affected rather by the upper class;

and the soldiers who swagger so jauntily in tartans are more like to have grown up in corduroy breeks. But for this fact, I should have laid down, as warning to strangers, that the "garb of Old Gaul" cannot be donned to advantage without youthful familiarity. The wearing of such a costume, indeed, needs some practice. A Highland battalion of trews stationed at Southsea became adopted into a kilted regiment some twenty years ago, when a corporal and file of men were detached from the latter as instructors for the neophytes how to carry their new honours un-blushingly, so as forthwith to be christened the "South Sea Islanders" by an *h*-less populace. The London Scottish Volunteers should wear the kilt by right of having Highland blood or Highland property; and it is enviously whispered that their qualification in most cases may be the possession of a tartan paper-knife.

It is, of course, the prowess of our Highland regiments that has made their dress as dear in Scotland as once over half of it this was hated and despised. The tartans are dyed by the blood of a hundred battlefields, as by memories of green braes and purple moors. Crude and *criant* may be some of their colourings, but not more so than is the tricolour or the Union Jack. Even if the kilt in its present form were more or less a modern invention, it is at least older than the Stars and Stripes, and we know what passionate loyalty that gaudy pattern can call forth. The other day, I forgathered with a Lowland Seaforth Highlander, fresh from South Africa, to whom I communicated a report that the War Office thought of putting him into trousers. "They daren't!" he cried, his eye ablaze with all the fire of Killiecrankie, where his progenitor might have chosen for the nonce to be equipped in the light-est running costume.

Strange how the Celtic leaven rises in the stodgy composition of British na-ture! What is this infectious quality it has? We are Saxons in business, and well for us it is so; but in hours of ease and sentiment we hark back to the race older on our mother earth. English settlers in Ireland notoriously become *Hibernis Hiberniores ipsis*. English workmen in Welsh quarries, it is said, learn to speak Welsh rather than their comrades English. In the long run the stolid Teuton grows to be proud of his lighter strain. I who write can trace my descent with unusual clearness back to a Norman adventurer whose progeny appears to have settled for a time in the Breadalbane Highlands, but long ago came down to opener straths—

> The mountain sheep were sweeter,
> But the valley sheep were fatter.

The alliances of my kin were for generations with the English-speaking Lowlands, where their neighbours had cause to look on the wild Highlandmen as an Amer-ican backwoodsman looked on Mohawk or Shawnee warrior. My forebears "had no use for" kilts, if some perhaps for dirks and claymores. I know of only one re-cent strain of Highland blood, and that at second hand through England, to make me a Celtic quadroon, so to speak. Yet there is many a Scot, with no more claim to Highland lineage than mine, who cannot see the tartan even in a Princes Street shop-window, or hear the pibroch wailing over forgotten graves of his father's foes, without a certain stir of spirit which a biological philosopher might explain as waves of molecular disturbance propagated through the nerve centres by vague emotional combinations organised in the earlier experiences of the race. Boswell confessed to the same weakness, and what had he to do with the Highlands?

LOOKING UP THE PASS OF KILLIECRANKIE, PERTHSHIRE

KILLIN, HEAD OF LOCH TAY, PERTHSHIRE

Where were we before launching forth into such a chequered digression on the "lad wi' the philabeg"? In the Atholl country, by Loch "Tummel and banks of the Garry." Above the Pass of Killiecrankie, the pedestrian who does not shun a thirty-miles walk to Braemar may turn off through Glen Tilt, with its gloomy gorges and snowy falls. But the coach-road to the Cairngorm Highlands goes from Dunkeld to Blairgowrie, then northward by the Spittal of Glenshee, the highest highway in Britain, at one point over 2000 feet, whose "Spittal" was a Hospital or Hospice that made a Highland St. Bernard's. I once sought to hire a horse at an inn on this road, but the landlord explained how it had gone off with "a man called Morell Mackenzie, who seemed in an awfu' hurry." That locally unknown celebrity was in haste to an illustrious patient on Deeside, an errand that would breed much bad blood in another country.

The first stage of the journey is lowland rather than highland, its chief feature being a chain of small lochs, stocked with perch, on one of which stands Cluny Castle, cradle of the "Admirable Crichton." Blairgowrie, with Rattray for its tiny Westminster, rivals Crieff as the second town in Perthshire, but is not so much a place of resort, laying itself out rather as an understudy of Dundee by its flax-spinning mills on the Ericht; and it seems a miniature of that longest and busiest of towns, the German Elberfeld strung out along the Wupper valley. Wildly romantic still is the walk up the Ericht, whose shaded pools and rapids, above the town, come down through a grand gorge overlooked by Craighall, one of several candidates for the honour of having sat to Scott as "Tullyveolan." From this gap in the Highland line a short branch puts us on the main line of the Caledonian Railway, which competes with the North British as route to Aberdeen.

Other Caledonian branches lead off to charming glens on the old Highland line, now facing east towards the lowlands of Forfar and Kincardine. But of Alyth, Edzell, Lochee, one need only say that they lie among sweet and noble scenes as well worth visiting as others better known to tourist fame, and that even prosaic Kirriemuir, Mr. Barrie's "Thrums," is a base for long moorland tramps into Deeside, over a part of the Highlands as yet innocent of railways.

CHAPTER VII

"ABERDEEN AWA'!"

THERE seems no general name to fit a part of Scotland which has a very marked character, that lowland shelf lying beyond the Grampians along the Moray Firth, where the counties of Aberdeen, Banff, Moray, and Nairn are comparatively flat on the north side, but on the south rise into grand mountains. The "back end of the Highlands" would not be a dignified title; "Moray and Mar" is not an inclusive one, nor is "Deeside and Speyside." One seems driven to indicate this as the district of which Aberdeen is the capital, environed by the "four nations," Angus, Mar, Buchan, and Moray, a division of local mankind copied by her university from Paris.

Angus *alias* Forfar, and Kincardine *alias* the Mearns, are lowland counties whose streams come down from a Highland background to a coast-line of broad sandy links on the Tay estuary, and weatherworn sandstone cliffs facing the open sea. We might linger here by notable names beyond Dundee—Arbroath, with its ruined Abbey, the scene of the *Antiquary*; Montrose, that Flemish-like town that has belied its Cavalier name by rearing such sons as Andrew Melville, the reformer, and Joseph Hume, the economist; Stonehaven, seat of the Barclays of Ury known in so different ways; and Brechin, with its Cathedral and Round Tower, neighboured by castles old and new. In this countryside settled the head of W. E. Gladstone's family, which, however, had moved from some *Gledstone* or "Hawk's rock" in the south of Scotland to make fortunes in England by trade. Sir Thomas, the great Liberal's brother, was a sound Conservative, of whom is told that at an election, seeing a son of the soil anxious to salute him, he stopped his carriage, and accepted a grasp of the horny hand, qualified by "For the sake o' yer brither!"

By the wild glens of the North and South Esk let us pass into Braemar, mountain region of Mar, the very cream of the Highlands, whose highest summits, Ben Nevis left out of account, are grouped in the south of Aberdeenshire. A generation ago Ben Nevis had not been crowned by revolutionary surveyors, and Ben Macdhui was still held monarch of Scottish mountains, keeping his state among the Cairngorms, that here have half-a-dozen truncated peaks over or hardly under 4000 feet, Ben Muich Dhui, as Gaelic purists would have us call it, Brae-riach, Cairntoul, the Peak of Cairngorm, Ben-a-bourd, and Ben A'an, heads of the grandest mountain mass in the British Isles. This is the native heath of sturdy Highland stocks, Farquharsons, Macphersons, and M'Hardys, Durwards, Coutts, and Stuarts, of whose exploits and traditions more than one book has been written. The folklorist will not be surprised to find how the legends of Braemar re-echo those of other lands. Here a crafty female Ulysses disables a giant and plays off on him a joking name that puts the stupid fellow to a loss in calling for help. Here a Mac-Tell wins his liberty by shooting at a mark placed on the head of his wife, with an arrow in reserve for the tyrant, in case his first aim should not be true. Here an outlawed David in tartans lays his sword on the throat of a sleeping Saul, then awakens him to reconciliation. Here a squire of low degree comes by his high-born lass in the end; and the youngest of three brothers of course wins the race of fortune, though handicapped like a Cinderella.

DUNNOTTAR CASTLE, KINCARDINESHIRE

This majestic crown of Scotland was chosen as the home of our late Queen, but not then for the first time had Braemar and its Castleton to do with royalty. If all tales be true, here was the cradle of Banquo's race, he to whom the fateful sisters promised a long line of kings, himself cut off as foretaste of so many violent ends. Malcolm Canmore, son of Duncan, had a seat at Braemar, where he often lived with his Saxon wife. He is said to have founded the autumn gathering, now tamed into a spick and span show of holiday Highlanders, but in old days a grand hunting party, more than once an assemblage for serious purposes. Taylor, the Water Poet, on his "Penniless Pilgrimage," after being duly rigged out in tartan, was taken by Lord Mar to the Braemar Hunt, when under mountains to which this Cockney declares that "Shooters' Hill, Gad's Hill, Highgate Hill, Hampstead Hill" are but mole-hills—

> Through heather, moss, 'mongst frogs and bogs and fogs,
> 'Mongst craggy cliffs and thunder-battered hills,
> Hares, hinds, bucks, roes are chased by men and dogs,
> Where two hours' hunting fourscore fat deer kills.
> Lowland, your sports are low as are your seat,
> The Highland games and minds are truly great!

It was under cover of the Braemar hunt of 1715, such a gathering as a generation later had Captain Waverley for eye-witness, that Mar hatched the Jacobite rebellion against George I., of which Scott aptly quotes—

> The child may rue that is unborn
> The hunting of that day.

When the Pretender's standard was raised at the Castleton, a hollow of rock by the Linn of Quoich, known as "the Earl of Mar's Punchbowl," is said to have been filled with several ankers of spirits, gallons of boiling water, and hundredweights of honey, a mighty brew in which to drink success to that unlucky enterprise. In 1745, also, the sons of Mar gave their blood freely to the cause of the Pretender, though this time their lords were rather on the Whig side. Jacobite sentiment remained strong in the district up to our own time. In 1824 was buried at Castleton Peter Grant, who passed for being 110 years old, and probably the last survivor of Culloden. To his dying day he would never drink the Hanoverian king's health, yet this constancy seems somewhat marred by the fact that, like Dr. Johnson, he accepted a pension from the usurping line. In our time all devotion to memories of Prince Charlie have been transferred to the sovereign lady who here would have lived as a private person, so far as possible, but was sore hindered by the snobbish curiosity that mobbed her even in the village church. Not that Highland loyalty is always enlightened, if we may believe a story told by Mr. George Seton of one Donald explaining to another the meaning of the Queen's Jubilee: "When ye're married twenty-five years, that's your silver wedding; and fifty years is your golden wedding; and if your man's deid, they ca' it a Jubilee"!

OLD MAR BRIDGE AND LOCHNAGAR, ABERDEENSHIRE

Braemar, indeed, with its bracing air and glorious mountains, is not for every tourist. Hotels are few and dear; there is little accommodation between cot and castle; ramblers are not made welcome in the deer forests around; and a country-side of illustrious homes cannot be left open to all and sundry. When royalty be in residence, there are no doubt keepers on the watch who have to guard something better than game; and the trespassing stranger may find himself under observation as strict as that of Dartmoor or Portland Island. In the promised elysium of socialism both palaces and prisons may be turned into hydropathics; and Braemar, 1000 feet above the sea, makes a princely health resort, with no want of water. But access to this backwater of travel is itself somewhat prohibitive to the strangers who would scamper over Scotland in six days. The railway from Aberdeen comes no farther up the Dee than Ballater. The direct access to Castleton is that of a long coach drive by the Spittal of Glenshee. Pedestrians have the best of it in rough tramps up Glen Tilt or Glen Clova from the south, or from Aviemore on Speyside, over a pass 2750 feet high, and with a chance of losing their adventurous way in Rothiemurchus Forest, where Messrs. Cook's coupons are of no avail. Once at the village capital of the district, one can visit most of its lions on pony-back, the Falls of Corriemulzie and of the Garrawalt, the Linn of Dee, Glen Cluny and Glen Callater, and even the top of the mighty Muich Dhui, thus ascended by Queen Victoria. But the Cairngorms show their jewels rather to him who, like Byron, can roam "a young Highlander o'er the dark heath," climbing "thy summit, O Morven of snow," and getting cheerfully drenched among the "steep frowning glories of dark Lochnagar."

If peer or poet could hasten from these royal Highlands, Byron's restless muse might rejoice in the motor cars that now connect Braemar with the fortunate Deeside railway. Down the strath of Dee, we descend to the lowland country by beautiful gradations. Past the old and the new Castles of Braemar, past Invercauld, Crathie, and Abergeldie, by the "Rock of Firs" and round the "Rock of Oaks," is the way to Ballater, a neat little town about a railway terminus, that makes it more of a popular resort. On the other side of the river are the chalybeate wells of Pananich, one of those unfamed spas held in observance by country folk all over Scotland. It was at a farmhouse here that Byron spent his Aberdeen school holidays; and happy should be the schoolboy who can follow in his steps, forgetting examinations and cricket averages. But alas! for the Aberdeen citizen who, on trades' holidays, seeks this lovely scene when it is veiled in mist and pelting showers. Him the Invercauld Arms receives as refuge; him sometimes a place of sterner entertainment. There is also a temperance hotel. Over the Moor of Dinnet, the railway takes us to Aboyne, another pleasant resort on Deeside, along which we find hotels for tourists and sportsmen, a hydropathic for health-seekers, a sanitorium for consumptives, and thickening villages which, on the lower reaches, become the Richmonds and Wimbledons of Aberdeen.

The Granite City of Bon Accord, with its old Cathedral and Colleges, if for a little overgrown by that upstart Dundee, comes after Edinburgh and Glasgow in dignity, well deserving such attention as Dr. Johnson gave to its lions. It has shifted its site from the Don towards the Dee, between whose mouths it almost touches the sands, and golf and sea bathing are among its pleasures, while in an hour the Deeside railway runs one up into the Highlands. The old town has here dwindled to a suburb, the new one laid out with striking regularity and solidity, relieved by such nooks as the Denburn Gardens, across which Union Street reaches by the tower of the Town Hall to Castlegate and the Cross, where a colossal statue of the last Duke of Gordon and an imposing block of Salvation Army buildings represent a contrast of old and new times.

The Aberdonians, as is known, pride themselves on a hard-headedness answering to their native granite. The legend goes that an Englishman once attempted to defraud these far northerners, but the charge against him was scornfully dismissed by an Aberdeen bailie: "The man must be daft!" By the rest of Scotland, Aberdeen is looked on as concentrating its qualities of pawkiness, canniness, and thrawnness; the Edinburgh man cracks upon it the same sort of jokes as the Cockney upon Scotland in general. The accent and dialect of this corner, strongly flavoured with Norse origin and sharp sea-breezes, are quite peculiar. Norse origin, I have said—and this has been held the main stock; but a recent anthropological examination seems to show that even in seaward Buchan only a minority of the school children are fair-haired. This sketch has nothing for it but resolutely to forswear all such upsetting inquiries, which nowadays go so far as to deny that any part of Scotland was purely Celtic, and may some day prove us the original strain of Adam, whose migration from Paradise to replenish the whole earth would be quite consistent with a birthright in "Aberdeen awa'!"

Aberdeenshire is on the whole a matter-of-fact county, by industry rich in "horn and corn," not without its pleasant nooks, and on the south rising into those royalest Highlands. Buchan, the most Aberdeenish part of Aberdeen, has a grandly rugged coast, with the cauldron called the Buller of Buchan, and the Dripping Cave of Slains for famous points, till lately much out of the way of travel, but now a railway opens the golf links of Cruden Bay, between the old and the new Slains Castles, whose lord, as Boswell observed, has the king of Denmark for nearest north-eastern neighbour to the High Constable of Scotland. Beyond, at this bleak corner, come the fishing towns of Peterhead and Fraserburgh, where Frasers are as thick as blackberries, their name, along the coast, being no distinction without a *tee*-name (*agnomen*) by which a prosperous fisherman may sign his cheques, or an ill-doing one be haled before the sheriff.

Inland, Aberdeen is rather the country of the gay Gordons, no real Hielandmen, but emigrants from the south, of whom it is not for me to say good words, inasmuch as I am kin to their hereditary neighbours, which is as much as to say enemies, the Forbes. Yet, "in spite of spite," one must admit that the Gordons flourish here, as on their native borderland, in Poland, in Russia, indeed all over the world. The "Cock of the North" has cause not to crow so boldly as of yore; and regiments cannot now be raised by bounty of a Gordon Duchess' kisses; but no less than three noble houses of the name have seats in this region, lordliest among them Gordon Castle, the northern Goodwood.

BALMORAL, ABERDEENSHIRE

The interior of this promontory has a prevailing aspect of prosperous commonplace; but here, too, are patches of romance and superstition. Turriff, for instance, looks as quiet a little town as any in the kingdom, yet at the Trot of Turriff was shed the first blood of our civil wars. A pool in the river has a wild legend of family plate thrown into it in those troubled times and found in guard of the devil by one who dived for its recovery. This is a legend of Gicht, the home of Byron's mother, that also has the subterranean passage of tradition, explored by so many a piper, whose strains were heard dying away underfoot till they went silent in what uncanny world! Near Gicht, Fyvie Castle contains a secret chamber which must not be opened on pain of the laird's death, and a stone that weeps for any approaching calamity to his house. There came a new laird from London, a man of metropolitan scepticism, nay, even a teetotaller, who regaled his scandalised neighbours with zoedone and such like. He was reported to have given out an intention of opening the secret chamber, but when pressed to do so in presence of certain local dignitaries, he turned it off with a laugh. Mark the sequel: this gentleman died suddenly very soon afterwards, so he might have opened the fateful chamber *whatever*. One of the treasures of the castle, a scrap of faded tartan from Prince Charlie's plaid, reverently preserved under a glass case, was being exhibited to me by the parish minister, when he felt himself tapped on the shoulder by the laird: "Did I hear you say the *Pretender*?" — a softened form of Lady Strange's rebuke for the same lapse, "*Pretender*, forsooth, and be dawmed to ye!" Another family in this district is believed, and believes itself, never to have thriven since its head was cursed by a Macdonald massacred in Glencoe. These are but samples of the old-world ideas that turn up in the soil so carefully tilled by Johnny Gibb of Gushetneuk.

Maybe the reader has never heard of Johnny Gibb—then the loss is his. This book is well known in Scotland as a head of the "kailyard" school that has flourished here since the days of Galt, though only of late some caprice of taste gave it a vogue in the south. The examples most popular in England do not always commend themselves to Scotsmen, who find one and another aspect of their character overcharged to move the sighs or grins of barren readers. At home is better appreciated such a writer as William Alexander, who, risen from herd loon to editor of an Aberdeen paper, knew his countryfolk thoroughly, and depicted them with an art that never oversteps the modesty of nature. One can hardly press Johnny Gibb on a stranger, weighted as he is with an uncouth dialect and with a serious stiffening of Disruption principles. But, to my mind, if Dr. John Brown had not written *Rab and his Friends*, William Alexander's *Life among my ain Folk* would be the flower of the kailyard: a collection of humble Aberdeenshire idylls, as seen by a shrewdly humorous eye, which can soften in not overstrained sentiment when it regards the "little wee little anes" and "wee bit wifickies" that draw from sons of a hard soil such endearing diminutives so characteristic of their wind-bitten speech. If I am not mistaken, George Eliot's *Scenes of Clerical Life* may have set a copy for these round-hand pages, not to be taken as lessons in spelling, for only too faithfully do they reproduce the local dialect.

STRATH GLASS, INVERNESS-SHIRE

Johnny Gibb deals with the essence of Presbyterianism, as distilled in Aberdeenshire Strathbogie during the non-intrusion controversy. But this part of the country is, in fact, much divided as to religious sentiment. About Aberdeen, the old Episcopal church is still rooted in the soil, elsewhere in Scotland rather a greenhouse plant. The Covenanters made war upon this prelatic city, and in its county Montrose brewed the storm that swept down upon Whigamore strongholds. Hereabouts it was Presbyterian divines who, after the Revolution Settlement, had sometimes to be inducted at the bayonet's point upon unwilling parishioners; then Cumberland's soldiers marching to Culloden could find plenty of sport in burning non-juring meeting-houses. The Roman Catholic element is still strong also, especially in the Highland part, many of the clans, from Aberdeen across to Skye, having stuck to the old faith. The Frasers have two heads, him of the Lovat branch a Catholic, but his namesake of Saltoun a Protestant. Blairs College on Deeside is a notable Catholic seminary, containing fine portraits of Queen Mary and Cardinal Beaton. The Roman Cathedral of Aberdeen has no cause to hide itself, but stands up boldly among its Free Church neighbours. In some parts of Scotland, a Papist is looked on askance, but in this northern belt, the two creeds have come to a *modus vivendi*, the parish minister perhaps saying grace before dinner and the priest returning thanks.

On the same shoulder of Scotland a similar contrast is shown in the matter of climate. The point of Buchan ended by Kinnaird Head has the name of being the coldest part of the kingdom, but farther up the Moray Firth, the counties of Moray and Nairn are so situated and sheltered as to be more genial than most of England. Forres, which Shakespeare vainly imagined as a bleak and blasted heath "fit for murders, treasons, stratagems," has in fact the mean climate of London, cooler in summer, warmer in winter; and the whole district vies with East Norfolk for the honour of being Britain's driest corner, so that the Forres Hydropathic, with its miles of pine-wood walks, makes both a winter and a summer resort, while a light and porous soil supports fat farming.

The country has many beauty spots also, even among its lowland features, swelling to the Highlands of Brae Moray, from which Wolves of Badenoch once swept down upon its folds as Roderick Dhus upon the Forth's "waving fields and pastures green." The Findhorn, in whose valley Gordons and Cummings have met lovingly, Professor Blackie calls "one of the finest stretches of dark mountain water and picturesque wood in the Highlands." Mr. Charles St. John is eloquent in praise of this river, where he made so careful studies in natural history. Rising in a wild solitude, it leaves the open ground to hide its charms among noble forests and beneath steep cliffs, at whose foot the angler may have to run for his life, its sudden spates now pressed up in a gorge a few feet wide, then making a bore-like wave on such a dark basin as that of the old Bridge of Dulsie, "shut in by grey and fantastic rocks, surmounted with the greenest of grass swards, with clumps of the ancient weeping birches with their gnarled and twisted stems, backed again by the dark pine trees. The river here forms a succession of very black and deep pools, connected with each other by foaming and whirling falls and currents, up which in the fine, pure evenings you may see salmon making curious leaps." Another notable reach shows the grounds of Altyre with its heronry. From these wooded gorges, so rich in finned and feathered life, the river emerges on a tamer plain, to enter the sea by the Sahara of Culbin, a singular coast-line, where cultivated fields have been long ago overwhelmed by sandhills, banks of shingle, and piles of stones, all barren but for patches of bent and broom, sheltering huge foxes, hares, and rabbits, that sally forth to prey upon the farms behind, like any Highland chieftain. Moray and Nairn thus present a fine variety of scenery, dotted by ancient mansions like Darnaway Castle, with its hall that holds a thousand armed men, and Cawdor Castle, which one legend makes the scene of Macbeth's murder. No part of Scotland indeed, has more ruined shrines and strongholds than the old *Moravia*, a name once extending beyond the present bounds of Moray *alias* Elgin.

Elgin, the town, built of a warm, yellow sandstone that helps it to a cheerful look, may call itself a city in right of what seems to have been the noblest Cathedral in Scotland, violated by wild Highlandmen when this lowland strip too much invited plunder and ravage. The town has other ruins to show, besides those of Pluscarden Priory some miles off, and of Spynie Palace on the way to Lossiemouth, Elgin's rising bathing-place, whose name should be familiar to readers of George MacDonald's novels. A little farther along the coast, Nairn, which a Scots king boasted for so long as to have one end in the Highlands, the other in the Lowlands, is now able to hold itself up as the "Brighton of the North," recommended by a mild climate, and by golf-links on the shore, not perched on diabolic downs, as behind the Londoner's resort.

Gouty southrons may well find their way so far north, but they do ill to pass by the recesses of this country, now that the Highland Railway cuts straight across from Aviemore to Inverness. Grantown above Speyside, indeed, is much sought as a high and dry health resort. Another place that begins to put in a claim to the same favour is Tomintoul, at the south end of Banff, the loftiest village in the Highlands, a hundred feet or so higher than Buxton, and with a chalybeate well that would work fashionable cures if it could only get a London doctor to patronise it, while the sub-Alpine site and the mainly Catholic population might help to give an illusion of *Swillingheim-am-Fluss* or *Argent les Eaux*. A very illustrious author expressed the picturesqueness of Tomintoul by calling it the "dirtiest, poorest village in the whole of the Highlands," but that was a generation ago, and the Tomintoulers are not likely to insist on perpetuating such a compliment, as Aberdeen solicitors to this day take the higher style of Advocates, because once so addressed by King James. A more famous spring, as yet, of this region rises in a distillery which does not want a *vates sacer*—

> Fairshon had a son who married Noah's daughter,
> And nearly spoilt ta Flood, by drinking up ta water,
> Which he would have done, I verily believe it,
> Had ta mixture been only half Glenlivet.

But we have jumped over Banff, which may resent being taken for an appendage of Aberdeen,—long, narrow strip squeezed in between Moray and Mar, as it runs up from its northern cliff face, set with fishing villages, to the grand Highlands of Deeside. Banff has a bad name among Scottish counties for a certain fault of morals which has been charged upon all Scotland, though as a matter of fact it attaches only to some parts, and pleas may be given in excuse: for one, the custom of such irregular unions as under the name of "handfasting" were long winked at in this corner; for another, the accommodating Scottish law that wipes out by legal marriage a transgression too lightly treated by local opinion, as not by Jean Armour's lover when, now and then, his song turned out a sermon. In other respects Banff may pose as a homespun Arcadia. Some twenty years ago, when I knew it, there were not thirty policemen in the whole county, and the county town was hard put to it to confine prisoners for a single night. The only familiar crime was that wont to be solemnly indicted before the Sheriff as "Making a great noise, opposite, or nearly opposite the Free Church Manse, cursing and swearing, and challenging to fight," *i.e.* in the blunter English of southern police courts, being drunk and disorderly; then it would be a point of legal acumen not to fine the almost always repentantly avowing offender more than he was likely to have at command. The authorities stood in dread that some Englishman or the like would break the law more seriously, as happened when a vagrant conjuror with an Italian name, but speaking in a strong Whitechapel accent, conjured a pair of boots into his illegal possession, and had to be sent all the way to Elgin at the expense of the county. Later on, Banff got a jail of its own opened, which I one day visited and found the only captive sociably doing a job of work for the keeper's wife. One case of theft, indeed, was not unknown, that of boys brought into illicit relations with apples or the like; but when an urchin was sentenced to be whipped for such puerile weakness, the small police force, with the fear of his mother in their eyes, struck, or rather refused to strike, and I believe the culprit went scot-free.

The absence of vulgar crime is still more marked in the Highlands, where, but for whisky and religious zeal, there would be little need of magistrates. "Ye see, if they stole anything, they couldn't get it off the island," a Bute cynic once explained to me; but on the mainland opposite, I have known the ladies of a family leave their bathing dress hanging over the hedge by the roadside for weeks together. It was only on the grand and gallant scale that John Highlandman made a confusion between *meum* and *tuum*. But a distinctly litigious disposition in trifles keeps northern lawyers from starving among clients who, like Bartoline Saddletree and Peter Peebles, often cherish a strong amateur interest in law. In Dandie Dinmont's country, we know, a man was "aye the better thought o' for having been afore the Feifteen."

Now that everybody subscribes to an Encyclopædia, it may not be necessary to remind readers how the Scots law is founded on the Roman, and how the practice of courts differs north and south of the Tweed. The administration of justice in Scotland seems now an example to England, whatever it may have been in the past. Feudalism died slow here. Baron courts continued to be held to our own day, though shorn of such unjust privilege as that by which the lord's bailie decided questions between himself and his tenants. There was a time when only high treason was withheld from the jurisdiction of these private Solons. Then they lost power to adjudicate in the "four pleas of the crown," —murder, rape, robbery, and arson, unless in the case of the slayer taken red-hand or the thief *infang* with the stolen property in his possession within the barony bounds. So late as 1707 Lord Drummond was good enough to "lend" his executioner to the city of Perth. After Culloden, hereditary judges like the Baron of Bradwardine were wholly deprived of the right of *furca et fossa*, the drowning of female and hanging of male offenders. Yet a generation ago the dispensers of minor justice in certain towns were the "bailies" of the superior, whom in one case I have known to be an Australian squatter and his distant deputy a respectable carpenter, while in such a town as Dalkeith, the Duke of Buccleuch appointed an able lawyer as permanent magistrate. The adoption of the Police Act brought this state of things to an end; and the baron's judicial rights, if not formally abolished, have practically dwindled out of existence.

The part of police magistrate and county court judge is doubled by the sheriff, an official whose title may be a stumbling-block to Englishmen, and still more to inquiring foreigners like Count Smalltork. Nothing is apter to perplex our Continental neighbours than the irregularities of our constitution, the overlapping of boundaries, the general want of such symmetrical and consistent arrangement as recommends itself to the Latin or the well-drilled Teuton mind. What a pitfall for the foreign student of our institutions lies in the fact of a sheriff being an honorary dignitary in an English county, an elected constable in an American one, but a paid and permanent judge north of the Tweed! The shire reeves here were in feudal times hereditary lieutenants of the Crown, who, as the baron handed over judicial authority to his clerkly bailie, appointed legal representatives, still entitled Sheriffs Depute, also known as Sheriffs Principal, as they have come to be. These well-paid offices are prizes of the bar, held by successful advocates in Edinburgh, who only in special cases or by way of appeal are called to judgment. The everyday work of minor justice, civil and criminal, is done by resident paid officials, called Sheriffs Substitute, each, in his own district, wearing a halo of authority as "the Sheriff," usually an advocate who has resigned the risks of practice to devote himself to this safer if less ambitious career, as is the case with the French magistracy. There are also Justices of the Peace, as in England, but these do not come so much before the public.

It need hardly be said that such a professional judge, assisted in important criminal cases by a jury, and checked in civil suits by right of appeal to his principal, makes a clearer fountain of justice than the Great Unpaid of an English Bench, who with the best intentions as to fairness must often depend on their clerk for law. In some points of procedure, too, the Scottish system sets a good example to the English. Prosecutions are not left in private hands, but are conducted by a public official. The Procurator-Fiscal is the Attorney-General of the Sheriff's Court, also performing the duties of Coroner without the meddling of a jury or reporters, though in late years public inquests in certain cases of death have been introduced into Scottish practice. Petty offenders are disposed of by the Sheriff off-hand. More serious charges he remits to the consideration of the Crown officers in Edinburgh, who decide before what court the prisoner shall be tried. The first step is his being brought to private audience of the Sheriff, who, taking care that he do not prejudice his cause, invites him to tell his story, often the only way of getting at the real facts. Another practical arrangement is that of a "pleading diet," at which criminals with no defence have a chance of submitting to the law and being sentenced with as little ado as may be.

A PEEP OF THE GRAMPIANS, INVERNESS-SHIRE

While certain crimes, made heinous by the law of Moses, are still marked on the Scottish statute-book as to be punished with Draconian severity, and while in "good old days" the gallows, the lash, and the branding-iron were as freely used as south of the Border, the administration of the law here has come to be notably mild. Executions are rare, as, indeed, are cases of premeditated murder. In criminal trials, a Scottish jury numbers fifteen, and their verdict is that of the majority. Perhaps a deeper sense of the issues of life and death begets a stronger reluctance to send a fellow-man to the scaffold, and often prompts the verdict of "Not proven," by which so many a criminal goes free yet hardly stainless.

From Aberdeen to Inverness there are three railway routes over an entanglement of Highland Railway and Great North of Scotland branches that have their main knot at Elgin. One line runs from Banff along the Moray Firth, giving fine views across to the opposite shore of Cromarty. Another turns up the Spey, and by this beautiful strath would bring us into the heart of the Highlands. The Speyside line considerately does not hurry passengers through its picturesque environments. There is a legend about this railway that the town council of Elgin—no wiser in their generation than Oxford and Cheltenham—sent up to London a deputation to oppose it in Parliament, when a Cockney crier made such strange work of the names Elgin and Craigellachie, that the worthy citizens sat on unconscious that the bill was being passed without question.

The Speyside line has ways of its own, or had in former days, when I once remonstrated with a clerk who had given me, unasked, a return ticket, and he drily answered, "Ye needn't take a return unless ye like; but it's cheaper"—as it was, by five shillings! At one stage of our journey, the meeting of a Presbytery or some such function swelled the company in the single carriage to nearly a score, which so much exercised the mind of an elder that I heard him remark to a minister, "Doesna this remind ye, sir, of the saying of Daniel the prophet, '*many shall run to and fro*'?" As if exhausted by its unusual burden, the train stopped some couple of hours at Craigellachie, giving one time to make a "Spey cast," but for the want of license and tackle. At the end of nearly a day's journey from Banff, I reached the Boat of Garten, too late for any southward train that evening. Like other "boats" and "bridges" of the Highlands, this has a snug little inn, enlarged I fancy since then, when it had only one good bedroom, in which more than one crowned head has lain to rest. A friend of mine was occupying this when a telegram announced the arrival of the Empress of the French. Of course he turned out, then the people of the house sought his advice in adorning the chamber. He found them hastily fastening up over the Empress' bed their most striking work of art, which happened to be a picture of the battle of Waterloo! Much more like Celtic courtesy was the conduct of William Black's Highland veteran, who scrupled to wear his tartan trews before a Frenchwoman, for fear of reviving sore memories.

CHAPTER VIII

TO JOHN O' GROAT'S HOUSE

Unless for that modern knight-errant, the cyclist, speeding to achieve the quest of John o' Groat's House, the far northern Highlands seem as unduly neglected by tourists as the southern mountains of Wales. Yet across the Moray Firth, that half insulates the north end of Britain, lie charms and grandeurs none the less admirable for being somewhat out of the scope of tourist tickets. The best face of this region it turns to adventurers who brave the Hebridean seas; but also it has winning smiles and impressive frowns for those who on the east side follow the Highland line to its Pillars of Hercules.

The railway to the far north begins by running westward from Inverness to round the inner basin of the Moray Firth at Beauly, indeed a *Beau lieu*. Here, beside the ruins of a priory, is a seat of Lord Lovat, whose shifty ancestor, after Culloden, lurked for six weeks in a secret chamber of Cawdor Castle, but was finally run down in a hollow tree after adventures trying for the age of fourscore and four. The falls of Kilmorack make perhaps the finest point in a district full of attraction. Gilliechrist is noted for a grim story that does not go without question: in the church here a congregation of Mackenzies is said to have been burned alive, to the sound of the bagpipes, by their Christian enemies of Glengarry, a memory of ancient manners which Wordsworth laments as "withering to the root." One of Lord Lovat's hiding-places was an island in the river, that afterwards became a summer retreat of Sir Robert Peel; and its romantic cottage was for a time the home of the two Sobieski or Allan brothers who made a mysterious claim to represent the Stuarts, and were treated with royal honours by some Scottish families. They were a stately pair, after a somewhat theatrical style, taking the part of silent Pretenders in the Highland dress, on which they published a sumptuous volume. In later years, when both were well-known figures in the Reading-room of the British Museum, they, or at least one of them, came down to lodgings in Pimlico, where I have heard pseudo-majesty calling for his boots from the upper floor like a dignified Fred Bayham.

All this part of the railway is set among varied beauty, as it bends away from the western mountains and curves about the heads of the deep eastern firths. Beyond Beauly, it crosses the neck of the peninsula called the Black Isle, on which stand the ex-cathedral city of Fortrose, and Cromarty on the deep inlet guarded by its cave-worn Sutors, where one can ferry over the mouth of this Cromarty Firth to the farther promontory, ended by one of Scotland's several "Tarbets," name denoting an isthmus or portage. Cromarty no longer exists as a separate and much-separated county, of which Macbeth seems to have been Maormor or satrap. Before the boundary adjustment in our generation, several Scottish shires had outlying fragments islanded within their neighbours' bounds, an arrangement probably due to the intrigues of interested nobles; but this one was all *disjecta membra*, the largest lying away up in the north-west corner of Ross, with which environing county Cromarty is now incorporated. The county town, at the point of the Black Isle, still flourishes in a modest way, after shifting its site so that the Cross had to be bodily removed. It has reared at least two notable sons, one that literary Cavalier Sir Thomas Urquhart, who so well translated Rabelais while a prisoner in the Tower, whence he published other ingenious works that but feebly represent his industry, for some hundreds of his manuscripts, lost at the battle of Worcester, went to such base uses as lighting the pipes of Roundhead troopers. The other was Hugh Miller, the stone-mason's apprentice, who rose to be an esteemed author, a geologist of note, and editor of the *Witness*, that full-toned organ that lifted with no uncertain sound the testimony of the Free Church.

This end of Scotland, like the south-west, has been strongly Whig in its sympathies. Even its Highland clans were often led by their chiefs to support the Protestant succession. It was a Mackay who commanded for King William against Claverhouse; the Munroes did service to King George against the Pretender; and President Forbes of Culloden kept the Mackenzies, or many of them, from joining the prince, who at his mansion spent a last quiet night on Scottish soil. Hugh Miller tells us how the Cromarty folk watched the smoke of Culloden across the Firth, of their rejoicing for Cumberland's victory, and of their savage exultation over Lovat's head. Religious enthusiasm here was kin to that of the Covenanters. To the south, as we have seen, lies a belt of Catholicism; and some glens of the Highlands shelter knots of Episcopacy; but when the Gael does take to Presbyterianism, he likes it hot and strong. This was the diocese of the "Men," those inquisitorial elders who played such a severe part in church life of older days. The Free Church movement found great acceptation in the Highlands, so much so that in many parishes the Old Kirk has been almost deserted. And the Free Church in the far north is still largely officered by a school of ministers, who, fervidly rejecting the conclusions of criticism and latitudinarian liberality, are known as the "Highland host," by humorous inversion of a phrase that once applied to an instrument of the prelatical party. The recent broadening of this body's base has here been fiercely resisted, some congregations even coming to blows over Disruption principles. There was a time when the Sabbath could be said not to come above the Pass of Killiecrankie; but now the northern Highlands are the fastness of a Sabbatarianism that dies hard all over rural Scotland. In Ross, the late Queen Victoria had the unwonted experience of being refused horses for a Sunday journey by a postmaster incarnating the spirit of John Knox; then it is understood that Her Majesty gave directions he should in no way suffer for conscience' sake. There were "godly" lords in these parts, to whose influence Hugh Miller attributes this temper of faith; and here was the diocese of that "Black John" the "Apostle of the North," whose field-preachings stirred the bones of martyrs to old prelatic tyranny.

THE RIVER GLASS NEAR BEAULY, INVERNESS-SHIRE

It is no wonder that Hugh Miller became a champion of the Free Church in its pristine glow. Alas! his promising career was cut short by his own hand. It is believed that the trial of reconciling the Mosaic geology with advancing science proved too much for his brain. Had his lot been cast in our generation, divines of his own beloved communion would have taught him more accommodating interpretations, that might have helped to a longer lease of usefulness one of Scotland's many self-taught sons, whose *Schools and Schoolmasters* remains the best book on this countryside.

At Dingwall, the little county town of Ross, which, like the Devonshire Torrington, has been fondly thought to resemble Jerusalem in site, a short branch line turns westward to Strathpeffer, the Scottish Harrogate, thriving apace since it got a railway. Till then its clients were chiefly local, many of them seeking an antidote to more potent waters distilled hereabouts; but now in the later part of the season it is crowded with visitors from both sides of the Border. Strathpeffer has varied advantages to bring patients all the way from London. It boasts the strongest sulphur water in the kingdom, also such an effervescing chalybeate spring as is rarer in Britain than in Germany; it has adopted peat baths, douches, and other balneological devices from the Continent; while a remarkably good climate helps it to distinction among northern spas. It is sheltered by mountains from the wet and windy west; then its show of flourishing crofts, originally granted to a disbanded Highland regiment, attests a genial summer; and beside the Pump-room Highland Eves tempt the drinkers with tantalising piles of strawberries, forbidden by the faculty as plum-pudding at Kissingen; but it is to be feared that British invalids are less docile to *Kurgemäss* rules. The village lies in a valley begirt by charming scenery of "dwarf Highlands" about the course of the Conon and other streams. Hugh Miller worked here as a mason lad, and his "recollections of this rich tract of country, with its woods and towers and noble river, seem as if bathed in the rich light of gorgeous sunsets." The long summer evenings light up patches of heather over which is the way to such beauty spots as Loch Achilty, the Falls of Conon, and the Falls of Rogie, that have been compared to Tivoli. Close at hand is Castle Leod, famed for enormous Spanish chestnuts that give the lie to Dr. Johnson; and farther off are other ancient mansions, Brahan Castle, whose gardens were laid out by Paxton; Coul with its fine grounds, and the spectral ruin of Fairburn Tower. Above the village the wooded ridge of the Cat's Back leads to a noble view from green Knockfarril, where is perhaps the best of the "vitrified forts" so common in the far north. Rheumatic patients would once celebrate their cure by dancing a Highland fling before the Pump-room, a saltatory exercise said to have originated in the experience of a kilt among midges. To prove themselves sound in wind and limb, Sassenach visitors might ascend Ben Wyvis, the "Mount of Storms," a ten-miles tramp or pony ride. There is no difficulty on the way unless a bog at the bottom, that must be skirted in wet weather; and the prospect from the top is rarely extensive in proportion to the trouble of reaching it: on a fine day may be seen the mountains of Argyll, of Braemar, of Sutherland, and of Skye, perhaps grandly half revealed through distant haze or thunderstorm.

MOOR OF RANNOCH, PERTHSHIRE AND ARGYLLSHIRE

At Dingwall diverges also the branch line to Lochalsh, the ferry for Skye. This takes one through a real Highland country, where at Auchnasheen goes off the coach route to Loch Maree, which some judge the finest scene in Scotland. Less smiling than Loch Lomond, it lies more wildly among naked pyramids of quartz, Ben Slioch the most conspicuous point of them, but this lake has the same beauty of wooded islets at the lower end, where a group of half-drowned hillocks "form a miniature archipelago, grey with lichened stone, and bosky with birch and hazel." On one of these are the ruins of a chapel of the Virgin Mary, who was perhaps godmother to Loch Maree. Beyond it open the sea-inlets Torridon, Gairloch, and Loch Ewe; and the coast northwards by Ullapool and Loch Inver is pierced by deep fiords and overlooked by grand summits, worn down from Himalayan masses of old. On the road from Garve to Ullapool, beside the strath looking down to Loch Broom, an oasis of greenery enshrines the Measach Falls of Corriehalloch, a stream tumbling through a deep-bitten chasm, which some have pronounced the grandest Highland scene in the *genre* of that Black Rock ravine mentioned below. If we are ever to reach John o' Groat's House let us turn away from the transparent waters of this coast and from the gloomy glories of Skye. The sportsmen to whom these northern wilds are best known would not thank any guide of idle tourists, and such a guide must be pitied in his task of repeating epithets.

From Dingwall the railway holds up the side of the Cromarty Firth by a country of Munroes and Mackenzies, who have taken all the world for their province. A notable natural feature here is the chasm of the Black Rock, through which a stream from Loch Glass leaps in a series of cascades gouging out an open tunnel that sometimes is only a few yards wide at the top, whence one looks down upon waters foaming into gloomy linns, an American cañon in miniature, its edges bristling like the Trossachs, its mouth thus described by Hugh Miller:—

> "The river—after wailing for miles in a pent-up channel, narrow as one of the lanes of old Edinburgh, and hemmed in by walls quite as perpendicular, and nearly twice as lofty—suddenly expands, first into a deep, brown pool, and then into a broad, tumbling stream, that, as if permanently affected in temper by the strict severity of the discipline to which its early life had been subjected, frets and chafes in all its after course, till it loses itself in the sea. The banks, ere we reach the opening of the chasm, have become steep and wild and densely wooded, and there stand out on either hand giant crags, that plant their iron feet in the stream; here girdled with belts of rank, succulent herbs, that love the damp shade and the frequent drizzle of the spray; and there, hollow and bare, with their round pebbles sticking out from the partially decomposed surface, like the piled-up skulls in the great underground cemetery of the Parisians.... And over the sullen pool in front we may see the stern pillars of the portal rising from eighty to a hundred feet in height, and scarce twelve feet apart, like the massive obelisks of some Egyptian temple; while in gloomy vista within, projection starts out beyond projection, like column beyond column in some narrow avenue of approach to Luxor or Carnac. The precipices are green, with some moss or byssus, that, like the min-

er, chooses a subterranean habitat—for here the rays of the sun never fall; the dead mossy water beneath, from which the cliffs rise so abruptly, bears the hue of molten pitch; the trees, fast anchored in the rock, shoot out their branches across the opening, to form a thick tangled roof, at the height of a hundred and fifty feet overhead; while from the recesses within, where the eye fails to penetrate, there issues a combination of the strangest and wildest sounds ever yet produced by water: there is the deafening rush of the torrent, blent as if with the clang of hammers, the roar of vast bellows, and the confused gabble of a thousand voices."

Turning away from the sea, the line soon strikes it again at the ancient borough of Tain, on the Dornoch Firth. Near the head of the inlet we cross into Sutherland, and soon by the gorge of the Shin come to Lairg, port of the mail-cars that cruise into far corners of this county. The southern land, whose name tells how it was once counted part of nakeder Caithness, has truly northern features of mountains and open moors, lakes, "waters," "straths," and the "kyles" of its coast, those deep narrow sounds taking their Gaelic name from the same root as Calais. Three of its five sides are washed by the sea. The interior is chiefly given up to deer and sheep, with here and there an oasis of moorland farm, rescued from the heather as Holland from salt water, and only by ceaseless industry held against Nature's encroachments. Too much of the land, indeed, makes "a wilderness of brown and ragged moorland," whose "monotonous features" are "masses of wet rock and dark russet heather, black swamps, low and bare hills, and now and again the grey glimmer of a stream or tarn" among heights "dulled with hurrying showers and glittering out again to the sun."

The fish of its inland waters is one of Sutherland's richest harvests. Its lakes are legion; one large parish alone is said to contain hundreds of sheets; and the coming and going of anglers keeps up the good roads and fair inns of a thinly-populated region, from which have been swept away the traces of homes made desolate by the "Sutherland evictions." Loch Shin, running half across the county from Lairg, is the longest lake, about which man has waged feeble war with the sternness of Nature; but the wildest scene is Loch Assynt, near the west coast, tapering among a group of grand mountains such as the Sutherlandshire Ben More and the three-peaked mass of Quinaig. This remote nook seems neglected by authors, yet a picturesque novelist might here find material for a second *Legend of Montrose*, whose last adventure brought him to be captured by Macleod of Assynt and confined in the Castle of Ardvreck. As for the features of the west coast, behind which rise so wildly weather-worn crags above glacier-planed glens and fiords, like those of Norway on a smaller scale, they are thus summed up by Mr. John Sinclair in his *Scenes and Stories of the North of Scotland*:—

"The Gaelic word 'Assynt' is a compound and signifies 'out and in.' If so, like almost all place-names in the Highlands, it is most fitting and felicitous. Indeed it applies admirably, not only to the district so called, but to the entire west coast of Sutherland from the borders of Ross-shire to Cape Wrath itself. Looking, for instance, at the map, we can still see in the endless contortions of the shore, as we used to do when children, the figures and profiles of men and beasts—not one of them in any degree like to any other. There are brows flat and high on the headlands; eyes large and small in the lochs and tarns; noses Roman, Grecian, *retroussé*, on the rocky capes; bay-mouths wide and narrow, open and shut, drooping in sadness, curving upward in joy; chins which are impudent, and chins which are retiring; cheeks smooth and furrowed, shaven and bearded; and in all these you can clearly see, if you have any discernment at all, grumpy grandfathers and grinning fools, laughing children and scolding dominies, gaping crocodiles and snarling monkeys, weeping maids and wistful lovers. The surface of the country inland from the shore is extremely varied, rugged, and wild, but full of interest and charm for healthy and buoyant natures. If you believe, as I for one do, that in order to see the beauties and taste the sweets of land and water there is needed not only sight but *insight*, which is something far more and better, you will find at every turn of the highway new matter of surprise and admiration. Island-studded bays like Badcall, picturesque retreats like Scourie; deeply indented lochs like Laxford, the 'Fiord of salmon'; distant views of a mountain-chain of peaks; long successions of rocky knolls crowned with brushwood and heather—these are a few of the elements which go to make up the panorama between Assynt and the Kyle of Durness. When at length you look down over the brindled cliffs of Cape Wrath; when you behold its rugged masses of God-made masonry; when you hear the thunder-throb of the waves in its vaulted caverns; when you gaze to south and west and north over the hungry heaving sea, you can but look and marvel and adore."

The north coast, with its Cave of Smoo and its Kyles of Durness and of Tongue, is also grandly broken. The east shore, along which the railway runs to Helmsdale, is rather a strip of fields and woods. In the south-east corner lies Dornoch, which enjoys the distinction of being the smallest county town in the kingdom, literally a village, with a restored Cathedral as proof of city dignity, and on the site of its Episcopal palace a prison that has been closed for want of custom among the honest Highlanders. There has been little crime here since the last witch was burned on British soil in 1722 at Dornoch. What brings strangers to Dornoch, now that it has a railway branch, is its golf-links, extending for thousands of acres on the seashore; and this far-northern understudy of St. Andrews offers a remarkably good autumn climate, often mild up till Christmas. Not much bigger is Golspie, with its sea-girt pile of Dunrobin, seat of the ducal family that, owning most of Sutherland, and having incorporated the title and estate of Cromarty as well as the English peerages of Stafford and Gower, can hold up its head as the largest landowner in Britain. With a thousand or so people of its own, Golspie has a good hotel, from which strangers may visit the Dunrobin Glen and waterfall, the traces of gold-working that once promised to pay in this neighbourhood, and Ben Bhraggie conspicuously crowned by Chantrey's statue of the first Duke of Sutherland.

THE ISLES OF LOCH MAREE, ROSS-SHIRE

Above Helmsdale, the Ord ridge makes the Caithness frontier, round the end of which winds what is literally a highroad into our northernmost county, described by Pennant as more terrible than the Penmaenmawr track that used to be the bugbear of travellers to Ireland. The road has been improved, but the railway is here forced away from the sea, seeking an entry into Caithness farther inland. The southern part of this county is still Highland, where the train runs on miles and miles over unbroken stretches of heather; then farther north these fall away into a windy expanse of hollows and ridges, in which Nature would seem to have come short of material for ending off our island with picturesque effect; the central part has even been called the most forlorn wilderness in Britain. Caithness, like other countrysides, has been "improved" in our time; but still it shows wide, cheerless prospects of bog and waste, with peat stacks more frequent than trees, and scattered, turf-walled houses having their thatch bound on by straw ropes and weighted down by stones to keep them from being blown away. Verses signed by the well-known initials, "J. S. B.," set in a frame of honour at John o' Groat's House, describe the bareness and bleakness of these poor fields, fenced by

> Flagstones and slates in a row
> Where hedges are frightened to grow;

and

> Shrubs in the flap of the breeze,
> Sweating to make themselves trees.

The most flourishing production of Caithness appears to be the flagstones, layers of mud and fish bones pressed together ages ago, which its quarries send forth to pave more genial regions. Its waters, too, grow a valuable crop, as one may know who has ever seen the multitudinous herring-fishing fleet set sail from Wick in the long summer twilight. Angling can be had in a chain of some dozen lochs drained by the Thurso river that runs through the county from south to north, at the mouth of which over 2500 salmon were once netted in one haul. In the south, if heather were edible, the folk should be fat; and below darkly naked cones, we find glens such as Berriedale, in parts rich as well as romantic, like a miniature Switzerland of which Morven is the Matterhorn.

Here again we have a duodecimo edition of Highlands and Lowlands bound together. In the north-east the people are tall and sturdy, with plain marks of Scandinavian origin, like their *sters* and *dales*. On the south and west rather, we find clans bearing such names as Mackay, Sutherland, Keith, and Gunn, the last certainly a Norse tribe who can wear only an adopted tartan. Most illustrious of all were the Sinclairs, that held the now dwindled Earldom of Caithness, one of those Norman families settling themselves so masterfully all over Scotland. From this farthest point of the kingdom, hundreds of them followed their Earl to Flodden, and hardly one came back to tell the tale of that "Black Monday," since when, it is said, no Sinclair will cross the Ord ridge on a Monday. Another sore loss fell on the clan a century later, when a certain Colonel Sinclair, heedless of what foreign enlistment regulations had then taken shape, led a regiment of his clan to serve Gustavus Adolphus against Norway, but, attacked by Norwegian peasants in a narrow gorge, more than half of them were crushed beneath rocks hurled down from above, as the French soldiers in Tyrol, or the Turks in defiles of the Kurdish Dersim. The monument on the spot records the death of fourteen hundred kindly Scots, which appears an exaggeration; but it is said that not a score escaped with their lives. Many other grim and gory tales might be told of this race, as some are in Mr. John Sinclair's book above mentioned. The shells of castles fringing these shores have as often as not had a Sinclair lord at one period or other, like Castle Sinclair, almost crumbled away, while the older Girnigo, on to which it was built, still stoutly defies the weather. To-day the most outstanding branch of the family is that of Thurso, first distinguished in a new field by Sir John Sinclair's *Statistical Account of Scotland*, and by his improvements in the county; then by the author of *Holiday House*, and by more than one dignitary of the English Church. This family is notable for stature as well as wisdom. I forget whether it was Catherine Sinclair's father or brother who was said to have three dozen feet of daughters; and when he put down a new pavement—probably from his own quarries—opposite his house in Edinburgh, it was readily nicknamed the "Giant's Causeway." The main branch of the Sinclairs, whose titles at one time, says Sir Walter, might have wearied a herald when they were not so rich as many an English yeoman, is represented near Edinburgh by the ruins of Rosslyn Castle and the monuments of that beautiful chapel—

> Where Rosslyn's chiefs uncoffined lie
> Each baron for a sable shroud
> Sheathed in his iron panoply.

The railway, forking for the only Caithness towns, Wick and Thurso, with their ports Pulteneytown and Scrabster, does not give a fair view of the county. Its most impressive features, as at our other Land's End, are to be looked for in its rim of brown cliffs, tight-packed layers of flagstones, their faces "etched out in alternate lines of cornice and frieze," here dappled by hardy vegetation, there alive with clamorous sea-fowl. Like the granite, slate, and serpentine edges of Cornwall, these sandstone rocks have been carved by wind and water into boldest shapes of capes and bays, dark caverns, funnels, overhanging shelves and gables, swirling "pots" and foaming reefs, isolated stacks lashed by every tide, broken teeth bored and filled by every storm, and the deep chasms here called *geos*, that sometimes lead down to beaches rich in fine and rare shells, for one, "John o' Groat's Buckie," akin to the cowries of the tropics. In the damp crevices, also, grow rare herbs such as that "Holy Grass" found by Robert Dick of Thurso, one of Mr. Smiles's "discoveries" in the species of self-helped naturalists. More truly than of Cornwall, it may be said that Caithness seldom grows wood enough to make a coffin. Where Cornwall comes short of Caithness is in the numerous castles, not all of them left to decay, that on the verge of those northern precipices might often be confounded with Nature's own ruins. It was only about the beginning of the eighteenth century that such strongholds could be deserted for snugger mansions. Here, in 1680, was the scene of our last private war, when the head of the Breadalbane Campbells invaded Caithness with a small army, that overcame the Sinclairs, it is said, by the wily stratagem of causing to be stranded on their coast a ship freighted with whisky to drown the enemy's prudence and resolution.

MOOR AND MOUNTAIN, ROSS-SHIRE

Traces of older inhabitants are very frequent in Caithness, its moors thickly strewn with hut circles, standing stones, tumuli, and those curious underground excavations known as "Picts' Houses," which appear to have been dwellings rather than burial-places. One usual feature of such burrows is the cells and passages fitting a smaller race than our noble selves, who must crawl on hands and knees in grimy explorations not likely to be undertaken by the general tourist. Hence there is reason to suppose that Scotland and other countries have been inhabited by a stunted race of aborigines, like the dwarfish Ainos of Yesso or the pygmies who turn up in various parts of Africa. Mr. David MacRitchie, an antiquary who has paid special attention to so-called Pictish remains, is doughty champion of a theory which connects the dimly historic Picts or Pechts and the legendary Fians with the whole fabulous family of fairies, elves, goblins, brownies, pixies, trolls, or what not, who are represented as dwarfish and subterranean, issuing forth from their retreats to hold varied relations of service or mischief with ordinary men. The name of the Fians, belonging to Ireland as well as to the Scottish Highlands, and fitly represented in the dark doings of Fenians, may point to Finland, where small Laplanders still exist in flesh and blood. The "good people," who long haunted Highland and Lowland glens,—but it seems they cannot abide the scratching of steel pens or the squeaking of slate pencils,—were apt to be tiny, of retiring habits, and in the way of disappearing underground. So the fairies may have been real enough, for all the scorn of that "self-styled science of the so-called nineteenth century." Scott, who seems well disposed to the theory, tells us of stunted, servile clans, such as the M'Couls, who were hereditary Gibeonites to the Stewarts of Appin. In our own time Hebridean herds have been found encamped inside beehive hillocks of turf such as opened to take in the captives of fairy adventure. As for the objection that such beings sometimes appeared as giants rather than dwarfs, it will be remembered how a similar transformation came quite easy to Alice in Wonderland, how *omne ignotum pro magnifico* is very apt to hold true in a misty climate, and how visions of the spiritual in this country have often had an origin disturbing to the senses—

> Wi' tippenny we'll fear nae evil,
> Wi' usquebaugh we'll face the devil.

But neither Mr. MacRitchie, in his *Fians, Fairies, and Picts* and other writings, nor any of his brother ethnologists, has much to tell us about John o' Groat, whose house is the shrine of so many cyclists, wheeling piously from the Land's End, a road of more than nine hundred miles at the shortest, through hundreds of villages, scores of towns, and dozens of cities or places of fame. All that way they come to see a low grassy mound and a flagstaff in front of an hotel, a mile or two west from the pointed stacks of Duncansbay Head. The story goes that this John was a Dutchman by descent, whose family, split into eight branches, kept up meeting for an annual feast; then to avoid squabblings for precedence, John hit on the idea of an octagonal table in an eight-sided house, with eight doors and eight windows, in which, let us trust, his kinsmen were not at sixes and sevens. Here we may have some hint of such a contest for chieftainship as is not unknown among Highland clans, else the folk-lorists must find this a hard text to expound. Three, seven, and nine are all mystic numbers; five is time-honoured in the East, as four in the Western world; two and ten have a practical importance; six bears with it a sense of satisfaction, as do a dozen or a score; thirteen and fourteen fit themselves to legend and superstition; even four-and-twenty blackbirds have been sagely interpreted as the hours of the day and night; but what can one say of eight in tale or history? It might take a mathematician to make a myth here. Maybe the points of the compass, doubled for the sake of emphasis, are at the bottom of it. Perhaps there is some political allusion to James VI.'s Octavian board of administrators. Or may some printer, short of copy, not have tried his hand at composing an octavo legend? Possibly the story is more or less true, in which the Scotticised Dutchman is further stated to have flourished as owner of a ferry to the Orkneys. The suggestion that his fare was a groat must give way before the fact of Groat being apparently a real Dutch name. Nor is it "past dispute" that here geese are bred from barnacles, as asserted by sundry authors, among them that tourist of Cromwell's time, Richard Franck, who seems to have made his way so far, and gives us much quaint information about divinity, scenery, and fishing, spoilt by a most affected style, by slap-dash spelling of names, and by an evident "scunner" at his model Izaak Walton.

One thing seems certain, that John o' Groat was a humbug if he gave out this non-existent house of his for the northernmost point of our mainland, as stiff-kneed cyclists fondly reckon. That honour properly belongs to Dunnet Head, the lofty line of red cliffs stretching to the east of Thurso Bay, hollowed out by billows that shake the lighthouse on the farthest point, from which one looks to the Orkneys over the "still vexed" Pentland Firth. I wonder if that modern John o' Groat be still to the fore, who some twenty years ago was presented with a testimonial for his constancy in carrying across the mail during the lifetime of a generation. He belonged to a school of ancient mariners who had the knack of smelling their way about the sea, whereas our modern Nelsons, it seems, don't know where they are till they have gone down into their cabin and worked out a sum. I once crossed with this "skeely skipper," and was much struck by his method of navigation. A thick fog came on half-way across a tide that races at ten miles an hour; then to clear his inner light, he had up a glass of grog, through which he took frequent observations. Every now and again he stopped the engines and bawled out into the fog without any response; but when at last a muffled hail came back, we were within a hundred yards of Scrabster Pier. On another occasion, he is said to have hit it off still more closely, carrying away the pier-head as a proof of his straight-steered course.

But here we must turn back, lest a darkless summer day tempt us to cross to Orkney, and on to the much-battered Shetlands by the stepping-stone of the Fair Isle, whose name, like that of the foreign Faröe Isles, denotes not beauty but sheep. This muggy and windy archipelago, indeed, is hardly Scottish ground, but an ex-Danish possession, held in pledge by us for a princess's dowry that seems like to be paid on the Greek Calends. Its people indignantly decline to be called Scotchmen. And though our Thule has grand and fine features of its own, too often wrapped in fog, they are hardly such as go to make up the character of Bonnie

Scotland.

CRAGS NEAR POOLEWE, ROSS-SHIRE

CHAPTER IX
THE GREAT GLEN

THE Highland Line is an oblique one, in the main facing south-east; and in much the same direction, between the head of deep inlets, extends the cleft of some threescore miles that cuts the Highlands into near and off halves, the former far the harder worked as a tourist ground, the latter retaining more of its Celtic poverty, while not less richly endowed by nature. From either side smaller glens and straths, each the "country" of some clan, debouch into Glenmore, bed of a chain of lochs and streams linked together as the Caledonian Canal, their varying levels made navigable by the locks that come easier to a Sassenach tongue. This canal is now nearly a century old. In the century before its trenches were opened, King George's soldiers had islanded the farther Highlands by a road between three fortified posts, in the centre and at either end of this Great Glen, thus used as a base for dominating and civilising a region over which the fiery cross ran more freely than the king's writ. The northernmost of the three, Fort-George, above Inverness, is still a military station, serving as depot for the Seaforth and Cameron Highlanders.

Inverness is called the capital of the Highlands, though it lies on an edge of Celtic Scotland, at the north end of the Great Glen, and near the head of the Moray Firth. This is not a Gaelic city, whose inhabitants had at one time the fame of speaking the best English in Scotland, or, for the matter of that, in England, a merit sometimes traced back to a colony of Cromwell's soldiers. Of late years, to tell the truth, the speech of Inverness has hardened and vulgarised somewhat in the mouths of a very mixed population; yet still in some of the secluded glens of the county may be heard a tongue not their own used with a melodious refinement unknown within the sound of Bow Bells.

Smart, cheerful, and regularly built, Inverness has the air of a lowland town, spread out on a river plain, across which fragments of the Highlands have drifted from the grand mountains in view, as the Alps from Berne. The Ness has the distinction of being the shortest river in Britain, shorter even than London's New River; but its course of only a few miles, from Loch Ness to the Moray Firth's inner recess, is enough to make it a resort for big salmon and small shipping. Hector Boece records a former great "plenty and take of herring," which vanished "for offence made against some Saint." Sheltered from the winds of the east and the "weather" of the west, the district has a genial climate where, indeed, the air often "nimbly and sweetly recommends itself unto our gentle senses." Shakespeare, not having the advantage of *Black's Guide*, says little about the scenery around, which has been much described in *Wild Eelin*, William Black's last and not his worst novel, though it has the deplorable fault of bringing in real personages not less thinly disguised than Inverness is as Invernish.

INVERNESS FROM NEAR THE ISLANDS

The famous Castle still stands by the river-side, in its modern form serving as a court-house and prison for ungracious Duncans made both drunk and bold; while the grounds of its "pleasant seat" are a lounge for honest inhabitants, kept in memory, by a statue of Flora Macdonald, how Prince Charles Edward's men blew up the old blood-stained walls. Opposite, across the river, is the modern Cathedral of the Episcopal Church, here a considerable body which once had a soul of Jacobite sentiment. Inverness shows several fragments of antiquity, most revered of them that palladium Clach-na-Cudain—"stone of the tubs," now built into the base of the restored Town Cross. A little way up the river its "Islands" have been adapted as a unique "combination of public park and natural wilderness, of clear brown swirls and eddies under the overhanging hazels and alders, and open and foaming white cataracts where artificial barriers divert the broad rush of the river." This beauty-spot of wood and water no stranger should fail to seek out; then not far beyond he may gain Tom-na-hurich, "hill of the fairies," which makes a picturesque cemetery, commanding what a pre-Wordsworthian writer describes as "a boundless view of gentlemen's seats, seated generally under the shelter of eminences, and surrounded by wooded plantations." Another fine prospect can be had a mile or so behind the station from the heights called "Hut of Health," on which have been built extensive barracks.

The hotels of Inverness are not too many to accommodate the crowds that flit through it in the tourist and shooting season. It has two annual galas, when accommodation may be hardest to find for love or money. The first is the "Character Fair" in July, so called because then some half a million changes hands over dealings in wool on the security of the dealer's character, not a fleece being brought to market, nor even a sample, unless of human brawn and beards well displayed in the brightest of tartan and the roughest of homespun. The second is the Northern Meeting in September, gayest and smartest of those gatherings by which the old Highland games, dress, and music are kept up. But ah! this touch of local colour is too like the artificial bloom on a faded cheek. The glow of tartans here revived by what a German might call "Sunday Highlanders," is but a Vanity Fair. The stalwart athletes, some of them "professionals," who exert themselves to make a London holiday, have little more of Arcadian simplicity than the fine folk who look on. The clansmen forget old feuds; the chiefs no longer command the old loyalty; the greyness and greed of our practical world are settling down over the Highlands, conquered by gold, as hardly by southron steel.

If the pensive tourist seek a purer vision of the past, let him go out to the lonely station of Culloden Moor, some half a dozen miles from Inverness. From the great viaduct that here typifies modern enterprise, he may hold up the Nairn to the roughly overgrown field on which are half buried those pre-historic stones of Clava, monuments of a past beyond Scott's ken. Then, crossing the river and mounting the heights, he comes on the commonplace road that will lead him over Drumossie, where the romantic cause fell hopelessly when Cumberland's redcoats mowed down and bayoneted its jealous, sullen, and weary champions, more than a tenth of them dying here for the Prince who, according to one story, fled basely, but others report him as forced from the field. Fir plantations and fields have now clad the wild nakedness of this tableland; but by the roadside are seen the mounds beneath which lie each clan together, still shoulder to shoulder, and the monumental cairn that is yearly hung with votive wreaths by a certain perfervid Jacobite. If these men gave way before disciplined valour and artillery, if their own martial spirit was marred by quarrelsome ill-temper, let us remember how many of them joined or rejoined the cause when it was as good as lost, after the Jacobite squires of the south had held back from its first flush of success. The next time the Cockney be moved to his sneer about bawbees, let him consider how neither bribes, nor threats, nor torture could tempt these poor Highlanders to betray their prince in his desperate wanderings with a price set on his head. And let us all forget, if we can, the cruelty with which the victors followed up that last rout of sentimental devotion. One poor fellow took hundreds of lashes on an English ship of war, without opening his mouth to confess how he had ferried the fugitive to a safer isle. Such stories of humble fidelity are too much forgotten by historians who bear in mind how the heads of certain houses—father and son—ranked themselves on opposite sides with a politic eye to escape forfeiture, whether James or George were king. The most romantic case, if true, is that of the Macintosh in the royal ranks, said to have yielded himself prisoner to his own wife, who had taken his place at the head of the rebellious clansmen. Another family manœuvre turned out luckily for a Lowland peer who, as preparation for taking the field with the Pretender, treated himself to a foot-bath which his prudent wife made so hot that her valorous spouse could not boot nor spur for many a day, and thus was kept out of political hot water. The same story, indeed, is told of another couple, whose sympathies were divided the opposite way on.

Where are the sons of the scattered clans? Many of them peacefully settled among law-abiding Lowlanders, many of them gone to America, where among other mountains, on fruitfuller straths and by mightier streams, they often cherish their Gaelic and their kilts, sometimes against sore pricks of climate and mosquitoes, sharper than the ancestral itch of dirt and poverty. In one district of Nova Scotia alone, there are said to thrive three thousand of those Macdonalds whose offended pride hung back from the clash of Culloden. Before the '45, emigration to America had already begun with the colony settled in Georgia by General Oglethorpe; even earlier indeed hardy Highlanders and Orkneymen were in demand for service in the wilds of Hudson's Bay; but after Culloden the exodus became considerable, increasing as the chieftains, turned into lairds, found idle and prejudiced dependants only in the way of improving their estates; and "another for Hector!" came to mean a fresh clansman shipped across the Atlantic to see Lochaber no more. Harsh as it was, the wrench proved often a blessing in disguise, when the last look at those misty Hebrides had softened into a tender memory with the farmers of New Glengarry or ice-bound Antigonish. Our day saw two Prime Ministers of Canada who, if kept at home, might have been carrying the southron's game-bag, as one of them perhaps did in his bare-legged youth.

TOMDOUN, GLEN GARRY, INVERNESS-SHIRE

Perhaps the most remarkable Highland-American has never been duly brought into the light of history, as neither has that mysterious soldier of fortune Gregor MacGregor, "Cacique of Poyais," who made such a stir in two worlds, but is now hardly remembered unless by the mention of him in the *Ingoldsby Legends*, and the banknotes of his bankrupt kingdom, treasured by collectors of curiosities. Did the general reader ever hear of Alexander MacGillivray, who was born at once a Highland gentleman and a Red Indian chief? His career, which I hope to write some day, if once able to bridge over certain gaps in my information, makes an extraordinary mixture of romance with very opposite features, better fitting the vulgar idea of a Scot.

Some time during the Jacobite disturbances, one Lachlan MacGillivray emigrated from Inverness to the Southern States, where he became a prosperous Indian trader, and, perhaps in the way of business, married a "princess" of the great Creek Confederacy. Alexander, the son of this mésalliance, was well educated and brought up to trade, but early in life betook himself to his mother's people, among whom his attainments as well as his birth gave him influence. Rank, by Indian law, as by "Lycian custom," being inherited on the spindle side, before he was thirty he had been recognised as chief of the Creeks, and for many years played a leading part in their fitful politics. Little is known of his rule beyond the main facts, our clearest accounts of him being derived from a rare book written by another young adventurer, the Frenchman Leclerc Milfort, whose story, in plain English, seems not to be always trusted.

According to himself, Milfort, having also wandered among the Creeks, was chosen by them as their war chief, an office separate from the civil headship of an Indian tribe. Then the Scotsman and the Frenchman appear to have governed the Creeks for years, making a congenial disposition of power, the one the head, the other the hand, of a powerful though somewhat unstable body politic. MacGillivray had no stomach for fighting, was even a coward, if Milfort is to be believed; but he was crafty, resourceful, and of a clear Caledonian eye to the main chance. Milfort found him living in a good house, with herds of cattle and dozens of negro slaves. Another source of profit he had in a secret partnership with a firm of brother Scots at Pensacola, to which he directed the trade of the Creek nation, jealously intrigued for by their British and Spanish neighbours. The Revolutionary War had nearly caused a rupture between these Creek consuls. MacGillivray's sympathies were with the British; Milfort had no scruple in fighting against the Americans, but when French troops came to take part in the struggle, he was disposed to side with his compatriots. His colleague, however, persuaded him to remain neutral; and by this Scotsman's influence, the Creeks seem to have been kept from throwing into the scale the weight of their war parties. The canny chief entered into a maze of tricky negotiations with the various bordering Powers, pretending to each to be in its special interest, receiving bribes from all, throughout, as far as his dealings can be traced, "true to one party, and that is himself."

The States having secured their independence, the eagerness of American settlers to press over the Creek bounds had almost brought about an Indian war with the great republic. Scenes of bloodshed took place on the frontier; and if MacGillivray was cunning and not warlike, he showed the civilised virtue of humanity in sparing and rescuing captives. Peace was negotiated by an Indian deputation which he led to New York. A secret article provided for his being appointed a general in the U.S. service, with a pension of $1200. At the same time, or soon afterwards, the wily chief accepted similar distinctions and payments from the British and the Spanish Governments, and between them he must have enjoyed a considerable income for steadily promoting his own interests, while impartially betraying all his rival employers in turn.

But the arrangement which he brought about with young Uncle Sam roused the Indians against him. A rebel leader appeared in one "General" Bowles, who, originally a private soldier, in the course of many dubious adventures more than once played the pretender among the Creeks. A civil war raged in the Confederacy; MacGillivray at one time was driven to flight; but, still backed up by Milfort, he succeeded in partly restoring his power, though not with the same firmness. In the middle of his tortuous policies, he died at the age of fifty, leaving a son, who was sent home to Scotland, where old Lachlan is said to have been still alive in Inverness-shire. It was his half-breed nephew, William Weatherford, who, later on, led the last struggle of the Creeks against American encroachment.

As for Leclerc Milfort, he was left for a time struggling against Bowles and other rivals for authority. According to his own story, the French Revolution brought him back to France, where he laboured to persuade Buonaparte how easily an empire might be won in America. It is said that the First Consul was taken by the idea, and that in 1801 a small French expedition had even been prepared to conquer the Creek country under Milfort's guidance. But vaster plans interfered with any such scheme, and in 1803, Louisiana and the great South-West were sold by France to the United States. The ex-chief had a chance to gratify his taste for fighting at home, when France was invaded in 1814; but he did not return to resume the authority of which he boasts in his book, so rare that I have never seen a copy except my own. If one only had all the truth about these two white adventurers, what a strange romance it would make!

The Highlands may be all the more prosperous for the new husbandry that drove so many of their sons to seek fortune in distant lands, often to find fame. It might be well for the people to have such enterprise roughly forced on a conservative spirit which scowled at the introduction of potatoes, turnips, and other improvements to their backward culture. What their good old days were in truth may be guessed in the smoky huts where they still love to pig together, stubbornly refusing to adapt themselves to an order in which sheep are found more profitable than men, and deer than sheep. The big sheep-farmer from the south makes more of the land than the easy-going crofter; yet the smallest drop of Celtic blood cannot but stir to see a clansman touching his hat for tips from southron stockbrokers, and serving as obsequious attendant to the American millionaires who enclose his native heath. Naturally the Highlander is a gentleman, for all his faults, with instinctive courtesy to soften his somewhat sullen pride. More than once I have had a tip refused by a Highland servant, as nowhere else in the world unless in the United States before their social independence, too, began to be demoralised by the largesses of successful speculators, who, after piling up dollars by "rings" and "corners," find they can buy less observance for their money at home than by corrupting a race declared by Mrs. Grant of Laggan, herself reared in America, "to resemble the French in being poor with a better grace than other people."

A SHEPHERD'S COT IN GLEN NEVIS, INVERNESS-SHIRE

RIVER AWE FLOWING TO LOCH ETIVE, ARGYLLSHIRE

The Highlander was a born sportsman as well as a gentleman, who by his paternal chiefs would not be called closely to account for every deer and salmon that went to eke out his frugal fare. Now he can shoot or fish only in the way of business, the very laird making two ends meet by letting out his moors and streams to a stranger, in whose service the sons of warriors play the gamekeeper and gillie, with more or less good will, loading the gun and carrying the well-stocked luncheon basket, perhaps not always very hearty in hunting down those Ishmaelite brethren who do a little grouse-netting on their own account for the supply of London tables by the 12th of August. Sometimes the Gael takes revenge by being able to hint his scorn for the sportsmanship of these new masters; but as often, to do them justice, they will not give him this poor satisfaction. A well-known southron humorist tells a story which needs his voice to bring out the point, how he missed a deer, to the disgust of the keeper, and how, trying to conciliate this worthy by admiration of a fine head, he got the dry answer — "It's no near so fine as the one ye shot this morning — a-a-at!"

Deer-stalking is a sport that still demands manly skill and hardihood, however many menials can be hired to mark down and circumvent the great game. So much cannot always be said of other shooting, when the noble sportsman entrenches himself behind fortifications to which the fierce wild fowl are driven to be shot down by gun after gun placed in his hands. Sport, that was once a bond between classes, becomes more and more a monopoly of the rich. The very meaning of the word suffers a change in our day from the doing of something oneself to a performance where most of the activity is by paid assistants or "professionals." One good feature of Highland sport is in not lending itself to the collection of gate-money from a mob of lookers-on; but the dollar-hunting and *coup*-landing chieftain need not expect to be loved by those whom he would fain bar out of his solitary playground.

I, too, have lived in Arcadia, and was duly entered at this craft, not that I ever took very heartily to it, or that a big capercailzie, then a *rara avis* in Highland woods, ran much more risk from me than from Mr. Winkle. But I know the free joy of tramping over wet moors behind dogs, shooting for sport and not for slaughter, lunching off bread and cheese, or a cold grouse, with fingers for forks, and coming home to a dinner won by one's own hands. That old-fashioned muzzle-loading work is scorned by the present generation who, indeed, pay such rents for moors and coverts that they have some reason to be keen after a big bag. Well I remember a true Nimrod's scorn for the first great noble in our part of the world who *sold his game!* We children in the nursery would be fed on grouse and salmon to use up what could not be sent away as presents; and, for my part, I have never quite got over a stickjaw conception of these expensive dainties.

There was a Highland shooting which in those days seemed a paradise of schoolboy holiday. It belonged to a well-known Scottish peeress married to a French nobleman, on whom it was thrown away, though their son grew to be of a different mind. Thus it came on a long lease into the occupation of keen sportsmen of my family, who naturally did not care to build for their inevitable successors. The "lodge" was a short row of white cottages, the centre one turned into a parlour, the others into bedrooms; and as youngsters grew up, extra accommodations were provided in the shape of a tent and iron shanties, the whole group backed by a thin clump of wind-blown firs visible some dozen miles away on the bare mountain side. All through the summer months it made an encampment for a band of kilted youngsters, "hardy, bold, and wild," taking in the Highland air at every pore, with miles of moor and burn for their playground, which they knew not to be haunted by the victims of Druid rites. Not that more sophisticated guests were unknown at this eyry of eyases. The great little Earl Russell, at that time, if I am not mistaken, Prime Minister, was tenant of a neighbouring moor. One day he had come over for a sociable beat, broken in on by a messenger, hot foot across the heather, bearing a huge official envelope superscribed with the name of a ducal colleague. The statesman requested a private apartment in which to examine this communication, but the only closet available was a bedroom, where he opened the cover to find—a caricature of himself from *Punch*!

I have been led away by a grumble at the self-indulgent and well-appointed sportsmen who in this generation invade my native heath. But, however much they make themselves at home here, we chuckle to think that they at least cannot tune their ears to the native music. For what says the poet—

> A Sassenach chief may be bonnily built,
> He may purchase a sporran, a bonnet, and kilt;
> Stick a skean in his hose—wear an acre of stripes—
> But he cannot assume an affection for pipes.

Another comfort taken by the dispossessed son of the mist is in hearing the weather abused by strangers, who may as well stay at home under shelter of their Twopenny Tubes and Burlington Arcades if they are afraid of rain. Dr. Johnson was not, and a gentler critic of his time observed that the Highlanders minded snow "no more than hair powder." In the warm south of England, I once caught a cold which stuck to me all summer and seemed like to settle on my lungs. Late in autumn, in a kill or cure mood, I went down to the dampest side of the Highlands, got wet from morning to night, and in a week my cough had gone like dew from the heather. But nature's hydropathy does not always work so well, even on seasoned constitutions. The severest loss of our Volunteer force, as yet, on British soil, has been from that soaking royal review at Edinburgh, when Highlanders were killed and crippled by a long railway journey in drenched clothes, even though at the way-stations matron and maid brought them patriotic offerings of dry hose, with which at least to "change their feet."

Now let us turn to the tourist, who has neither lust nor license to ruffle the least feather of grouse or gull, but calls forth angry passions when his red guide-book or her sunshade come scaring the prey stalked by lords of Cockaigne and Porkopolis. He and she, by coveys, swarm in various directions from Inverness, but chiefly by the Caledonian Canal, that highroad of pleasure, as once of business, between the North and the South Highlands. Had we seen this road "before it was made," we should find little difference to-day, unless for a few more modern mansions that have swallowed up many a lowly home, still, perhaps, marked by patches of green about the ruined mountain shielings where, as on Alpine pastures, Highland *Sen-*

nerin made butter and cheese through the long summer days. A steamboat carries one right through the Great Glen, beneath mountain giants, clad in nature's own tartan of green and purple chequered by brown and grey, with bare knees of crag, and streaming sporrans of cascade, and feathers of fir-wood, too often wrapped in a plaid of mist, or hidden by a mackintosh of drenching rain. Else, against the clear sky-line, one may catch sight of a noble stag on the hill head, displayed like its crest, sniffing motionless at the steamer far below, unconscious of an unseen enemy stealing up the rearward corrie with heart athrob for his blood, which, at the pull of a trigger, may or may not stain the heath.

From its port below Craig Phadric, believed to have been the stronghold of a king older than Duncan, then past the hill bearing his name, the Canal soon takes us through the fertile strath into the wilder Highlands. The first stage of that grand panorama is through deep Loch Ness, where on one side Mealfourvonie towers like a hayrick, round which goes the way to those remote Falls of Glomach, called the noblest in Britain, and on the other are more easily reached the Falls of Foyers, chained and set to work by an Aluminium Company that did not tremble at the rhapsody of Christopher North:—

"Here is solitude with a vengeance—stern, grim, dungeon solitude! How ghostlike those white, skeleton pines, stripped of their rind by tempest and lightning, and dead to the din of the raging cauldron! That cataract, if descending on a cathedral, would shatter down the pile into a million of fragments. But it meets the black foundations of the cliff, and flies up to the starless heaven in a storm of spray. We are drenched, as if leaning in a hurricane over the gunwale of a ship, rolling under bare poles through a heavy sea. The very solid globe of earth quakes through her entrails. The eye, reconciled to the darkness, now sees a glimmering and gloomy light—and lo, a bridge of a single arch hung across the chasm, just high enough to let through the triumphant torrent. Has some hill-loch burst its barriers? For what a world of waters come now tumbling into the abyss! Niagara! hast thou a fiercer roar? Listen—and you think there are momentary pauses of the thunder, filled up with goblin groans! All the military music-bands of the army of Britain would here be dumb as mutes—Trumpet, Cymbal, and the Great Drum! There is a desperate temptation in the hubbub to leap into destruction. Water-horses and kelpies, keep stabled in your rock-stalls—for if you issue forth the river will sweep you down, before you have finished one neigh, to Castle Urquhart, and dash you, in a sheet of foam, to the top of her rocking battlements.... We emerge, like a gay creature of the element, from the chasm, and wing our way up the glen towards the source of the cataract. In a few miles all is silent. A more peaceful place is not among all the mountains. The water-spout that had fallen during night has found its way into Loch Ness, and the torrent has subsided into a burn. What the trouts did with themselves in the 'red jawing speat' we are not naturalist enough to affirm, but we must suppose they have galleries running far into the banks, and corridors cut in the rocks, where they swim about in water without a gurgle, safe as golden and silver fishes in a glass-globe, on the table of my lady's boudoir. Not a fin on their backs has been injured—not a scale struck from their starry sides. There they leap in the sunshine among the burnished clouds of insects, that come floating along on the morning air from bush and bracken, the licheny cliff-stones, and the hollow-rinded woods."

At the head of Loch Ness our boat takes to locks again at Fort-Augustus, now turned into a Catholic monastery, arms yielding to the gown. Hence, if the rain persistently blot out all prospect, we might hasten on by branch railway to the West Highland Line, passing near those geological lions called the "parallel roads" of Glenroy. Else we thread the water between the heights of Keppoch and Glengarry, marked by the cairns of many a forgotten feud, and through Loch Oich and Loch Lochy come to cross the West Highland Railway at Banavie, where the Canal descends to sea level by a staircase of locks like that at Trollhatta on the not less famous waterway from Gothenburg to Stockholm.

Loch Oich, the smallest of the chain into which the Garry comes down from its basin, has an authentic legend as retreat of Ewen Macphee, perhaps the last British outlaw above the rank of a lurking poacher or illicit distiller. Early in the nineteenth century he enlisted in a Highland regiment, from which he deserted, and though captured and handcuffed, made a romantic escape to his native wilds of Glengarry. After camping in the woods till the hue and cry after him had died out, he settled on an islet of Loch Oich, where he took to himself a wife and reared a sturdy brood. For long he played Rob Roy on a small scale, "lifting" sheep and helping himself to game, while he enjoyed the sanctity of a seer's reputation. When a southern landlord bought the property, he established a not unfriendly *modus vivendi* with this tackless tenant, who introduced himself to the new owner by sticking his dirk into the table as title-deed to his island—"By this right I hold it!" But by and by the minions of the law pressed upon his retreat; and in spite of a resolute defence, in which his wife handled a gun like a modern Helen Macgregor, he was arrested for sheep stealing, and taken to prison, where he pined away after a long life of lawless freedom. Bales of sheep skins and tallow, found hidden about his fastness, were evidence of how he had lived at the expense of his neighbours, a feature too much left out of sight in modern regret for the picturesque old times.

Banavie—that seems to be a kilted cousin of Banff, and forebear of the Rocky Mountain paradise an American geographer presumes to spell *Bamf*—is close to Fort-William, the southernmost of the three military posts that bridled the Great Glen. In Stuart days this was Inverlochy, scene of that battle between Montrose and Argyle. It is now a town of snug hotels, over which rises the proclaimed monarch of British mountains, his gloomy brow often crowned with mist and his precipitous shoulders ermined with snow at any season. But if the weather favour, from the Observatory Tower at the top, one has the far-spread prospect masterly laid out by Sir Archibald Geikie:—

> "While no sound falls upon his ear, save now and then a fitful moaning of the wind among the snow-rifts of the dark precipice below, let him try to analyse some of the chief elements of the landscape. It is easy to recognise the more marked heights and hollows. To the south, away down Loch Linnhe, he can see the hills of Mull and the Paps of Jura closing the horizon. Westward, Loch Eil seems to lie at his feet, winding up into the lonely mountains, yet filled twice a day with the tides of the salt sea. Far over the hills, beyond the head of the loch, he looks across Arisaig, and can see the cliffs of the Isle of Eigg and the dark peaks of Rum, with the Atlantic gleaming below them. Farther to the north-west the blue range of the Coolin Hills rises along the sky-line, and then, sweeping over all the intermediate ground, through Arisaig and Knoydart and the Clanranald country, mountain rises beyond mountain, ridge beyond ridge, cut through by dark glens, and varied here and there with the sheen of lake and tarn. Northward runs the mysterious straight line of the Great Glen, with its chain of lochs. Thence to east and south the same billowy sea of mountain-tops stretches out as far as eye can follow it—the hills and glens of Lochaber, the wide green strath of Spean, the grey corries of Glen Treig and Glen Nevis, the distant sweep of the moors and mountains of Brae Lyon and the Perthshire Highlands, the spires of Glencoe, and thence round again to the blue waters of Loch Linnhe."

Hitherto the drenched tourist has been too ready to hasten away towards drier Saxondom by steamboat or rail from the end of the Caledonian Canal, ignorant what choice spots may hereabouts be lingered among, such as that "Dark Mile," which some have found better worth seeing than the Trossachs, and Glen Nevis that, opening as a lush valley, mounts by rushing falls into recesses of wild magnificence. Now the West Highland Railway takes one on through Glenfinnan and the Lochiel country, where Charles Edward raised that last standard of rebellion, against the prudent judgment of the Cameron chief whose loyal pride yet followed it to Culloden, and where a tall column records how a later Cameron fell as gallantly in the service of the established dynasty. Thus we come to Arisaig on the west coast, and to Mallaig opposite Skye, in which a book that draws to its end must not venture to enter upon the most gloomily grand aspects of Highland scenery. All this, like the country above the Moray Firth, comes under the head of "counsels of perfection"; but every conscientious Highland tour takes in Inverness, on the round made by the Highland Railway and the Caledonian Canal, the most perfunctory minimum being the Trossachs trip, which might be extended to pass by Oban and the Clyde.

A CROFT NEAR TAYNUILT, LOCH ETIVE, ARGYLLSHIRE

CHAPTER X

GLASGOW AND THE CLYDE

At the junction of salt and fresh water navigation, beside Fort-William, the tourist begins a new stage of his journey, if in haste, speeding by the West Highland Railway through beautiful glens and over bleak and bare moorlands to come on the Clyde at Helensburgh. The older pilgrimage is by steamer down Loch Linnhe to Oban, past Ballachulish, where, if the Saxon can get his tongue round its name, he may land to visit "dreary dark Glencoe," whose grimly sublime seclusion seems in keeping with its tragic memories and with its legendary fame as birthplace of Ossian.

Oban, "Charing Cross of the Highlands," which Cockneys sometimes confuse with Holborn, and which in thick weather may rather suggest the Tilbury Docks, had in Dr. Johnson's day one "tolerable inn," now multiplied into a forest of hostelries, "a huddlement of upstart houses," above which the shell of an unhatched Hydropathic looks down on darker ruins of the "Land of Lorne." Here the not impecunious traveller might tarry long to visit the islands around or the lochs and falls inland. Turning his back on the cloudy Atlantic, he may take the Caledonian Railway by Loch Awe, Loch Tay and Loch Earn, and thus be wafted to Perth, Edinburgh, or Glasgow, while at Tyndrum it is open to him to make a cut across to the West Highland Line. But his most beaten path is still a watery one, on to the Crinan Canal, and through it to Ardrishaig, where he enters on the safe and luxurious navigation of the Clyde.

This is not a guide-book that can afford to expatiate in small print on all the aisles and monuments of this grand estuary, with its lochs opening like side chapels. The stranger will do well to halt almost wherever he pleases, and at a dozen resorts has a choice of steamboats plying up and down *the* water, as a Glasgow man calls it, even as his ancestors named the Esks and Avons which for them were alone familiar. The butterfly tourist, if he get a fine day or two, may settle on Tarbert, the isthmus of Cantire; or at Inveraray, the ducal village-capital of Argyll; or at Dunoon, its largest town; or at Rothesay, the Swindon Junction of this inland voyaging; or at the Cumbraes, whose minister prayed for "the adjacent islands of Great Britain and Ireland"; or at one and another of those snug bathing-places that almost line the shores. The gem, the *bouquet*, the crown of all Clyde scenery is, of course, Arran, to know which *non cuivis contingit*. But if he can find quarters in some airy hovel with rats running about the roof, or on some shake-down of an hotel annexe, and if the rain clears up over Goatfell, the reader will not regret taking my word for the exceeding loveliness of glens and corries, which have inspired painters, poets, and even guide-book makers.

GLENCOE, ARGYLLSHIRE

Many writers have described Clyde voyaging. To save myself trouble, let me borrow from the ingenious M. Jules Verne, who in his *Rayon-Vert* gives a remarkable account of this region and its inhabitants. It is always well to see ourselves as others see us, especially through the eyes of a famous story-teller. This story of his is intended to be amusing, and he appears to succeed in being funnier than he knew by reading up Sir Walter Scott and other works of fiction, then "combining his information."

The time is the present day; the scene opens on the Clyde; the *dramatis personæ* are as follows: Two old bachelor brothers, Sam and Sib Melvill, have been avowedly "lifted" from those chieftains of the southron clan Cheeryble. They live together in kindly one-mindedness; they take snuff out of the same box; they quote Ossian in alternate stanzas, also Scott, and such good old Scottish proverbs as "let us leave that fly tranquil on the wall." They especially agree in spoiling their niece, Miss Helena Campbell, who, like other heroines of fiction, is beautiful to behold, and like other Scottish damsels of rank, does her hair up in a snood, believes in valkyries and "browines," then, though as good as she is charming, has a most troublesome obstinacy in getting her own way. This is a rich family, who have a town house in Glasgow and a cottage near Helensburgh, opposite the promontory always spelt "Rosenheat," a cottage of much gentility, with a tower, a terrace, and a park. Over a large household rule two faithful retainers of the olden time, (1) the "intendant" Partridge, who always sports tartan in the form of a kilt "above the philabeg," with blue bonnet, cow-skin brogues and other trappings of a Highland butler's livery; (2) a venerable housekeeper, who, like all housekeepers in the Highlands, bears the title of "Luckie," but is also styled Dame Bess, and addressed by Partridge as "Mavourneen," that well-known Scottish term of endearment, while her masters invariably summon her by crying "Bet! Beth! Bess! Betsey! Betty!" each word taking up a line, so as to make what printers call "fat" and what French authors, from the great Dumas downwards, must find very convenient for stretching out "copy."

Though Sam and Sib are Glasgow aristocrats, they seem so far in touch with the great metropolis as to take in the *Morning Post,* in which one day Miss Campbell reads an account of a wonderful green ray shed by the unclouded sun at his setting on an open sea horizon. Nothing will serve this wilful young lady but at once setting out to behold such an optical phenomenon. Gifted as she is, our heroine can have passed no high standard of geography, but her uncles explain to her that Oban is the nearest place at which an open sea view can be had. *Va pour Oban!* she exclaims. The sly uncles agree on the trip, all the more readily as they are aware how at Oban happens to be sojourning a certain Aristobulus Ursiclos, on whom they have their eye as an *excellent parti* for their ward.

The household is at once thrown into a confusion of packing, for by seven o'clock next morning it is necessary to be in Glasgow to catch the Oban steamer *Columba,* which seems rather a roundabout route for residenters at Helensburgh. At this early hour the party punctually embark, to be carried admiringly down the scenery of the Clyde, though, indeed, the faithful steward and housekeeper, always in attendance, shake their heads in sad harmony at every stage over the engines and smoke stacks that are overshadowing good old Highland customs, the sole example of which here given is unhappily referred to the Orkney Kirkwall. Messrs. MacBrayne have no cause of complaint as to praise of the steamer and her accommodations; but the proprietors of Murray's *Guide*, with which the party are provided rather than Black's, might find ground of action in the French printers' libellous misspellings of names. That work is duly drawn on for notices of Dumbarton Castle, of Greenock, of ruined strongholds, and of the distant crests of Arran and Ailsa Craig. The passengers hold stiffly aloof in groups, except of course some French tourists, who bring their native sociability with them; but there is none of the British *morgue* about Partridge, when he claps his hands in applause at the sight of a tower ruined for the MacDouglases by his young mistress' clan. They sail safely through the Kyles of Bute, past Ardrishaig, by the Crinan Canal, then up the Hebrides archipelago to Oban, where they install themselves, regardless of expense, in the best rooms of the Caledonian Hotel, awaiting the first fine sunset to catch the green ray.

At this *ville des bains*, not more than "a hundred and fifty years old," in August crowded with bathers, who do not satisfy French ideas of propriety by a bathing costume *souvent trop rudimentaire*, our friends soon fall in with Aristobulus Ursiclos, a mere Lowlander, who wears no kilt but, on the contrary, aluminium spectacles and such like, and having graduated both at Oxford and Edinburgh, is a scientist *pour rire*, not to say a prig and pedant of the darkest dye, seizing every chance to lecture on meteorology, mineralogy, chemistry, astronomy, in short *de omni re scibili*. It goes without saying that Miss Campbell at first sight takes a strong dislike to this false hero, who at once sets about playing the superior person over such a childish fancy as the green ray, also excites her contempt by his awkwardness at the British game of "crocket." Equally of course, a true hero has already been provided, a ram caught in one of the handy thickets of romance as due sacrifice to Hymen. This is Oliver Sinclair, a young and sympathetic artist, who sends notes of his travels to the celebrated *Edinburgh Review*, but at present has nothing more pressing on hand than to attach himself to the party.

The episodes of the story henceforth turn upon repeated efforts to see the green ray, always baffled by the weather or by some clumsy interference of Mr. Aristobulus, who can never understand when he is not wanted, though able to rebuke his companions' enthusiasm for the sea by instructing them that it is merely a chemical compound of hydrogen and oxygen with 2½ per cent of chloride of sodium. In vain they hire a carriage-and-four to drive to the "village of Clachan," and on to one of the outlying islands, from which there is a clear sea view, at Oban, as we know, blocked by the island of "Kismore."

After weeks of disappointment and bad weather, the whole party take steamer for Iona, where they put up at the "Duncan Arms," feasting daily upon a truly Scottish *menu* of haggis, hotch-potch, cockie-leekie, sowens and oat cake, the Highland Cheeryble brothers pledging one another in pint stoups—containing four English pints, we learn—of "foaming usquebaugh," also in a drink called "whisky," with strong beer, "mum," and "twopenny" flavoured with a *petit verre* of gin. A Scottish breakfast, it appears, is a slighter meal, consisting of "tea, butter, and sandwiches." This good cheer is so engrossing that only after a few days they recall the fact of there being some ruins on Iona, which are then visited and described at much length, with all due enthusiasm on the part of the author. Dr. Johnson declares the man little to be envied whose piety would not grow warmer among the ruins of Iona. That man is soulless Aristobulus, who excites our heroine's indignation by the cold-blooded manner in which he would peep and geologise among so sacred monuments, hammering off a piece of a cross to examine it as a mineral specimen. Worse, just as she was about to see the green ray, this unlucky spoil-sport lets off a gun, scaring up a cloud of gulls to obscure the for once bright sunset.

GARELOCHHEAD, DUMBARTONSHIRE

Miss Campbell is determined at any cost to shake off such a hateful suitor. She hears of another island called Staffa, from which a still opener view can be had. Nothing will hinder that in the frequented port of Iona a "Cowes-built" yacht is waiting to be hired. The obedient uncles charter her forthwith, engage a brass-bound captain and a crew of six men, provision her suitably, and sail off for Staffa, which, as the author explains, is at no great distance. Aristobulus, with his hammer and spectacles, is left behind, henceforth dropping out of the story.

Our heroine, having had the geological marvels of Staffa explained to her, is so delighted that she proposes to buy the island. Their yacht blown away before a storm, the passengers encamp in a cave and go through perilous adventures, for the scenery of which the guide-book comes in useful. Oliver Sinclair, whose life Helena had been the means of saving at his first appearance on the scene, now in turn rescues her in most romantic style; and the young pair are so taken up with each other that they almost forget all about the green ray in search of which those long-suffering uncles have been dragged so far. At last comes one clear glorious sunset, lighting up a panorama of sea line that could not but have excited admiration even in "the most prosaic merchant (*negotiant*) of the Canongate." As the sun disappears, all the party behold the long-sought wonder, all but the hero and heroine, who are too intent on the rays lit in each other's eyes by a "light that never was on sea or land." After this, there is nothing left but "Bless you, my children," and a sumptuous marriage in "St. George's Church, Glasgow," transported for the occasion, apparently, from Hanover Square. All which, if one skip the guide-book passages, makes a very striking account of Scottish manners and customs, but prompts some doubt of the author's accuracy when he comes to deal with such more remote regions as the moon or the bottom of the sea.

It seems a rule with French writers to be careless about the local colour of their foreign scenes. Well known is the haughty answer of Victor Hugo to the Englishman who ventured to remonstrate with him on his Lords "Tom Jim Jack," and other ornaments of British aristocracy. He at least spared Scotland, — or was it he who translated the Firth of Forth by *le premier du quatrième*, as another *traducteur* elevated "a stickit minister" into *un prêtre assassiné*? If it be true that Dumas' chief "ghost" was by origin a Scotsman named Mackay, that voluminous romancer was ill-served in the wild work made for him of British topography. D'Artagnan, landing at Dover, found our posts "pretty well served," so well, indeed, that starting at 2.30 P.M. he rode to London in four hours, then on to Windsor, followed the king to a hunting-ground two or three leagues beyond, and galloped back to Buckingham House, all before nightfall, a feat that beats Dick Turpin and John Gilpin. When Charles I. exclaimed *"Remember!"* with his dying breath, he was of course addressing that *preux chevalier* Athos, hidden below the scaffold; and what Athos should remember was how the king had stowed a million of money in two barrels under the vaults of the Abbey of Newcastle. In due time Athos goes to turn up this deposit, then from Monk's camp at Coldstream on the Tweed, he and the General stroll over to Newcastle in the course of half an hour or so. Athos of course comes off successful in this midnight quest, but not so Monk, who, as M. Dumas first informed us, was kidnapped by D'Artagnan in the midst of his army and carried off in a fishing boat from Coldstream to Holland, to be laid bound before his lawful king, brought back after all in time to prevent Athos from exterminating a company of Scottish soldiers in defence of his million. The whole series of those Three Musketeers' adventures contains many such curious side lights on the history of our country. In a comic opera, of course, one need not read up for examinations; yet Scribe's *Dame Blanche*, bearing to the *Monastery* and *Guy Mannering* much the same relation as Thackeray's *Rebecca and Rowena* to *Ivanhoe*, should not have opened with a rustic Scots couple hard up for a godfather to their child, nor ended with the sale of an estate that carried with it a peerage and a seat in Parliament.

Perhaps, after all, Scottish writers may be trusted for a more faithful picture of their own country; and one would commend the reader rather to Sarah Tytler's *St. Mungo's City* as a truthful and taking tale of Glasgow life, including a trip on the Clyde under characteristic circumstances. Only this trip is not one to be suggested to strangers, since it is an incident of Glasgow Fair, that concentrated week of more than Bank Holiday-making, when the great city of the West disperses itself to its waterside resorts so recklessly that in the familiar rainy weather churches as well as police stations may have to be thrown open to thousands of roofless and hundreds of senseless guests. Let the Sir Charles Grandisons of the south, and the Miss Ophelias of the States mix themselves rather with the Trades Holidays' bustle of Edinburgh, or the 12th August distraction of Perth station.

> "The steamer (as our author describes this popular excursion), fluttering with flags from stem to stern, was pushing down the river on the sunny yet showery summer day, preceded and followed by many similar vessels, through the labyrinth of shipping from every part of the world—past wharves and warehouses deserted by toilers—past the yards, well known to ship-builders, with skeleton ships on the stocks, where the sheds were forsaken and the din mute. Down and down the living freight went, till green pastures and ripening cornfields began to smile under the very frown of the hills rising in the distance. Here was the heart-shaped rock of Dumbarton, with the castle where Wallace had lain a prisoner. There were the crowded roofs of Greenock, clustered under its own storm-cloud, hanging over the city churchyard where Highland Mary was laid to rest. Yonder ran the Tail of the Bank, by which fleets have ridden at anchor, where Colin's solitary ship was seen through the morning mists by the sharp eyes of the loving gude-wife, so fain to tell that her man was 'come to town.' This was the entrance to the loch by whose shore the race of Macallum More slept soundly. Across the river the warning white finger of the Cloch Lighthouse bade belated crafts beware. Roseneath was fair as when Jeanie Deans landed under the guardianship of the Duke's man. At Toward Point the tenderest of Highland tragedies lingered with the memory of the old clan Lamont. At last the twin islands of Bute and Arran came full in sight, and Goatfell rose, brown and grey and russet—not

purple as yet—unrivalled from the sea, and held up a rugged face
to the fleecy clouds."

GLEN SANNOX, ISLE OF ARRAN

Reversing this route, and shortening it by train from Greenock, we come to St. Mungo's City, by Liverpool's leave, the second in Britain, yet none of your mushroom Chicagos, but a good old Lanark borough that has spread itself far over two counties, since the days when its Broomielaw harboured a few small craft, and its Fair was confined to the Green, on which the Earl of Moray encamped before crushing Queen Mary's cause in half an hour, at the battle of Langside, its field now within the extended municipal bounds. In her time Glasgow was already known as the Market of the West, showing the rudiments of a varied fabrication in its plaiding, and in such a "Glasgow buckler" as the adventurous Queen would fain have carried when she wished she were a man to "lie all night in the fields," and swagger mail-clad along the crown of the causeway.

Max O'Rell and other moderns have said very unkind things of Glasgow; but all the early travellers extol the prettiness, pleasantness, and cleanness of this city on a once limpid river, qualities not so apparent nowadays. Along with too many most squalid slums, Glasgow has fine features in her ancient Cathedral, in her lofty Necropolis, in her picturesque Trongate, in her noble University Buildings elevated above the West End Park, and in her central square with its forest of illustrious effigies, "an open-air Madame Tussaud's." But these monuments are not so remarkable as the wealth and manifold industry of which signs abound on every hand, drowning the rustic charms noted by Defoe and Burt. In the Commonwealth days Richard Franck had dubbed Glasgow the "non-such of Scotland"—"famous and flourishing"—on whose "beautiful palaces" and warehouses "stuft with merchandise" he expatiates in his conceited style. Even the crabbed Matthew Bramble was "in raptures with Glasgow." Pennant twice calls this "the best built of any second-rate city I ever saw," and tells how Glasgow had been "tantalised with its river," soon to be deepened into such a highway of traffic.

By the middle of the eighteenth century Glasgow had not 20,000 inhabitants, but she began to make her fortune fast while the rest of Scotland rather sullenly prepared to exchange thistly patriotism for more profitable crops. Rum and tobacco were the foundation of a prosperity that came to be checked by the American Revolution; then the long-headed worthies of the Saltmarket took up cotton, and cotton was weighed down by iron, and iron was set afloat as well as wood; and a host of other trades sprang up, among them that Turkey-red dyeing that is for Glasgow what its purple was for Tyre.

On Glasgow Green, we are told, James Watt thought of the steam condenser that was the great practical step towards starting such merry-go-roundabouts here at Fair time, and so many wheels on which the progress of the world has spun with such acceleration "down the ringing grooves of change." If the first model of a steamship was made in Edinburgh, the first passenger paddle-boat that plied in Britain was that between Greenock and Glasgow in 1812. Glasgow, not quite so large as Edinburgh in James Watt's lifetime, had then begun to give the capital the go-by, even before she became environed by a wilderness of "pits and blast furnaces that honeycomb and blacken the earth, and burn with a red glare throughout the night for many a mile around," where another writer describes daylight showing "patches of sour-looking grass surrounded by damp stone walls; gaunt buildings soot-begrimed and gloomy; and an ever-increasing blue-grey mist pierced by tall chimneys." St. Kentigern, whose *petit nom* was Mungo, could hardly now identify the site of his hermitage among noisy Clyde ship-yards and busy streets, noted by jealous neighbours as too familiar with

> The merchant rain that carries on
> Rich commerce 'twixt the earth and sun.

LOCH TRIOCHATAN, ENTRANCE TO GLENCOE, ARGYLLSHIRE

The relations between the two chief cities of Scotland have been a little stiff since Glasgow rose so high in the world, as how should a laird of old pedigree, crippled by forfeitures and mortgages, not look askance from his castellated turrets on the spick and span buildings of an upstart millionaire neighbour, the one standing on his name and title, the other on his shrewdness, honesty, and strict attention to business rather than the graces of life. One suspects Sarah Tytler to be no west-countrywoman, from her kindly hits at Glasgow cotton lords and iron lords, with more money than they always knew what to do with, a generation ago; yet she loudly extols their generosity and public spirit; and in our time Bailie Jarvie's successors have distinguished themselves, like their rivals at Manchester and Liverpool, by a liberal patronage of art, proof of which may be seen in the new Corporation Gallery that is a legacy of the last Exhibition. Edinburgh wits are not so scornful now towards Glasgow cits, as in the days when Kit North—himself a Paisley body—joked his coarsest at the expense of the "Glasgow Gander," and Aytoun told scandalous tales of the Glenmutchkin Railway and the Dreepdaily Burghs.

In spirit and sentiment, the two cities have not always seen eye to eye. Auld Reekie often showed herself a bit of a Tory, the ladies of the family having even a tenderness for Jacobitism and philabegry, since Rob Roy lived not so close to their gates, and they knew the Dougal Cratur only as a red-nosed porter or town-guard of bygone days: thus the Red Indian, beneath whose war-paint the western settler could see no good unless mark for a bullet, might be hailed as a noble savage in Boston or New York. But Glasgow has always been Whig, with grey homespun for its own wear rather than the tartans it manufactured in the way of business. It would have as little dealing as might be with the Pretender, an unwelcome guest who took it on his way back to the Highlands, and forced the citizens to rig out his ragged army with coats, shirts, and bonnets. In the troubled days of early Radicalism, again, the city of the west seethed with sedition, almost breaking out into revolt.

Glasgow was also markedly Presbyterian from an early date, and its monuments may well be crowned by one to John Knox. Its Cathedral is said to have been defended by pious craftsmen against an iconoclast mob; but in this reformed fane, under Charles I., met the Covenanting Assembly whose denunciation of prelates counts as the second Reformation. Even in the days when they dealt in rum, the Glasgow folk were noted as sober and douce, their morals, indeed, being pushed to austerity. Episcopal ministers and other bad characters were driven out of St. Mungo's bounds, when its licensed preachers became chosen from the "High flying" party of the Church. Theatrical performances were here held in horror after these had ceased to be banned in the capital. And as for the Sabbath-keeping that was the sacrament of old Presbyterianism, hear what Mr. H. G. Graham, in his instructive *Social Life of Scotland in the Eighteenth Century*, has to record of Glasgow:—

> "To secure proper observance of the Sabbath, compurgators,
> or 'bumbailies,' patrolled the streets and wynds on Saturday
> night to see that by ten o'clock all folk were quietly at home; and
> if incautious sounds betokening untimely revelry issued from be-

hind a door, or a stream of light from chinks of a window-shutter betrayed a jovial company within, they entered and broke up the party which dared to be happy so near the Lord's own day. On Sabbath, as in other towns, the seizers or elders, in their turn, perambulated the streets during divine service, and visited the Green in the evening, haling all 'vaguers' to kirk or session. The profound stillness of the Sabbath was preternatural, except when the multitudinous tramp of heavy shoes came from a vast voiceless throng of churchgoers. In these streets of which the patrols 'made a solitude and called it peace,' at all other hours no persons passed, no sound was heard, no dog dared bark. In the mirk Sabbath nights no lamp was lit, because all but profane persons were engaged in solemn exercises at home. During the day the window-shutters were, in strict households, just opened enough to let inmates see to walk about the room, or to read the Bible by sitting close to the window-panes."

Times have changed in Glasgow, for here Sunday trams came to be suffered before they desecrated Edinburgh. A certain *vieille roche* minister of Arran, not yet forgotten, who used to startle strange worshippers by addressing them, "O ye towrists and eemissaries of the deevil!" was also, if all tales be true, in the way of warning his flock that they grew wicked as Glasgow folk, and almost as bad as them of Edinburgh—the superlative profligacy of London being no doubt taken for granted. But some such moralist seems to have met his match in two Glasgow urchins whom he rebukefully catechised: "Whaur will laddies gang that play themselves on the Sabbath?" With real or assumed innocence one of the boys answered, "Tae the Green!" Then, on the stern corrector more fully explaining the drift of that question, he heard the lad exclaim, "Rin awa,' Jock; we mauna listen to the bad man sweirin'!"—an attitude now largely taken towards extreme Sabbatarians, even in Glasgow.

The more liberal spirit of contemporary Glasgow is largely due to its popular minister of half a century ago, Norman Macleod, who infected the Scottish Church with much of his own heartiness and width of mind. Many good stories are told of him, such as, a generation earlier, crystallised rather round the eminent personality of Dr. Chalmers, also a Glasgow minister. One, which Macleod used to tell of himself, seems an essence of the national character as developed under modern influences. This burly West Highlander, along with a reverend brother of feebler physique, having taken boat among the Hebrides, they were caught in such a storm that one of the boatmen proposed the ministers should pray; but "Na, na," said another; "let the little ane pray, but the big ane maun tak' an oar!" He has also told with much gusto how, in the early days of his ministry, he was put to the test of orthodoxy by a deaf old woman, who, adjusting her ear-trumpet, screamed at him, "Gang ower the fundamentals!" Another story, not so likely to be quite true, but representing a very human side of his nature, refers to a notorious Glasgow murderer, who capped a cold-blooded crime by treating himself to the services of this approved divine on the scaffold. It is said that the ghostly counsellor was so sickened by the man's cant, that on his last words, "Good-bye, Doctor: we shall meet again in the next world!" Macleod could not refrain from ejaculating, perhaps in the less emphatic Greek, "God forbid!"

GLEN ROSA, ISLE OF ARRAN

Good Words, the popular magazine founded by Dr. Norman Macleod, made a powerful solvent of Presbyterian severity, introducing into family life stories for Sunday reading, along with broader views that called forth loud protests from more orthodox theologians. Another such influence was the novels of Dr. George MacDonald, in which he tossed and gored Calvinism with much acceptance, when formal statements of his doctrine would have been recognised as having *foenum in cornu*. The "Kailyard" Muse so much in vogue of late quite openly flirts with the carnal man, cuts up the Shorter Catechism to make curl-papers for more "up to date" sentiments, and grinds down the forefathers' faith for picturesque local colour. This generation hardly yet recognises a turn of the tide that floats such fiction into popularity. The plain fact is, which some do not love to hear stated, that the Churches of Scotland are passing into a transition state of unstable compounds, that would have horrified their old doctors. The absolute has thawed into the relative, and some of the once so solid landmarks of faith are already evaporating out of a fluid state into a very gaseous one. It is hard for hereditary believers to measure their drift from cast-off moorings; but the many Scotsmen living out of Scotland see, as a stranger does not, how the currents are setting. And even to an outsider who takes any interest in theology, it must appear that the logical turn formerly devoted to dogmatising on the darkest mysteries is now exercised rather in explaining away the standards and confessions once held so sacred, still nominally in honour, but no more consistent with actual belief than the foregoing mixed metaphors are with each other.

CHAPTER XI

THE WHIG COUNTRY

Scorched and blasted as much of the ground about Glasgow is, this city lies hard by some of the finest and most famed scenes of Scotland, to be easily reached by land or water. Even busy Paisley, nurse of poets as well as of weavers, has a point of high antiquarian interest in its restored Abbey Church; and a stretch of moorland rises behind smoky Greenock, with its monuments to James Watt and to "Highland Mary." Not to speak of land-and sea-scapes "down the water," up the river, Clydesdale shows us on what green banks and braes Glasgow once stood, which may yet spread its octopus arms about Cadzow and Bothwell Castles and the Tower of "Tillietudlem." There has been talk of harnessing to industry those rushing Falls of Clyde, the upper linn, Bonnington, a miniature of Niagara that is already slave to the Philistines. Below this fall, the mills of New Lanark record the well-meant industrial experiments of David Dale and his son-in-law Robert Owen. In a cave near the Stonebyres Fall, young William Wallace took hiding after he had slain the English sheriff at Lanark, where now the hero's statue stands over the church door, strangely arrayed in a kilt that gives him somewhat the aspect of that snuff-shop Scotsman. Wallace came from the Renfrewshire Ellerslie, and many of his guerilla exploits were in this west country, though his noblest monument has found a proper site near Stirling. Ayr, town of "honest men and bonnie lasses," cherishes other legends and memorials of him, here almost forgotten in the renown of Robert Burns's birthplace near the mouth of his "bonnie Doon." An hour's stroll along the seashore from Ayr brings us to that humble cottage, better neighboured by "Alloway's auld haunted kirk" than by the pretentious classical monument that so ill fits Scotland's "barefoot Muse." Then from this coast to Dumfries, the valleys of the Ayr and the Nith are sown with memories and needless monuments of the poet who spoke the people's heart. Above Nithsdale, in the south of Lanark, rise the Lowther Hills, that for height might call cousins with some Highland Bens. Here stands Leadhills, the highest village in Scotland, birthplace of Allan Ramsay; and near the wider pass, through which went the old highroad to the south, may be sought out the "sudden and immense depths" of the Enterkin, renowned by Defoe and by Dr. John Brown, as gloomy scene of an encounter between persecuting dragoons and the armed Covenanters, who had many a fastness in this hill-country.

THE FALLS OF THE CLYDE, LANARKSHIRE

The "Scott country" has its brightest associations in chivalric war. The "Burns country," which is also the Wallace country and the Bruce country, has been the cradle of the strongest Scottish sentiment, as of the most popular movements. Long before Burns was born, it got the familiar name of the Whig country, as congenial soil for those aspirations after both political and religious freedom that have gone so far in shaping our constitution. Burns, it will be noted, had sucked in the political better than the religious spirit of the region; though he confesses that "the Muses were all Jacobites," and once in a way he fires up with—

> The Solemn League and Covenant,
> Cost Scotland blood,—cost Scotland tears,
> But it sealed Freedom's sacred cause.

Here first arose the nickname Whig or Whiggamore, as its opposite Tory did in Ireland, both of them originally no compliments. A Whig of our time is taken to be an eminently sober and staid, not to say lukewarm politician; but the first Whigs were fierce and dour enthusiasts, one derivation of the name connecting it with *whey*, as what should hint at sour-faced sectaries. In the mouth of an Episcopalian, Whig meant a Presbyterian, while a moderate Presbyterian used the word to stigmatise those extremists whose doctrine was made white-hot by the *perfervidum ingenium* natural to this nation. Moderate Presbyterian is a relative term, Presbyterianism in general having been such a rebound from Popery and Prelacy that it sought to hold itself *toto coelo* apart from them, and in small matters as well as in great went to antipodes of opposition, so that in some parts of Scotland, at this day, heathen rites and customs are unwittingly better preserved than those of Catholic Christendom. But indeed it was an Irish Orangeman who, being asked for a death-bed profession of faith, desired to be furnished with the heads of Roman doctrine, and "whatever they believe, I don't."

The south-west corner of Scotland, after being an early stronghold of the Reformation, was the native heath of those stern non-conformists who got the by-names of "West-country Whigs," "Wild Whiggamores," and so on, known also with good reason as "Hillmen," "Wanderers," "Martyrs," and in history specially as the "Covenanters." That Solemn League and Covenant of theirs had been accepted on both sides of the Border; but the English Independents came to flout it as no more binding than "an old Almanac," and to the Scottish Cavaliers it made a hated symbol of their long eclipse, while the right Presbyterian clung to it as an almost inspired standard of truth. When the reactionary measures of the Restoration brought back Prelacy to Scotland, hundreds of ministers gave up their homes and stipends to the more compliant "curates" that braved popular scorn for the sake of a living. This feeling was not, indeed, national; in the north, as has been shown, the adherents of Episcopacy held their own, and sometimes had to be forcibly ejected after the Revolution settlement. But in the "Whig Country" almost all the ministers left their cures, gaining in reverence what they lost in stipend. The most eloquent and zealous of them became, each in his sphere, nucleus of those conventicles and hillside gatherings that drew from the parish churches the cream of Presbyterian faith, along with some of the skim milk, for Covenanting youngsters would find a carnal savour in sermon-going that involved a chance of open-air adventure. Jock Elliot or Kinmont Willie might have proved religious enough, when hard knocks was the exercise of the day. Scott gives the Covenanting preachers credit for tam-ing the wild moss-troopers who had been recalled to activity on the Borders by the troubles of that time. But fanaticism was the main alloy in the devotion of old men and tender women, whose sacrifices and sufferings for what they held the truth have endeared their memory to their children, nay, to all Scotland.

Scott has been accused of prejudice against the Covenanters, as represented in *Old Mortality*; but surely this charge is unjust. More than one of his ancestors stood out on that side in those unhappy times, a fact that would alone have bespoken his sympathy. To my mind—making a little allowance for stage effect—his novel gives a not unfair view of the two parties' manners and motives; and as a historian he thus describes the Covenanting conventicles, that left his countrymen with an acquired taste for field preaching, till such ministrations had degenerated into the scenes of Burns's "Holy Fair":—

> "The view of the rocks and hills around them, while a sight so unusual gave solemnity to their acts of devotion, encouraged them in the natural thought of defending themselves against oppression, amidst the fortresses of nature's own construction, to which they had repaired to worship the God of nature, according to the mode their education dictated and their conscience acknowledged. The recollection, that in these fastnesses their fathers had often found a safe retreat from foreign invaders, must have encouraged their natural confidence, and it was confirmed by the success with which a stand was sometimes made against small bodies of troops, who were occasionally repulsed by the sturdy Whigs whom they attempted to disperse. In most cases of this kind they behaved with moderation, inflicting no further penalty upon such prisoners as might fall into their hands, than detaining them to enjoy the benefit of a long sermon. Fanaticism added marvels to encourage this new-born spirit of resistance. They conceived themselves to be under the immediate protection of the Power whom they worshipped, and in their heated state of mind expected even miraculous interposition. At a conventicle held on one of the Lomond hills in Fife, it was reported and believed that an angelic form appeared in the air, hovering above the assembled congregation, with his foot advanced, as if in the act of keeping watch for their safety. On the whole, the idea of repelling force by force, and defending themselves against the attacks of the soldiers and others who assaulted them, when employed in divine worship, began to become more general among the harassed non-conformists. For this purpose many of the congregation assembled in arms, and I received the following description of such a scene from a lady whose mother had repeatedly been present on such occasions: The meeting was held on the Eildon hills, in the bosom betwixt two of the three conical tops which form the crest of the mountain. Trusty sentinels were placed on advanced posts all around, so as to command a view of the country below,

and give the earliest notice of the approach of any unfriendly party. The clergyman occupied an elevated temporary pulpit, with
his back to the wind. There were few or no males of any quality
or distinction, for such persons could not escape detection, and
were liable to ruin from the consequences. But many women of
good condition, and holding the rank of ladies, ventured to at-
tend the forbidden meeting, and were allowed to sit in front of
the assembly. Their side-saddles were placed on the ground to
serve for seats, and their horses were tethered, or piqueted, as it
is called, in the rear of the congregation. Before the females, and
in the interval which divided them from the tent, or temporary
pulpit, the arms of the men present, pikes, swords, and muskets,
were regularly piled in such order as is used by soldiers, so that
each man might in an instant assume his own weapons." — *Tales
of a Grandfather.*

We know what rampagious Tories were John Wilson and James Hogg, but
one was a west-countryman by birth, and the other a son of moorland hillsides;
and even they are found testifying to the cause of their kin. "The ancient spirit of
Scotland," exclaims the shepherd at *a Noctes,* "comes on me from the sky; and the
sowl within me re-swears in silence the oath of the Covenant. There they are —
the Covenanters — a' gathered thegither, no in fear and tremblin', but wi' Bibles
in their bosoms, and swords by their sides, in a glen deep as the sea, and still as
death.... When I think on these things — in olden times the produce o' the common
day — and look aroun' me noo, I could wush to steek my e'en in the darkness o'
death, for, dearly as I love it still, alas! I am ashamed of my country."

Alas! alas! indeed, for this rhapsody makes part of a fulmination against Catholic emancipation, a question on which such whiskified Protestants proved themselves too true sons of the Covenanters. The proscribed Whigs were not less hot
in testifying against all other creeds than in asserting their own spiritual liberty.
When the Government offered their consciences some measure of relief, the "Black
Indulgence" proved as hateful as persecution, which, indeed, they would willingly have directed against other sects, as against "right-hand deflections and left-
hand way-slidings" in their own body. The only sect of that day that would not
persecute was the Quakers, whose turn did not come; and Quakerism, as judged
by Wodrow, seemed but "a small remove from Popery and Jesuitism," or from
what one of his heroes styled that "stinking weed," Prelacy. On the other side of
the Atlantic Roger Williams for the first time had begun to preach religious toleration; but there the prevalent sentiment was expressed by a Puritan divine who
denounced "Polypiety as the greatest impiety in the world." Puritan or Prelatist,
it was the party in power on which rested the guilt and the shame of spiritual
tyranny. On the other hand, the suffering party may have entered into a renown
of virtues beyond their desert. A generation that hardly knows the *Fourfold State*
even by name, sees little in those martyrs but their wrongs, their harshness and
narrowness forgot, their own occasional crimes, their misspent zeal for "dogmas
long since dead, pious vituperation on antagonists long buried in dust and forget-

fulness; breathless insistence on questions which time has answered with a yawn."

A HIGHLAND VIEW

At least the westland Covenanters bore manfully the scourge which they looked on as an instrument of righteousness, but for the time laid on the wrong shoulders. Their enthusiasm was not to be damped by the scenery of their secret gatherings. Boldly they took the sword against a conformity dictated by dragoon colonels, by selfish statesmen, and by such a sacred majesty as Charles II.'s. If only they had added to their faith the practical spirit of the English Roundheads, who did not neglect discipline for doctrine!

KILCHURN CASTLE, LOCH AWE, ARGYLLSHIRE

In the Whig country was borne highest that blue banner inscribed in letters of gold "For Christ's Crown and Covenant." At Lanark gathered to a head the first rising of 1666, easily crushed among the Pentlands when the rustic army had fallen back from the gates of latitudinarian Edinburgh. At Rutherglen, near Glasgow, began the second outbreak, stirred up by the brutal murderers of Archbishop Sharpe; then it was near Loudon Hill, where the counties of Lanark, Ayr, and Renfrew meet, that a half-armed congregation routed Claverhouse's guardsmen on the morass of Drumclog. This casual success was wasted on an army that, when a few thousand strong, dared to defy the forces of the three kingdoms. Torn by fanatical dissensions, paying more attention to loud-lunged preachers than to prudent officers, it met at Bothwell Bridge the fate that was a foregone conclusion. Cameron, leader of the "wild" or extreme party, was followed up and slain in that desolate moorland region, "without grandeur, without even the dignity of mountain wildness, yet striking from the huge proportion it seemed to bear to such more favoured spots of the country as were adapted to cultivation." In caves and remote cottages skulked the faithful remnant, while persecution raged unchecked for years. Dark and bloody are the memories of that "killing time," and the superstitious legends that attached themselves to the fame of the martyrs, to Cargill and Cameron, to Peden and others in whom Scriptural gifts of prophecy blended with Celtic second sight. Still darker stories were whispered of the persecutors, believed to have sold themselves to the devil that they might have power over the Lord's people; of "bloody Mackenzie," the Lord Advocate; of Grierson of Lag, in whose hands a cup of wine would turn to blood; of the calm cruelty of Claverhouse, charmed against bullets; of the ruthlessness of Dalziel, who, with Tartar manners brought from Russian wars, with his bygone dress and the outlandish beard unshaved since Charles I.'s execution, might well seem an infernal monster. But all the slaughters, the maddening tortures by boot and by thumbkins, the miserable imprisonments on the Bass Rock and in Dunnottar Castle, the mockery of lighter spirits among the populace, only went to harden Presbyterian endurance. The Covenanter wrapped tighter about him his blood-stained cloak of orthodoxy till that bitter wind blew over. Then the westland, so vainly harried and dragooned towards conformity, proved a hot-bed of strong Protestant and Presbyterian feeling, inspired by resentment as well as by religion, a lesson in the use of persecution that stops short of extermination.

The quartering of Highland clans was among those means of grace brought to bear on the stubborn Whigs, with whose scruples the Gael as a rule had scant sympathy. But the great western clan Campbell, neighbours of the Whig country across the Clyde, obeyed chiefs otherwise tempered, two of whom rank among the victims of Charles II.'s reign; and the House of Argyll continued to furnish champions for the Whig and Presbyterian interest. Over adjacent clans, the powerful Macallum More had too much played the tyrant; then it was hatred to the Campbells as much as loyalty to Charles or James that brought so many tartans round the banner of Montrose and Dundee. On the other hand, sore memories of that Philistine "Highland host" helped to keep the Whig country loyal in the later Jacobite movements. It was long before "wild Highlandmen," or dragoons, would be looked on with a friendly eye by the sons of the Covenanters. When the goodman one Saturday night had "waled a portion" that led him to corrupt the verse, "another wonder in heaven, and behold a great red *dragoon*"—he was interrupted by his wife, "I doot ye're making a mistake, John; there's no' many o' that sort gets in there!" but he had a sound answer ready: "Weel, woman, and doesna' it say it was for a wonder?" It was in another part of the country that some misquoting Mac could chuckle over a text which seemed to make it easier for a rich man to go through a needle's eye than for a Cam'ell to enter the kingdom of heaven.

Whatever they may have been in the past, no worse if more strong than their neighbours, the Campbells of Argyll have risen on the flowing tide of progress. The house lost nothing under that statesman who figures as Jeanie Deans's patron, nor under that host who so courteously entertained Dr. Johnson, though his wife would not speak to Boswell. The late Duke, a man of note in any station of life, was looked on as, in a manner, chief of the Presbyterian establishment, even when—so have times changed—he could not get one of his sons elected as member for the county. But long before his time this Church had ceased to be one and undivided, soon indeed showing strongly fissiparous energies, which, till our day, kept it "decomposing but to recompose."

More than once in these pages the writer has let the reader shy away from a thistly exposition, which we may here yoke to and have done with it. Nothing puzzles strangers more than the fact that till recently a Scottish parish would have three Presbyterian Churches, differing not at all in ritual, in discipline, or in such points of doctrine as are visible to the naked eye unprovided with theological spectacles. It would be difficult to give southron Gallios the faculty for splitting controversial hairs possessed by minds trained to subtleness on the Shorter Catechism; but an outline of the divisions of the Scottish Church may perhaps be made plain to the meanest capacity. At least I will try to be fair, which is more than have been all exponents of such matters. Like most Scotsmen, I have an hereditary bias in these controversies. One of my forebears was a Covenanter extolled among Howie's *Scottish Worthies*, who, after being persecuted under Cromwell for loyalty to Charles, came to be hardly dealt with for conscience' sake at the hands of that ungrateful king. I am proud to think of the ancestress who, urged to move him to safe submission, answered like a true Presbyterian wife, "that she knew her husband to be so steadfast in his principles, that nobody needed deal with him on that head; for her part, before she would contribute anything that would break his peace with his Master, she would rather choose to receive his head at the Cross." Other friends were not so scrupulous, "two ladies of the first quality" going so far as to send "a handsome compliment in plate" to the "advocate's lady," who had the honesty to return this bribe or ransom when she judged it impossible to save the prisoner's life. All the same it was saved, and he lived on till the Revolution year in a state of proscription, sometimes hunted into hiding, but throughout a most "faithful and painful" preacher, who "left many seals of his ministry," and steadily refused to put himself at ease by leaving the country, for, "in his pleasant way," he used to say "he would suffer where he had sinned." His son followed in his steps; and his grandson took a leading part in the early movement of dissent which is presently to be shown as legacy from the Covenanting spirit. But if the memory of these worthies weighs with me, I was brought up at an English knee, in a church that held them much mistaken; and I was confirmed by the Anglican Bishop of Gibraltar, within whose diocese the very Pope is a dissenting minister. Since then I have sat at the feet of teachers from whom may be learned that to know and to speak the truth of one's fellow-men is the only sure foundation for sound divinity. And perhaps an outsider may be in a better position for taking the altitude of even the most celestial bodies of faith.

The moving spirit of Presbyterianism has been a consciousness that Christianity claims to be something far higher than any human institution, the Court of Session, for instance, or even the British Constitution. Other countries seem more willing to make practical compromises between heaven and earth. One has heard of such a country, whose chief ambassadors of heaven are appointed with a ceremony in which the holiest influence is implored to direct a choice published weeks before in every newspaper as fixedly made by very mortal authorities, who may be notorious evil livers, open unbelievers, or what a sectarian journal has politely qualified as "non-co-religionists." But a religiously minded Scot has too much logic, not to say sense of humour, to take part in such a farce. For him the Gospel did not dawn from the eyes of Boleyns and such like; he took his Scriptures as a law rather than a title for rulers. His watchword has all along been Christ's headship of the Church, and his anathema the "Erastianism" that rendered to Cæsar what man owes to God alone. The later Stuarts were not Cæsars to wear any halo in his eyes; then all the more clearly he saw the futility of their lay Popedom. That "wisest fool in Christendom" was perhaps not so far out in his adage "no bishop, no king." But Scotland held its faith by the same title as he his crown; and he and his successors found faith on the whole stronger than loyalty. The dogmas of that faith are not the question. It was sadly coloured by the struggles of its origin, by the character of the nation as well as the stern scenery of the land, by persecution and by congenial Calvinistic logic brought back from exile, and by the troubles of the time in which Puritan influences were exchanged across the Border.

Scotsmen being, after all, but human, their serious and democratic view of religion was held with two different degrees of intensity, which took shape as the main parties of the Kirk. The one that came to be known as "Moderate" was hotly reproached with Erastianism, a less unwillingness to look on religion as a department of the Civil Service. The other had various nicknames, the "Wild Party," the "High-fliers," but we may as well call them the High Churchmen of Scotland, if it be borne in mind that they favoured Evangelical doctrine while clinging to a union of Church and State, in which the former was to be predominant. These were, in fact, the heirs of the Covenanters, who on strongly Protestant soil fought out the old quarrel between Pope and Emperor. And whereas the English High Church has been strongest among the priesthood, in the north, where presbyter is priest writ small, it is the laity that have rather fostered ecclesiastic zeal. To Buckle's representation of Scotland as a priest-ridden people, Mr. H. G. Graham rightly objects how it would be nearer the truth to speak of a people-ridden clergy.

The Revolution Settlement secured the victory of Presbytery over Episcopacy, quieting the contention of a century. But when Episcopal curates had been "rabbled" on what was a far from merry Christmas for them, the extreme wing of the Covenanters were by no means satisfied with King William's toleration of unsound belief, and would accept no status at the hands of an uncovenanted king. Long used to worship spiced with peril, hardship, and hatred, they held aloof rather than seceded as the Cameronians, a sect which, with its obscure sub-divisions of Macmillanites, Russellites, Harleyites, Howdenites, and so on, still has a feeble remnant of "Reformed Presbyterians," while the mass of it nearly two centuries later gravitated into the Free Church, then in part representing their principles. The militant youth of this body had been kept out of mischief by being embodied as the Cameronian Regiment, that fought sturdily against Jacobites, Papists, and other enemies of a Protestant succession, and still remembers its origin by carrying a Bible in every knapsack, and not suffering its band to play on the Sabbath.

But with changed times the Covenants began to lose their power as a watchword. Having parted from its hottest gospellers in the Cameronian following, then being cooled by milder spirits in Episcopal conformists, presently admitted to the new order on easy terms, the Kirk's clergy became more moderate, not much to the satisfaction of their congregations. The union of the kingdoms, carried through by crooked ways, and its benefits long hidden in ignorance, soon called forth all the "thrawn" aloofness of Scottish patriotism, for the nonce bringing Jacobite and Cameronian sentiment into one focus. One of the early acts of the united Parliament was to meddle with what has been a sorer question north than south of the Tweed, the patronage of livings. The right of patrons was now revived and confirmed by an Act making a "call" from the congregation unnecessary to the placing of a minister. The ministers themselves were more apt to sympathise with patronage as easier road to a benefice than the ordeal of popular election; but the people strongly resented the laird's placing of a pastor over them, even when this privilege was exercised with delicacy and conscientiousness, and there were cases like that in Galt's *Annals of the Parish*, when the presentee had to be inducted by military force. This grievance, then, became a standard in the battle between the Moderate and the High Party, patronage being looked on as Erastianism in retail, when its wholesale transactions in prelates and prayer-books were still angry memories.

With hatred of patronage was involved a zeal for Evangelical doctrine, which now began to take colour from other sources than Geneva, and to blur out beyond the rigid lines of Calvinistic logic. Early in the eighteenth century the Evangelical party got the name of Marrowmen, as rallying round a little book which, published in England, gained popularity north of the Tweed as the "Marrow" of Christian doctrine, when edited by Boston of the *Fourfold State*. The "Marrow" came to be condemned by a Moderate majority in the Assembly; then for teaching its doctrines and rebuking the general luke-warmness of the Church, the saintly Ebenezer Erskine was censured by his Presbytery, and finally suspended from the ministry, along with three sympathetic brethren, Alexander Moncrieff, William Wilson, and James Fisher. In 1733 these four suspended ministers formed themselves into the first Presbytery of the original Secession Church, with Fife as its focus and Erskine as its leading spirit, whose younger brother Ralph in some respects suggests himself as its Charles Wesley, giving scandal to severe members by his love of music and songs not David's.

RIVER COE, GLENCOE, ARGYLLSHIRE

The Seceders were, in fact, the Scottish Methodists, having an early ally in Whitfield, who, however, became a stumbling-block through his willingness to exercise Christian fellowship with the Erastian establishment; he professed it his duty to preach to "the devil's people," whereas the Seceders would monopolise him for "the Lord's people." Nay, more, if testifying scandal-mongers are to be credited, "that grand impostor" went so far as at Lisbon to "symbolise with Popery" by attending a Catholic Lenten service, where the Crucifixion was represented "in a most God-dishonouring, heaven-daring, ridiculous, and idolatrous manner." About the same time as the Secession, rather earlier indeed, was formed the Glassite sect, still seated at Perth; but they went off upon a narrow side track, and may be neglected in a general view of Scottish religious life. A generation later Pennant reports the population of Perth as 11,000, of whom 9000 still belonged to the Kirk, the rest being Episcopalian, Non-jurors (these chiefly "venerable females"), Glassites, and Seceders. Independents, Baptists, and such like came later on from England, but these exotic congregations are still a mere scattering, hardly found outside of large towns. Carlyle might have remembered such exceptions, when he dogmatised that "all dissent in Scotland is merely a stricter adherence to the National Kirk in all points."

The Secession Church soon began to disseminate itself, but almost as soon developed a tendency to disintegration. Over the question of the test exacted from municipal authorities the body split into Burghers and anti-Burghers, the latter strongly holding it inconsistent to use a form of oath as to "the true religion presently professed within this realm," when in their view the religion thus professed was far from the truth. This "breach" was acrimoniously maintained even when Test Acts had been abolished; then the Seceders underwent further fission into "Old Lights," "New Lights," and others claiming to represent the original doctrines of the Secession. Twenty years after that first schism, a kindred but independent sect had come to birth under the title of the "Relief Church," seeking relief for tender consciences from Moderate tyranny, while its leader, Thomas Gillespie, perhaps through association with English nonconformity, made some scrupulous exceptions to the former seceding platform, and some touch of innovation, as the use of hymns, upon the Presbyterian practice.

The reader need not be troubled with all the sunderings of sectlets, one or two of which still testify in out-of-the-way corners like "Thrums." This much may be noted, that Presbyterian differences have been not much exported from Scotland, though, indeed, American Churches still show some trace of fissions that began on this side the Atlantic. The root of such differences was usually a narrowly pent-up earnestness that looked not for truth beyond its own horizon; but the Scot abroad has more readily seen for himself the proper proportions of his own little Bethel in all Christendom. Then, of course, he does not carry beyond the Border that bone of contention, the joint connecting Church and State. The original Seceders had not been much concerned on that point; but a long course of abstinence from public endowments gave them new views, till the most conspicuous device on their banner came to be "Voluntaryism" — that is, the practical notion that ministers should be paid by those who wish to hear them.

While these dissenting sects were multiplying themselves, the Moderate party in the Church throve the more by their absence. During the philosophical eighteenth century the clergy declined upon "sanctified common sense," some of them, "a waeful bunch o' cauldrife professors," making easy accommodations with worldliness, science, and even free thought; and as, after the extinction of the Jacobite spirit, Scotland settled down to a course of material improvement, its official teachers waxed fat and lethargic, while the nonjuring Episcopalians for a time enjoyed the wholesome discipline of persecution. The popular theology indeed was never without champions in the Kirk pulpits. A collegiate church might have two ministers, representing either party and preaching against each other, as when, in Greyfriars Church, young Walter Scott, if not a "half-day hearer," sat alternately under Principal Robertson and Dr. Erskine, the Moderate and the Evangelical leaders. But if the warmer doctrine were cherished in the hearts of godly hearers, Erastianism dominated the Church courts of a generation in which Pitt's viceroy Dundas practically governed Scotland, and robed bullies like Braxfield sent to banishment political martyrs, inspired by the lurid glow of the French Revolution.

Then, the long war with Napoleon having ceased to stifle free thought and free speech, the Tory rule of Scotland had to face a rising demand for reform, a movement heated through the sufferings brought upon the working classes by shiftings of economic conditions after the peace, and by the bungling interference of Government with trade's natural course. The new sentiment found champions in a knot of Whig lawyers, whose weapon was the *Edinburgh Review*. The Church was stirred by sympathy with the popular cause, whose name had sprung from its loins. A religious revival came in on the flowing tide of Whiggism, and with the passing of the Reform Bill the Evangelical party began to recover their ascendency, led by the eloquent Chalmers, himself of Tory leanings and a convert from Moderate indifference. A by-product of this enthusiasm was the sect popularly but incorrectly dubbed the Irvingites, which found more acceptance about London than in Scotland.

The new fermentation soon proved strong enough to burst old bottles that had served for the moderate vintage of faith. The spirit of the Covenanters came to life in the "non-Intrusion Controversy," the gist of which was the right of the people to choose their own mouthpiece of edification. It is rare to find a new Scotch story; but here is one that has never yet appeared in print. I remember as a lad hearing from an old shepherd his account of such a dispute in his native parish. "There was a chiel' wi' a poodered heid cam' doun frae Edinburgh," was his account of the legal proceedings, "and he made the folk a lang clishmaclavering speech—ye never heard sic havers in yer born days! They needna' care what like a minister was pit in! It was a' the same doctrine, and the mahn made nae differ! But up gat an auld wise-like elder had sat in that kirk since he was a laddie; and says he, 'What did I hear the gowk saying? What is the big, blethering brute tellin' me?' says he. 'Does he mean for tae mak' a body believe that a saft, young, foozy, wersh turneep's as guid as a fine, auld Swedish one?' says he." Then this son of the Whig country looked up to heaven, and never can I forget the solemnity with which he declared, amid the silence of the eternal hills—"Mahn, it was a graund answer!"

BEN CRUACHAN FROM INVERLOCHY, ARGYLLSHIRE

The first step was the resuscitation of a claim that the patron's nomination fell through unless countersigned by a call from the people. The General Assembly passed an Act confirming this popular Veto, which for a time went unchallenged, patrons having learned to "ca' canny" in the exercise of their rights. But, after some years, the momentous Auchterarder case, where an obstinate patron persisted in forcing his nominee on an objecting congregation, brought about a collision between the laws of Church and State. A majority of the Court of Session, confirmed by the House of Lords, pronounced the Veto illegal. The Church accepted the judgment as affecting the temporalities of the living, but refused to ordain the intruded pastor. All Scotland was in a blaze of controversy; the very schoolboys took sides as Intrusionists and non-Intrusionists. In the Strathbogie Presbytery seven ministers were suspended by the Church for obeying the Court of Session, to whose bar were brought seven others for not obeying it in the Dunkeld Presbytery. A deadlock thus arose, out of which there appeared no escape but by secession, so long as the Government refused to recognise the strength of this popular movement.

A little patience would probably have brought relief by law; but the perfervid sons of the Covenanters were in no mood for patience. The "Headship of Christ" was in question, and no prospect of loss or suffering appalled spirits exalted in such a cause. This movement, it must be remembered, had small sympathy with the Voluntaryism of dissent. Its leaders as yet strongly maintained the connection of Church and State, only, in their eyes, the Church must stand above the State. The Free Churchman's attitude at the Disruption was a consistent one, entirely reasonable from the premises on which his Church based its teaching. He took the grand tone of the ages of faith; and there was something noble in his disdain for mandates of earthly law, which he treated as served by creatures of a day on the servants of the eternal Jehovah.

The Disruption took place at the General Assembly of 1843. The retiring Moderator, after reading a protest against the invasion of the Church's liberties, headed a procession to a spacious hall in the Canonmills suburb, where, electing Dr. Chalmers as their first president, the protesters constituted themselves the Assembly of what they maintained to be the true Church of Scotland. The Government had expected a secession of some score or two of hot heads; but nearly five hundred ministers went out of their churches and manses, giving up all for conscience' sake with a courage that at once roused a wave of generous sympathy. The building up of the new Church was set about with true Scottish energy, prudence, ay, and generosity. For when Cockney jesters sneer at Scottish poverty, they do not consider how ready this people is to spend its savings and sparings on what it believes a good cause. Mainly from the contributions of the poorer class was the Free Church sustained. Most of the rich and mighty were against it, some of them bitterly hostile, many landlords refusing ground for sites, so that at first preachers and congregations had often some taste of the Covenanters' sufferings in open-air worship. Very bitter was the feeling between the ruptured congregations and of the seceding ministers against the "residuum," that had to fill hundreds of empty livings in haste, not always with the most fitting candidates. This ill-wind blew good to not a few "stickit ministers," who had little hoped to wag their heads in a pulpit, and the old Adam in the Seceders found matter for much scornful criticism of those "residuary cattle."

Long before such animosity had died down, the new body had its churches, manses, schools, and colleges built and endowed on a scale that gave Scotland two Establishments instead of one. But its main strength was the fact of its commanding the allegiance of the most spiritually minded and intellectual among the people. Its very pride was no vainglory. English dissent is apt to take a socially humble and apologetic attitude. A Free Churchman never thought of himself as a dissenter, and could not be looked down upon from any point of view. In all parts of the country his Church took rank beside the Establishment; in some it gained an ascendency. In the Highlands especially, where the exaltation of warm Celtic blood goes to its highest, and where eloquent ministers have inherited the devotion once inspired by warlike chiefs, the "Auld Kirk" is often little more than empty walls and a stipend. There is a tale of graceless laddies boasting against each other of their reckless deeds. One brags of having been to the circus, which another caps by a visit to the theatre, but the third is bold to avow a darker crime, "I once went to the English Chaipel." As told in some parts of the country, this fable has a further climax of iniquity in the Established Church, erst so dear.

While the Free Church went on flourishing apart, the Establishment was moved to drop the main standard of so much controversy. Its General Assembly petitioned for the abolition of patronage, which was brought about so easily that most of the lairds interested did not choose to demand the compensation voted to them for their thorny rights of presentation. In principle nothing seemed to keep the Churches apart; but the Establishment had been drifting into a broader theology and a new toleration of liturgical worship, which separated it from an organisation more conservative in religious matters, yet a school of liberalism in politics that gave Mr. Gladstone his hold over Scotland. The "Auld Kirk" lost more and more its suspicion of prelatical ways. Men still alive can remember how Dr. Robert Lee was indicted for the introduction of an organ and a prayer-book. Now such scandalous innovations are perhaps the rule rather than the exception in parish churches, and instrumental music has crept also into Free Churches, where a generation ago the use of hymns was scouted as unscriptural. For a time some faithful worshippers in the city congregations insisted on conspicuously standing to pray and sitting to sing psalms, like their fathers; but even in out-of-the-way places now there is a gradual conforming to the customs once banned as English or Papist.

The Dissenters, meanwhile, had been touched by the spirit of the time. As far back as 1820, two of the chief sects came together again, their walls of separation, indeed, having long fallen down. After the Disruption a further movement of adhesion took place, and while some congregations remained hugging their microscopic differences, most of the dissenting bodies joined to form the United Presbyterian Church, which, by a century's practice rather than on original principle, has evolved the doctrine of Voluntaryism as the backbone of its communion, repudiating any interference of the State with the teaching of religion.

THE MORVEN HILLS FROM APPIN, ARGYLLSHIRE

Certain fragments of secession, for their part, had been attracted into the glowing mass of the Free Church. This Church, also, began to suffer change. When the original stalwarts, who made much of a theoretical relation of Church and State, died off into a minority, the second generation was found less concerned about "Disruption principles" than in sympathy with Evangelical doctrine. The position of Scottish Presbyterians out of Scotland, where their differences of constitution were idle words, helped to open shrewd eyes to the absurdity of three Churches, all professing the same main doctrines, yet standing as rivals to each other. As the heat of controversy grew cool, more friendly relations became possible, and the ministers of the one might fill the pulpits of the other. In certain parishes having a summer population, it would be arranged to keep only one Church open in winter. The waste of power in the three almost identical bodies could not but strike a practical people sooner or later. The Established Church seemed to flirt too boldly with deans and Oxford professors; but what hindered the Free and the U.P. Church from making a match of it? After long courtship and much discussion of settlements, their alliance was celebrated in 1900, and now these two organisations are merged under the title of the United Free Church.

This union was not consummated without hot opposition, a small remnant of the Free Church standing outside and claiming at law the disposal of the great endowments bestowed on certain principles now put into the background. As I write, the House of Lords still delays its decision on a question of momentous interest, which the Scottish Courts decided in favour of the main body. There can be no doubt that what has already got the nickname of the "Wee Free" Church better represents the views of its spiritual fathers. But if all Churches were brought to payment of ancestral debts, otherwise than in paper money of Creeds and Confessions, some theological Statute of Limitations would be required. Whatever be the result, it should prove a lesson against investing any Church in a suit of clothes sure to be outgrown or to go out of fashion. Perhaps the most remarkable feature of this particular case is, that almost for the first time in Scottish ecclesiastical history there has been talk of a compromise.

Another fragment had seceded some years before as the Free Presbyterian Church, their *raison d'être* being testimony against the Declaratory Act by which the Free Church Assembly had loosened the bonds of subscription, that its doctrine might run in harness with the slightly less stringent views of the uniting body. So, in more than one parish, instead of three may now be found four Presbyterian places of worship: the Established Church, the United Free Church, which often has practically taken its place, the Free Presbyterian, and a congregation belonging to that rump of the Free Church which denounced the Union. There were scenes of violence in the Highlands, where Free Churches came to be hotly defended against their new title by obstinate adherents of the order half a century old, during which Laodicean humorists had interpreted the bells of the Establishment as ringing out "I am the Old Kirk," to which the Free Church answered back in a deeper note, "I am the true old Kirk," but then the U.P. bell jangled back, "It's me! it's me!" As for the Episcopal body that now holds its head so high, only in the last century was it suffered to have a bell at all, long paying dear for its spells of forced supremacy.

A CROFT NEAR LOCH ETIVE, ARGYLLSHIRE

One weaned from the Church of his forefathers, yet not from what should be
the *quod semper, quod ubique et quod ab omnibus* of all beliefs, may venture to give his

opinion, without suspicion if not without offence, that the Free Church of Chalmers and Guthrie best represented the true soul of Scottish Presbyterianism and enshrined the strongest religious life of its first generation. But in our generation this body has generated an impulse that may lead to fresh flyting between two parties now unequally yoked together. It had one divine eminently pious, eminently learned, eminently loyal to his Church, unless in coming to certain modern conclusions that are more or less freely accepted by almost every mind qualified to judge. Him the more bigoted sort picked out as quarry for one of the heresy-hunts which make a favourite sport in the north. I heard the case against him put in a nutshell by one of the old women who were too much deferred to in this matter. "It might be true," admitted this mother in Caledonian Israel, "that Moses did not write the account of his own death; but if you began there where were you going to stop?" so she was clear for muzzling that troublesome scholar. He had been teaching his "unsound" views, without much observation, to a few students in an out-of-the-way corner. According to the milder laws of modern persecution, he was unwillingly driven into renown, into wide influence, and into the arms of an English University, that felt itself honoured in receiving such a scapegoat. All the more enlightened spirits of his own Communion are now ashamed of the silencing that sent him into famous exile. Many of them were ashamed of it at the time; and the majority against him was partly made up of men who knew that he spoke truth, but thought it not well that the truth should be freely spoken. The theologians who take this tone are no longer inspired by the virtue of the Covenanters, and have fallen away from the heritage of that great preacher that feared not the face of man, nor woman.

Enthusiasts like Knox are out of vogue in our day; but perhaps can be seen all the more clearly what we owe to the stiffness with which they stood out, that neither King nor Pope should bind the conscience, taught by freedom to claim its rights, too, against Parliament and Presbytery. Out of the troubles of the time when Scotland was a distressful country, somewhat given to "the blind hysterics of the Celt," came the resolute temper that has turned poverty to gain and is turning superstition to knowledge. At all events, no account of "Bonnie Scotland" is complete that does not take in the stern and wild, not to say grim and gloomy aspects often presented by the Whig country.

CHAPTER XII
GALLOWAY

THE Whig country included Galloway, that rough south-western corner that stretches its Mull towards Ireland in what Boece calls "ane great snout of crags." The whole promontory formed by the stewartry of Kirkcudbright and the county of Wigtown, once known as Upper and Lower Galloway, and then taking in parts of Ayr and Dumfries, seems to concentrate many of the qualities of Scotland, *Land und Leute*. This northern Cornwall lent itself of old as a scene for dark romance, whose combats glitter here and there through deepest mists of history. Its Attacott people, Picts or what not, mixed with Scots from Ireland and Gaels from who knows where, run to dark hair and the tallest forms of Britain, perhaps even of Europe, while their character is a blend of especially perfervid spirit. Though this corner was the first foothold of Christianity on the mainland, it long remained notable for untamed fierceness, like that of the northern mountain cats. So near England, it came to glow with a patriotism more fervent than its loyalty; and some of the doughtiest exploits of Wallace and Bruce were done upon its borders, not always indeed with the help of the Galwegians. Mr. S. R. Crockett, who in a generation too forgetful of *Guy Mannering* has come forward to give Galloway its fair share of fame, tells us how most of its gentry, as well as its long-limbed and hot-hearted peasants, threw themselves into the Covenant struggle, their "Praying Societies" throughout making camps of resistance and protest against the persecutors; and in quieter times the same enthusiasm has flared up into will-o'-the-wisp fanaticism bred among the moss hags. Later on, as we know from Scott, the wild coasts of Galloway reared a daring breed of smugglers to testify for what they called "fair trade" with the Isle of Man. That trans-atlanticised firebrand, Paul Jones, hailed from Galloway, to which he came back to threaten the mouth of his native Dee.

Whatever this people's hand finds to do, it has been apt to do it with might and main. What it chiefly finds to do in our day is the rearing of cattle, that seem to thrive best on the promontories of our island; then also Galloway has given its name to a hardy horseflesh, and pigs, too, are largely reared in this region. Such an authority as the author of *Field and Fern* judges no beef better than that which matches the brawn of Galloway men. And these tall fellows have the name of living to a good old age, as witness the Galloway story of a man of threescore and ten found "greeting" when his father had given him "his licks" for throwing stones at his grandfather.

A BIRCH-WOOD IN SPRINGTIME, BY LOCH MAREE, ROSS-SHIRE

ON THE RIVER AYR, AYRSHIRE

By this time the reader must have an inkling how the names Highland and
Lowland are but relative. The knobbed area of Scotland, which, as a native boast-

ed, would be as big as England "if ye flattened it oot," consists mainly of two uplands, that of the south smaller, greener, and less boldly mountainous, between which dips a more thickly peopled interval, at one point but forty miles broad from sea to sea, where only the rich river straths and the coast plains are right lowlands, never out of sight of sheep-dotted hills. Galloway is mainly a wild region of rocks, lochs, moors, and bogs, in the north rising to mountains almost as high as any in England. This ground seems too much neglected by tourists, who yet might find here and there smart hotels to their mind, oftener the more old-fashioned inns where they would have to do not with managers and foreign waiters, but with housewifely Meg Dods and decent servant lasses, now instructed by the spread of knowledge no longer to mistake a tooth-brush as an instrument for sharpening the appetite before dinner. We Scots have a grudge against southrons for the degree to which they have sophisticated the hotels on more frequented routes, especially in the matter of charges. The butterfly-travellers as well as the bee-travellers should have a grievance against their landlords (Limited) not so much for making hay while the holiday sun shines, as for the tyranny that tries to impose upon them boarding-house regulations at Piccadilly prices. My grudge at those exotic caravanserais is that they try to set all their guests "feeding like one," and draw out the chief meal of the day through that sweetest hour of the northern summer —

> 'Twixt the gloaming and the mirk,
> When the kye come hame.

This grumble and others one need not make in Galloway, where strangers not too pock-puddingish about being "done well," would find a hearty welcome and openings for exploring a country sacred through memories of patriots and martyrs, dotted with ruined shrines and with strongholds of Douglases, Kennedys, Gordons, who in their lifetime loved better to hear the lark sing than the mouse squeak. From Newton-Stewart, not yet wide awake to its capabilities as a tourist centre, one has half a day's walk northwards into the heart of the Galloway Highlands, where Merrick raises its heathery Pentedactylon above the lovely Glen and Loch of Trool, one of the fastnesses of Bruce's *Wanderjähre*. Another goal in these hills is Murray's Monument, commemorating one of Scotland's gifted herd-loons, who with homely schooling raised himself to be Doctor of Divinity and Professor of Oriental Languages. Three heights in Galloway bear the name of Cairnsmore, the highest Cairnsmore of Carsphairn, approached from the town of New Galloway by Loch Ken, Kenmure Castle, and the beautiful Glenkens. Passing beyond Carsphairn to Dalmellington, we can strike by rail into the native country of Burns, who at the Galloway spa of Lochenbreck wrote down his "Scots wha hae," meetly composed by him, it is said, on a wild ride through a stormy night.

The chief town of Galloway is Stranraer, port of the shortest sea-crossing to Belfast, by Loch Ryan; but the nearest point to Ireland is Portpatrick, where that saint could step across the Channel long before so much money had been sunk on an abandoned harbour. The lion of Portpatrick is the glen and ruin of Dunskey; as that of Stranraer the grounds of Castle Kennedy, nursing exotics that attest the mildness of this western shore. The Irish express trains dash also past the beauties of Glenluce and its ruins haunted by legends of Michael Scott the Wizard, of Peden the Covenanting prophet, and of that hapless Bride of Lammermoor, whose story seems to have been distorted as well as transplanted to the other side of the country. Luce Bay separates the Mull of Galloway from a broader promontory in which the lochs of Mochrum are perhaps the finest nook. Its southern point is the green "Isle" of Whithorn, where Scottish Christianity was planted by St. Ninian; and still stand fragments of the famous monastery sought by James of the Iron Belt, and many another penitential pilgrim. On the same branch line from Newton-Stewart, Wigtown rears above its bay a monument of that shamefullest tragedy of the Covenanting persecutions, when two women martyrs were fastened to stakes to be drowned by the tide. At the mouth of the Cree is Creetown, "Portanferry" of *Guy Mannering*, from which can be visited caves fit to shelter Dirck Hatteraick, and the ruins of Barholm, that claims to be "Ellangowan," and to have given concealment to John Knox. Gatehouse of Fleet is a picturesque place in the district illustrated by the Faed brothers' pictures, and sanctified by the preaching of Samuel Rutherford. Farther east, on its inlet, is reached the county town Kirkcudbright, church of St. Cuthbert, who would hardly know his own name as now pronounced *Kirkoobry*. Here we have an interesting museum of Galloway antiquities; and a few miles off is Dundrennan Abbey, poor Mary's last resting place in her troubled kingdom, whence she gave herself to the mercy of Elizabeth after her flight from Langside. The Kirkcudbright branch takes us back to the main line at Castle Douglas, near which stands the grim tower of a stronghold whose lords were once a terror to their own country, while over the Border English nurses would hush babes to rest with—

> Hush ye, hush ye, dinna fret ye:
> The Black Douglas shall na' get ye!

Like too many other noble Scottish names, this one has sadly degenerated, its last exploit to be proud of ending in the catastrophe that cut short Lord Francis Douglas's life on the first ascent of the Matterhorn; and his brother, the late Marquis of Queensberry, made some stir in the world, least unenviably perhaps by the Queensberry rules of boxing. Several members of the family have in modern days come to an obscurely tragic end, as if urged by the Nemesis of forgotten bloodshed. Their chief title, the Dukedom of Queensberry, had passed to the house of Buccleuch, along with the princely seat of Drumlanrig in Nithsdale.

The oldest bridge in Scotland leads over the Nith to the largest town of the southern counties, out of Galloway in the letter, but not in the spirit. Dumfries, originally the fastness of Frisian pirates whose stock would "go far," is set among famous sites and relics. In the Church of its Greyfriars, Bruce stabbed the Red Comyn, a deed "made siccar" by an ancestor of the Empress of the French. Near the town are the remains of Lincluden Abbey, "ruins yet beauteous in decay." To the south, on the Galloway side of the estuary, Criffel's cone rises above the walls of Sweetheart Abbey, built by John Baliol's widow as tomb in which her husband's heart should lie upon her own. On the opposite side stands another stately ruin, Caerlaverock Castle, where in the churchyard lies "Old Mortality," as "Jeanie Deans" rests at Irongray. To the north is Lochmaben, the castle, perhaps the birthplace, of Robert Bruce. But the name that first rises to memory in this

Nithsdale countryside is Robert Burns, tenant of Ellisland under that Dalswinton laird for whom is claimed the honour of the earliest steamboat experiments. Bruce, possibly born at Turnberry Castle on the Carrick coast, may have been an Ayrshire man like Burns, who came to end his broken life at Dumfries, now counting itself honoured by the sepulchre of one who thus wrote his own epitaph—

> The poor inhabitant below
> Was quick to learn and wise to know,
> And keenly felt the friendly glow,
> And softer flame;
> But thoughtless follies laid him low,
> And stained his name.

Scotland's heart warms to the memory of Robbie Burns, over whose sayings and doings in lifetime big wigs about Dumfries were shaken and grave eyes up-turned. As if in repentance for his hard life and troubled death, his countrymen will now hear no word against the poet, who could be severe enough on his own frailties. And if mortal ever deserved kindly judgment, it was he whose heart went out not only to his Jeans and Annies, but to his "auld mare Maggie," to a hare wounded by "barb'rous art," to dumb cattle left out in a storm, even to such a "poor earth-companion and fellow-mortal" as a field-mouse; he who would not willingly have crushed with his ploughshare a "wee, modest, crimson-tippit flow-er"; who had no hatred for the very enemy of mankind—"Wad ye take a thought and mend!" It is vain to deny or conceal that "he had twa faults, or maybe three," but fate indeed gave him hard measure. Had his sphere been a higher one, he would not have been the man he was; yet with a little ease, with wise friends to counsel "prudent, cautious self-control," with Pitt's port or even Byron's hock and soda-water instead of tippenny and usquebaugh among spell-bound tavern cronies, might he not have lived to draw as good an income from the Civil Service as Wordsworth, to become a douce elder of the Kirk, and to take a seat among the orthodox *bon vivants* of the *Noctes*? As it is, his humble birthplace draws more pilgrims than come to Stratford-on-Avon from all over the world, for—

> Who his human heart has laid
> To Nature's bosom nearer?
> Who sweetened toil like him, or paid
> To love a tribute dearer?
>
> Through all his tuneful art, how strong
> The human feeling gushes!
> The very moonlight of his song
> Is warm with smiles and blushes!

This singer of the people's joys and sorrows represents the soft side to a strong nature. From the scene of his last days it is but a step to Annandale, cradle of a neighbour genius that is Scotland's boast rather than her darling. Thomas Carlyle, who ascended into such a clear heaven of contempt for the "mostly fools" of his "swindler century," fell short of Burns in one highest point of wisdom. He knew himself hardly better than did his amazed contemporaries; and seems never to have guessed what short work some of his admired strong men would have made of one who preached the gospel of silence in such long-drawn screeds of rhetoric, rising often to a falsetto note. An unchristianised Calvinist and Covenanter; a poet "wanting the accomplishment of verse"; a painter in "hues of earthquake and eclipse"; a philosopher who "thought in a passion"; a Stoic who could not abide the crowing of a cock; an historian who "saw history in flashes of lightning"; a reformer "calling down fire from heaven whenever he cannot readily lay his hand on the match-box"; a painful preacher who has ministered more amusement than repentance; a prophet who could not recognise the master force of his own age; a ferocious moralist and a bitter humorist, this "great imperfect man" owes much of his renown to a gnarled eccentricity which at first scared away readers, but more to the ardour that has inspired so many minds rejecting both his premises and his conclusions. To some who receive *Sartor Resartus* into the canon of immortality, his idolatry of strength, so natural to the sedentary, bilious student, seems the weakness of his character, through which he was led to work up bloodshot halos for unscrupulous violence, from his fancy picture of Dr. Francia to his fond glorification of Frederick the Great, till at last he appears struggling to pervert his own moral judgment. A countryman of his who, but for another weakness, might have made himself better known, Patrick Proctor Alexander, has well exposed his obliquity of vision in a burlesque that shows as much wisdom as fooling; and to my mind the soundest judgment of Carlyle comes across the Atlantic from James Russell Lowell:—

"If not a profound thinker, he had what was next best: he felt profoundly, and his cry came out of the depths. The stern Calvinism of his early training was rekindled by his imagination to the old fervour of Wishart and Brown, and became a new phenomenon as he reproduced it subtilised by German transcendentalism and German culture. Imagination, if it lays hold of a Scotsman, possesses him in the old demoniac sense of the word, and that hard logical nature, if the Hebrew fire once gets fair headway in it, burns unquenchable as an anthracite coal-mine. But to utilise these sacred heats, to employ them, as a literary man is always tempted, to keep the domestic pot a-boiling—is such a thing possible? Only too possible, we fear; and Mr. Carlyle is an example of it. If the languid public long for a sensation, the excitement of making one becomes also a necessity of the successful author, as the intellectual nerves grow duller and the old inspiration that came unbidden to the bare garret grows shyer and shyer of the comfortable parlour. As he himself said thirty years ago of Edward Irving, 'Unconsciously, for the most part in deep unconsciousness, there was now the impossibility to live neglected—to walk on the quiet paths where alone it is well with us. Singularity must henceforth succeed singularity. O foulest Circean draught, thou poison of Popular Applause! madness is in thee and death; thy end is Bedlam and the grave.' Mr. Carlyle won his first successes as a kind of preacher in print. His fervour, his oddity of manner, his pugnacious paradox, drew the crowd; the truth, or, at any rate, the faith that underlay them all, brought also the fitter audience, though fewer. But the curse was upon him; he must attract, he must astonish. Thenceforth he has done nothing but revamp his telling things; but the oddity has become always odder, the paradoxes more paradoxical. No very large share of truth falls to the apprehension of any one man; let him keep it sacred, and beware of repeating it till it turn to falsehood on his lips by becoming ritual."

After all Carlyle was not wholly a typical Scotsman. His stock seems to have come from Cumberland, and his birthplace, not far from the Border, is one of Scotland's less bonnie *airts*. He was very Lowlandish, indeed, in some features: in his perfervidness, in his intolerance, in the coarseness of mental grain that chuckles over abusive nicknames, and in volcanic stirrings of sympathy that enabled him to appreciate Burns. He was above all himself, *Der Einzige*, as he proclaimed others, a most portentous and vigorous force in literature, that has been transmuted into different modes of intellectual motion. Whatever rank this coruscating star may eventually take in the firmament of fame, its spectrum is not that of Scotland. At the best, he represents but one side of his country's nature, as appears in his grudging and belittling view of Scott, who more fully unites the chequered elements of the national character.

In a generation much blinded by literary superstitions and idolatries, Scotsmen should faithfully testify to Scott as the truest genius of their country. With him for guide, we entered his beloved Borderland; he has seldom been far from us as we passed through its scenes and monuments, and still on the rhinns of Galloway and in the dales of Dumfries, his shade attends us; nor does it wholly vanish as we cross the Solway viaduct into "Happy England," pronounced by a recent American writer, after his lights, "a section more beautiful perhaps to the eye," forsooth, than Bonnie Scotland, but "certainly not one which appeals more forcibly to the imagination." Burns did something, Carlyle almost nothing, towards fusing angry memories of the past into one national sentiment. To the spells of that Wizard of the North we chiefly owe it that now "Highland and Lowland, all our hearts are Scotch!" as a romancer of our own time exclaims, who elsewhere recalls Stewart of Garth's story how, when a Highland regiment landed at Portpatrick after long exile, the kilted veterans flung themselves down to kiss the ground of Galloway, so far from their native heath.

THE END

Lector House believes that a society develops through a two-fold approach of continuous learning and adaptation, which is derived from the study of classic literary works spread across the historic timeline of literature records. Therefore, we aim at reviving, repairing and redeveloping all those inaccessible or damaged but historically as well as culturally important literature across subjects so that the future generations may have an opportunity to study and learn from past works to embark upon a journey of creating a better future.

This book is a result of an effort made by Lector House towards making a contribution to the preservation and repair of original ancient works which might hold historical significance to the approach of continuous learning across subjects.

HAPPY READING & LEARNING!

LECTOR HOUSE LLP
E-MAIL: lectorpublishing@gmail.com